BEAUTIFUL BRITAIN

WESSEX

BEAUTIFUL BRITAIN

WESSEX

Published by the Reader's Digest Association Limited, London for the Automobile Association,
Fanum House, Basingstoke, Hampshire RG21 2EA

WESSEX
was edited and designed by
The Reader's Digest Association Limited
for the Automobile Association,
Fanum House, Basingstoke, Hampshire RG21 2EA

This book contains material from
the following titles originally
published by Drive Publications Limited:
*Treasures of Britain, Discovering Britain,
Book of British Towns, Illustrated Guide to
Britain, Book of British Villages, Illustrated
Guide to Country Towns and Villages of Britain;*
and from *Folklore, Myths and Legends of Britain*
and *The Past All Around Us,* both published by
the Reader's Digest Association Limited.

ISBN 0-86145-517-7

Filmset by MS Filmsetting Ltd, Frome
Separations by Litra Ltd, Edenbridge
Printed by Blantyre Printing and Binding Co Ltd, Glasgow
Bound by Hazell Watson & Viney Ltd, Aylesbury

Printed in Great Britain

The map on the endpapers was produced by
Thames Cartographic Services, Maidenhead,
and is based upon Ordnance Survey material
with the permission of the Controller of
Her Majesty's Stationery Office, Crown
copyright reserved. A name printed on the
map in bold type indicates that the place
is featured in this book.

Cover photographs: Avebury by Patrick Thurston (*top*);
Stonehenge by Mike Taylor (*bottom left*);
Handfast Point by Nigel Cassidy (*bottom right*).
Introduction (*pages 6–7*): Bicknoller Hill by Malcolm Aird.

CONTENTS

There are many claimants to the title of the *real* Wessex. Lovers of Thomas Hardy's novels visualise the lonely heath and grey villages, which stretch over the immeasurable, surreal expanse of south-western England, bordered somewhere on its farthest reaches by the moors and craggy coasts of Devon and Cornwall. Students of history recall the Wessex of neolithic Britain, then the most populous part of the island. Defended from invading Saxon hordes by the legendary Arthur, 350 years later it was consolidated by Alfred into a mighty kingdom, with its capital at Winchester.

Though Winchester today is still romantically linked in the popular mind with its one-time fiefdom (and in honour of this historical attachment is included in this book), it has little to do with modern Wessex. Taking into account contemporary borders, the region now tends to include only Gloucestershire, Avon, Somerset, Wiltshire and Dorset.

But the cartographic and civil servants have not managed to tame or eradicate any of its regional diversity. The rolling chalk downs of Wiltshire give way to Gloucestershire's lush dairylands and the picture-perfect villages of wool-rich Avon, while the rural solitude of Hardy's Dorset is challenged by the secret valleys and bournes of Exmoor's Doone country. And pervading all is a profound sense of mystery – whether among the stone circles of pagan Avebury or Stonehenge, or within the sacred cloisters of Wells, at the top of Saxon Maiden Castle or on Christian Glastonbury Tor.

ABBOTSBURY

Dorset

8 miles northwest of Weymouth

St Catherine's Chapel, set on the summit of a steep 250 ft hill, commands the large and spread-out village of Abbotsbury. The chapel – built in the 14th century with thick stone walls, sturdy buttresses and a heavy, barrel-vaulted roof – overlooks the barns, thatched cottages and orange-stone houses that make up the village. Some of the buildings' stones came from demolished monastery sites, and the area's meadows and gardens abound in mullioned windows, age-blackened timbers, ancient stone roof-tiles, and paving on raised footpaths – most of them half-buried in ivy. It is likely that the chapel itself was spared from destruction by Giles Strangways, Henry VIII's Dissolution Commissioner, because it was a landmark for mariners. From the chapel, there are marvellous views out to sea and along the coast.

The Benedictine abbey which gave the village its name was founded in the middle of the 11th century. Today, with the exception of the half-ruined but imposing Abbey Barn, little remains of the abbey and its related buildings. The tithe barn was built in the 14th century, and measures 272 ft by 31 ft, with a sturdy, buttressed porch and hexagonal staircase tower. It is one of the largest buildings of its kind in Britain and, together with an adjacent pond, marks the nucleus of the abbey site. Nearby is the 15th-century Church of St Nicholas, which contains a marble monument of an abbot, dating from the early 13th century. To the west of the church are several large, post-Reformation houses – including Abbey House, Abbey Dairy House, the Old Manor House, and the Vicarage.

Abbotsbury lies in a sheltered, green valley about 1 mile from the coast. Just beyond the encircling hills is the northern end of Chesil Beach, a massive rampart of pebbles piled up over the centuries by strong tides and stretching 17 miles from Bridport to Portland. Behind the beach is a long, narrow and brackish lagoon, rather surprisingly called The Fleet, and for the past 600 years the western corner of the lagoon has housed a colony of swans, which feed on a rare grass in the area, *Zostera marina*.

Each May, when the birds are incubating their eggs, The Swannery opens to visitors. It is then, in their aggressive defence, that the birds show themselves to be every bit as wild as they are graceful. The 18th-century gardens on the Beach Road west of the village are also open to the public. Exotic plants and trees flourish in these sub-tropical gardens, and late spring brings an abundance of camellias and heavily perfumed magnolias.

A narrow, unsignposted road opposite the Ilchester Arms in Abbotsbury leads high up over Black Down Hill to the Hardy Monument – commemorating not Hardy the writer, but Admiral Hardy, Nelson's flag captain at the Battle of Trafalgar. The car park by the monument commands a fine panorama.

A mile-and-a-half to the northwest of the village is Abbotsbury Castle, an Iron Age earthwork set on a hill and covering some 10 acres, and a long barrow known as The Grey Mare, a single Stone Age burial chamber built of sarsens or sandstone boulders. It is an anomaly in these chalk lands, where free stones are scarce.

ABLINGTON

Gloucestershire

7 miles northeast of Cirencester

The trout-happy River Coln curls through Ablington, watering a woody dell in which rests a hamlet of stone-built houses. This is but one of a string of pearls along the Coln, among which the best known is Bibury, 1 mile downstream. Little seems to have changed in Ablington for centuries – except for the

old mill whose forecourt serves as a vestigial village square. It is now a private house with gardens leading down to a millstream where the banks are golden with daffodils in spring.

But the Victorian writer J. Arthur Gibbs – who chronicled Ablington life in his book *A Cotswold Village* – would perhaps applaud improvements made since this time. 'Farms are to be had for the asking,' he wrote then, 'and the country is rapidly going back to its original uncultivated state.'

Now disused barns have been converted to handsome homes, and the gardens around the old houses are immaculate. The Elizabethan Manor House, where Gibbs lived, has huge gardens stretching down to the river, but remains private behind high stone walls. Its doorway, dated 1590, features five elaborately carved heads – one of them Elizabeth I herself. The high gables of 17th-century Ablington House peer over another tall, dry-stone wall. Guarding the iron gate are two rampant stone lions that once graced the Houses of Parliament.

One of the most colourful characters in Arthur Gibbs's book was a gamekeeper named Tom Peregrine. He was based on a real-life gamekeeper, John Brown,

whose small cottage sits somewhat unsteadily on the slope above the hamlet.

ADLESTROP
Gloucestershire
4 miles east of Stow-on-the-Wold

Edward Thomas immortalised this village in his short poem *Adlestrop*, because his train stopped here briefly one summer afternoon.

> *The steam hiss'd. Some one clear'd his throat.*
> *No one left and no one came*
> *On the bare platform. What I saw*
> *Was Adlestrop – only the name.*

The station has gone, but the nameplate that caught Thomas's eye is now in the village bus shelter, with the poem inscribed on a plaque below.

Had Thomas left his train, he would have found a village of golden-stone houses, a Georgian mansion,

ADLESTROP *Made famous by a First World War poet, the village has grown, but still retains a sleepy charm.*

and a 13th- to 14th-century church. The mansion, Adlestrop Park, is in Gothic style with grounds landscaped by Humphry Repton. Neither the house nor gardens are open to the public.

The Church of St Mary Magdalene contains monuments to the Leigh family, who have owned Adlestrop Park since 1553. Thomas Leigh was the rector at the beginning of the 19th century and his granddaughter, the novelist Jane Austen, was a visitor to the rectory, now Adlestrop House. It dates from the 17th century, and stands among magnificent cedar trees. The schoolroom, school house and a cottage close by are 19th century.

Chastleton House, 3 miles north of Adlestrop, overshadows thatched cottages of Cotswold stone. This great mansion dates from 1603 and is in its original state, right down to the furniture. There is a secret room where one of the Royalist family hid from Parliamentary troops during the Civil War. In the garden of a nearby house are box bushes neatly trimmed into animal shapes.

AISHOLT
Somerset
3 miles south of Nether Stowey

Aisholt is an attractive village of thatched cottages, oak barns and a 14th-century church. Its name is taken from the ash trees of the Quantock Forest where the Saxons settled. The poet Sir Henry Newbolt lived here in the 1930s – his best-known poem is *Drake's Drum*. Another poet, Samuel Taylor Coleridge, had hoped to live here too, but decided against it, fearing that his wife would find the place too lonely.

A short detour north from the village leads along the side of Aisholt Wood and follows a small stream. You may be lucky enough to see red deer sheltering under the beech and ash trees.

IVYCHURCH *The Augustinian priory north of Alderbury is ruined, but sculptures and architectural details remain.*

Aisholt Common is the heart of the Quantocks, a high moorland plateau fringed by the dark green edge of Quantock Forest and dropping away to a deep valley which Coleridge called 'a deep romantic chasm...down a green hill'.

The common is best seen by walking around it, using the $5\frac{1}{2}$ mile trail laid out by the Somerset Trust for Nature Conservation. The walk starts from Birches Corner. Cuckoos, buzzards and stonechats can be seen flying low above the gorse, bracken and heather, with an occasional glimpse of red deer. And along the trail there are ever-changing views as the path, starting at 1000 ft, drops to 400 ft as it passes through the village of Aisholt, and then follows the edge of the Quantock Forest, finally climbing to 1260 ft at Wills Neck, the highest hill in the Quantocks. At one point it is possible to see three National Parks – Brecon Beacons, Exmoor and Dartmoor.

ALDBOURNE
Wiltshire
6 miles northwest of Marlborough

Aldbourne is one of the prettiest villages in Wiltshire, set 700 ft up on the Marlborough Downs. It has two focal points, The Green and The Square. The Green is a turf slope with an old, weathered stone cross in the middle and a framing of ancient cottages, Georgian houses and the Blue Boar pub, on whose site an ale and lodging house has stood since 1460 at least.

Standing above all, on a higher mound still, is the truly majestic Church of St Michael, a building that is a conglomeration of all kinds of periods from the Normans on; it probably stands on the foundations of an earlier, Saxon church. The interior is equally magnificent, and presents an extraordinarily vivid picture of Aldbourne's history. There is a superbly executed alabaster tomb of John Stone, a priest who died in 1524, and numerous monuments to Goddards and Walronds. An early Walrond was Ranger of Aldbourne Chase in the days of William the Conqueror. The Goddard monument of about 1616 shows husband, wife and four children in decreasing sizes; the three small boys, curiously, have beards and moustaches.

Nearby is the splendid tomb of two Walrond brothers – benign, bearded old gentlemen who also died at the beginning of the 17th century. One is described as a 'lover of hospitality and entertainer of many friends', and looks it. All the monuments, Goddards and Walronds alike, have had their praying hands knocked off, presumably by Parliamentarian troops during the Civil War. Also in the church are a pair of 18th-century fire engines, known affectionately as Adam and Eve. They served the village well through a number of serious conflagrations, the last in 1921, before going into honourable retirement.

Behind St Michael's along a rocky causeway high above the road, and around The Square are a number of good-looking Georgian houses, recalling the days when Aldbourne was an important place, noted for its bell-founding, the weaving of fustian – a coarse cloth – and its hats of plaited straw and willow. Many of the houses are in a local mixture of red brick and rough stone blocks, offset by dark pink, tiled roofs.

The Square is also a green, with a perfectly round pond at its centre. A notice board tells of the several occasions on which Aldbourne has been judged the best-kept village in Wiltshire, and beneath it there is a monument to a dog called Rover, 'a faithful worker for Savernake Hospital', who died in 1933. Rover used to carry a collecting box at Aldbourne's carnivals, and raised a lot of money for the hospital.

High on a ridge to the north is the little village of Baydon. No architectural gem, it has a fair share of modern buildings, but the views to the Marlborough Downs on one side and the Lambourn Downs on the other are breathtaking. The road that runs through the village is the great Roman Ermin Way, which linked the towns of Corinium (Cirencester) and Calleva (Silchester).

ALDERBURY
Wiltshire
3 miles southeast of Salisbury

Successive landlords of the Green Dragon, an inn by Alderbury's triangular village green, have been proud to point out that Charles Dickens used the inn as a model for the Blue Dragon portrayed in his novel *Martin Chuzzlewit*, published in 1843.

A little to the north of the village, though closed to visitors, lie the remains of Ivychurch, a 12th-century Augustinian priory, founded by King Stephen. Its prior and 12 monks ministered to the spiritual needs of royalty when they were in residence at Clarendon Palace. Stones from the ruins of Ivychurch were used to build the fountain and drinking-trough on the village green.

Another inn with a story is the Three Crowns, on the Southampton side of the hamlet of Whaddon. Its name is thought to recall the fact that Edward III hunted in nearby Clarendon Forest in 1357 with two captive guests, the King of France and the King of Scotland. Another theory is that the inn is named after the three kings of the Nativity.

St Mary's is a 19th-century church with a tall four-gabled tower and spire. Across the road is the driveway to Alderbury House, a late-18th-century residence, said to be built of materials from the bell-tower of Salisbury Cathedral after it had been pulled down in 1789.

St Marie's Grange, 1 mile to the northwest, is the home built in 1835 by the architect Augustus Welby Pugin for himself and his young bride. The house was much altered after Pugin returned to London to help with the design of the new Houses of Parliament. It was while staying at St Marie's Grange that Dickens wrote *Martin Chuzzlewit*.

On a ridge 2 miles southeast of Alderbury is an extraordinary eye-catcher called Eyre's Folly, or 'The Pepperbox'. It is one of the oldest follies in the country, a slate-roofed, six-sided structure built in 1606. It stands on 73 acres of open downs covered with junipers and is owned by the National Trust.

Trafalgar House, 2 miles south, was built in 1733 and presented to Lord Nelson's family in 1814, when it received its present name. It contains a 'Ganges' room, panelled with timbers from the man o' war of the same name which fought with Nelson's fleet at the Battle of Copenhagen in 1801.

AMESBURY
Wiltshire
7 miles north of Salisbury

The town of Amesbury is set in a bend of the River Avon, which is crossed by a five-arched bridge, known as the Queensbury Bridge and built in Palladian style. Amesbury Abbey is built on the site of the priory to which, according to Thomas Mallory, Queen Guinevere withdrew when she heard of King Arthur's death. The abbey was re-founded by Henry II in 1177, at which time it was altered to become cruciform with a central tower. It was later granted to Edward Seymour who became the Duke of Somerset. Gatehouses from his manor are still standing. The third and final house on the property was completed in 1840. West of the Avon, on the border of Amesbury Park, are the outlines of prehistoric earthworks which are named Vespasian's Camp after the Roman emperor, but date from a much earlier age. The large military and RAF camps near Amesbury include the important experimental flying base of Boscombe Down, where new aircraft are tested.

Two miles west of Amesbury is Normanton Down, one of the most remarkable barrow groups in Britain. Many of the barrows have been excavated in the past and the contents, mainly of the Early Bronze Age, show them to have been the graves of people of importance of the 'Wessex culture'; one of them, the Bush Barrow, contained gold armour and may well have been that of a paramount chief of his day. It seems certain that these barrows were placed here to be close to Stonehenge, which is surrounded for miles by a concentration of fine barrows. A few of those in this group have suffered some ploughing, but most stand to a considerable height. Apart from a single earlier long barrow, there are 26 round barrows of bowl, bell, disc and saucer types. Finds from the site are in Devizes Museum.

ANSTY

Dorset
6 miles north of Puddletown

Ansty lies in the heart of farming country. Along a narrow lane out of the village is a signpost to Wardour Castle, once the home of the Arundel family and now a girls' school. The old castle was destroyed during the Civil War, and 1 mile away from its ruins is the present 18th-century castle. Adjoining this is one of the most beautiful baroque Roman Catholic chapels in England; its splendid interior, rich in art treasures, was designed principally by Sir John Soane, James Paine and Quarenghi.

ASHLEWORTH

Gloucestershire
9 miles southwest of Tewkesbury

The Jelf family has lived by the River Severn at Ashleworth Quay since the 17th century at least. During the Civil War, an ancestor is believed to have ferried Charles I across the river and received, as a reward, a charter granting his family a perpetual monopoly of the ferry at this point. From that day to this, the Jelfs have been identified with the varying fortunes of the tiny riverside community.

In the 19th century, when the quay was the point where horse-drawn barges had to change from one side of the river to the other, to avoid cliffs upstream near Tewkesbury, it had two pubs. One of them, the Boat Inn, belonged to the Jelfs, and today the charmingly old-fashioned pub, having outlived its rival, remains within the family. However, the busy quay of a century ago now presents a picture of perfect tranquillity, disturbed only by an occasional angler.

Near the quay, another exceptional group of buildings, all medieval, clusters round the Church of St Andrew and St Bartholomew, which has some ancient herringbone masonry, dating from the early 12th century, and a 14th-century spire. Beside the church looms the immense 15th-century Tithe Barn, which is owned by the National Trust. This huge building has two vast doors on one side, to let loaded wagons in, and two much lower ones on the other side, through which they would roll out after their high loads had been removed and stored away in the barn.

An outstanding stone house, Ashleworth Court – occasionally open to the public – is set back on a lawn adjoining the churchyard. It was built in 1460 by the Abbey of St Augustine, Bristol, which owned the manor, and it has remained almost unchanged. At about the same time, the abbey also built Ashleworth Manor, a short distance away across the flat riverside meadows. This fine timber-framed house, discreetly enlarged in the 19th and 20th centuries, was the abbots' summer residence.

A noble avenue of poplars leads from the church to the main part of the village, set on higher ground to avoid flooding. At the centre is a large green with a fine stone cross – probably 12th century – its four-sided head showing a figure of Christ.

There are also some charming timber-framed cottages, and, on a rise behind the village, the Gothic-style mansion Foscombe, built in the late 19th century. For a number of years this elaborate mansion, with its fantastic turrets and tower, was the home of Charlie Watts, drummer in the Rolling Stones rock group.

ASHMORE

Dorset
5 miles southeast of Shaftesbury

Its pond is the pride of Ashmore, for the village is the highest in Dorset, 711 ft up on Cranborne Chase, and on the hilltops open water is a rare curiosity. The pond lies at the centre of the village, a huge circular mirror 40 yds across and 16 ft deep in the middle. It is said to have never dried up, even in the most severe drought. Mallard and muscovy ducks dabble on its surface, and reflected in its placid waters are an old stone barn, thatched cottages of grey-green stone and flint, the Georgian Old Rectory with its spreading cedar, and the wide downland sky.

No one knows how long the pond has been here, but it probably existed in pre-Saxon times, despite the Saxon name of the village recorded in the Domesday Book – *Aisemare*, meaning 'the pond by the ash tree'. In the last half century the pond has certainly never dried out; sometimes, in fact, the water rises even when there has been no rain – a phenomenon characteristic of chalk country, where rain drains away through the upper layers of rock and collects in underground reservoirs. Each year around Midsummer Day the villagers honour the pond in a ceremony,

called Filly Loo, of uncertain origin. A band plays from a platform in the middle of the pond and Morris dancers from all parts of southern England join the villagers for the occasion.

The largest farm in Ashmore surrounds the Victorian Gothic Church of St Nicholas, with its modern stone brackets shaped as various animals, Norman font and 17th-century altar. A Nonconformist chapel nearby was built in the 1830s. There are also a number of barrows, or ancient burial mounds, in and around the village.

Ashmore's many vantage points provide magnificent panoramic views. On a clear day the Isle of Wight is visible, some 40 miles away to the southeast, and the ridgeway road which leads to the village from Shaftesbury gives fine views across the downs and combes.

ATHELHAMPTON

Dorset

1 mile east of Puddletown

Walls and courts surround the medieval manor house of Athelhampton, which was built in the 15th century by Sir William Martyn, a lord mayor of London.

The 15th-century Great Hall is one of the finest in existence, with a timber roof, brass chandelier, linenfold panelling, minstrels' gallery and heraldic window glass. The house also contains secret staircases and a Tudor great chamber. The stables belonging to the manor are thatched and the Italian-style formal gardens contain a 15th-century dovecote, fishponds, fountains, pleached (interlaced) limes and clipped yew trees.

Several hauntings are attributed to Athelhampton House. During the 19th century sightings of a headless man were often reported, and a Grey Lady has been active in recent years. Another ghost – the Black Monk – was seen several years ago by the owner of the house. The Martyn family, who occupied the house in the 15th and 16th centuries, were devout Catholics and the ghost might have been that of an itinerant priest.

Sir William Martyn's crest of a chained ape holding a mirror can be found on some of the windows, and may account for the legend of a pet ape which was accidentally walled up in a priest's hole; its phantom, too, is alleged to roam the house.

HIGH WATER *At Ashmore on Cranborne Chase, ducks paddle on the pond, which is the highest in Dorset.*

MYSTIC STONES *Sheep graze contentedly around the boulders in the 4000-year-old ring at Avebury.*

AVEBURY

Wiltshire
6 miles west of Marlborough

Entering Avebury from any direction is like stepping back into the past. Before the centre of the village is reached, the road passes through an immense circle of brooding stones which stand like petrified ghosts of an age about which little is known. The circle was raised about 2300 BC, probably by the Beaker People. These settlers from the Low Countries take their name from the sophisticated pottery they made and often buried with their dead. The site was probably an open temple used in sun worship or fertility rites.

The heaviest stone in the outer ring weighs some 40 tons. Inside there are two incomplete circles. Only 27 of the original stones remain, although concrete plinths mark the gaps where stones have gone – often to be built into cottage walls in the village. In the 17th and 18th centuries, farmers used many of the megaliths for local building purposes, but some were recovered in a massive restoration of the site this century. The stones, called sarsens (meaning 'saracen' or foreign to the indigenous chalk), were hauled from the nearby Marlborough Downs, and all are naturally shaped. It is believed that they may represent human figures; the tall, narrow stones males, and the rough diamond shapes females. Surrounding the circle is a great earth bank – 1400 ft in diameter – which encloses 28 acres and is split into four parts by roads.

The centre of Avebury is a cluster of thatched cottages and farms, and a gabled Elizabethan house called Avebury Manor. The house contains collections of porcelain and antique furniture. The Church of St James, just outside the earthworks, combines Saxon masonry with broken fragments of stone from the prehistoric circle.

The Alexander Keiller Museum is reached through the churchyard and is named after its founder, who opened it in 1938 to house the material from his excavations at Windmill Hill, $1\frac{1}{2}$ miles to the northwest. This is a fortified camp of 2900 BC and a Bronze Age burial site of about 1700–1400 BC. The museum also includes objects from the West Kennet Long Barrow, Silbury Hill and Avebury.

AXBRIDGE

Somerset
2 miles west of Cheddar

This ancient town was made a borough before the Norman conquest in 1066. Its hub is a spacious square, off which there are many small old streets; the High Street contains several historic buildings, including King John's Hunting Lodge, a late-medieval building that has no connection with King John. It houses a museum in which are preserved the old stocks, a 'bull anchor' used in bull-baiting until the 19th century, and a money-changer's table dating from 1627. The Church of St John Baptist has a fine plaster nave ceiling dating from 1636 and some 15th-century monuments.

A mile to the north, just beyond Rose Wood, a track narrows into a 2 mile footpath leading across the Callow Hill and on to a lane that returns to the outskirts of Axbridge.

B

BADBURY RINGS

Dorset
4 miles northwest of Wimborne

A steep hilltop close to the Wimborne to Blandford road has been strengthened with two massive inner ramparts and a third, much slighter, enclosing them, to form the Iron Age hill-fort of Badbury Rings. The fort had two entrances and complicated defence works. It is likely to have been a large settlement in Roman times, too, since two major Roman roads meet here. One is the main road from Old Sarum to Dorchester, Ackling Dyke, and the other is the road from Bath to Poole. Ackling Dyke, a broad straight embankment, 40 ft wide and 6 ft high in places, is one of the finest stretches of Roman road in Britain. Setting off from Badbury Rings across downland, you can walk along it northwards for about 8 miles until you reach the B3081.

Badbury Rings is one of several places which tradition has identified as Mount Badon, the battleground where Arthur finally defeated the Saxons in 518. There, according to the ancient chroniclers, 'Arthur carried the cross of Our Lord Jesus Christ, for three days and nights on his shoulders, and the Britons were victorious'. The battle was said to have given Britain 21 years of peace which lasted until Arthur took up arms against his treacherous nephew, Mordred. Though Badbury Rings has the oldest claim, the battle has also been sited at Badbury Hill in Berkshire and at Badbury near Swindon in Wiltshire.

BADMINTON

Avon
10 miles southwest of Malmesbury

As you approach the rolling parkland of the Duke of Beaufort's 15,000 acre estate at Badminton, the place seems at first sight to be guarded by a series of forts and small castles. Closer scrutiny reveals that the forts are farm buildings, disguised by turrets and castellations; and the little castles are lodges with miniature round towers at each corner. These charming 'follies' date from the 1750s when the estate was decorated by the architect Thomas Wright. More of Wright's eccentric work can be seen on the edge of Badminton village. One cottage looks like an upturned boat.

The village centre is more restrained, as befits a village that was largely built to house estate workers. The main street flanks the gates of Badminton House, the cottages standing back at a discreet distance. Some are in terraces, some freestanding; some in stone, some rendered. They were built at different periods between the 17th and 19th centuries, but all share the same colour scheme – dark cream front doors, and battleship grey for the gates and low palings that surround many of the front gardens.

The 18th-century almshouses have leaded-light windows and are topped by pediments decorated

POOR BUT PROUD *The fine 18th-century almshouses at Great Badminton have mullioned windows and ornate pediments.*

with the Beaufort family crest. You enter the post office through a grandiose iron arch supporting a lantern; and to step inside the two delightful village shops is to return to the era of personal service.

Badminton House is an impressive Palladian mansion, which has been the home of the Dukes of Beaufort for more than 300 years. Visitors to the house can enjoy the collections of Italian, Dutch and English paintings and fine examples of carving by the sculptor Grinling Gibbons (1648–1721). Outside the house, the kennels of the Beaufort Hunt are also open to visitors.

The mansion also gave its name to a game. Guests on a wet afternoon in the 1860s found in the nursery battledores and shuttlecocks – crude rackets and corks with feathers in them – used by children. A string was stretched across the hall as a net, for a game of indoor tennis, and badminton was born. One of the guests took the game to India where, in Karachi in 1877, the first set of formal rules was drawn up.

The parish church of St Michael and All Angels is attached to Badminton House. Built in a Classical style in 1785, it is filled – as might be expected – with Beaufort memorials. Among them is a marble monument by Grinling Gibbons for Henry Somerset, the 1st Duke, who died in 1699. The effigy, brought here from St George's Chapel, Windsor, shows the duke in garter robes. The elaborate memorial is topped, 25 ft up, by a coronet on a tasselled cushion. The 2nd, 3rd and 4th Dukes are commemorated with monuments by the Flemish sculptor Michael Rysbrack (about 1693–1770).

The dukedom was created in 1682 in recognition of the Somerset family's descent from John of Gaunt, Duke of Lancaster. Naturally, they supported the Lancastrian cause in the Wars of the Roses, and were Royalists in the Civil War. Recent dukes have been great horsemen. The 10th Duke, who died in 1984, was known simply as 'Master' by his many friends. He was for many years Master of the Queen's Horse, and even in his eighties, rode to hounds several days each week as Master of the Beaufort Hunt. He created the three-day Badminton Horse Trials, a highlight of the competitive equestrian year, held each April.

Little Badminton is a smaller village on the estate, beside the western wall of the great park. Its cottages – several of them very old and some thatched – are scattered in a wide circle around a large green. The little Church of St Michael, dating from the 14th century, is shaded by large yews.

A handsome round dovecote stands at one side of the green; it is said to have 365 nesting boxes – one for each day of the year. A wicket gate leads into the beautifully wooded grounds, where visitors may walk.

BALLARD DOWN

Dorset

Headland at the east end of the Purbeck Hills and at the north end of Swanage Bay

The Dorset chalklands begin dramatically at Ballard Down, where the hills of the Isle of Purbeck meet the sea. Below Studland's small Norman church, a fingerpost indicates two paths. One climbs straight ahead, first by a lane, then through blazing gorse and

BATCOMBE *The village lies sheltered by the ridge of Batcombe Hill, and is approached by narrow, twisting lanes.*

stone-strewn cornfields southwards to the crest of Ballard Down. About 1 mile west is Nine Barrow Down with views of Corfe Castle 4 miles westwards. The other path – a more leisurely walk – descends eastwards towards the beach, turns to climb through Studland Wood, heavily scented with wild garlic and stinking iris, and finally emerges on the springy turf of the cliff top. Do not go near the edge, for these cliffs are dangerous.

Far below, chalk stacks rise dazzlingly from the sea. The great cliffs of The Foreland, 1 mile east of Studland, are penetrated by wave-pierced arches, and beyond lies Old Harry rock and, much eroded, Old Harry's Wife. Old Harry is a synonym for the Devil, and the area on the cliff top is known as Old Nick's Ground.

The path continues along the cliff top, with the green down and quietly grazing sheep to the right. At Ballard Point, 383 ft and 1 mile southwest of The Foreland, two seas come into view – to the north the great sweep of Studland Bay to Poole Harbour, and to the south the graceful crescent extending to Swanage and Peveril Point. The path then winds down into Swanage.

BANWELL

Avon

5 miles east of Weston-super-Mare

The village of Banwell was named after a millpond or well – no longer to be seen – that was said to possess healing properties.

A privately owned Victorian extravaganza, Banwell Castle, complete with battlements, turrets and all the standard features of a medieval fortress, stands guard over the southeastern approach to the village; but once past it, and over the brow of the hill, a more serene picture unfolds. Narrow winding streets lined with small cottages surround the church, the 'Cathedral of the Mendips', which dates from the 14th and

15th centuries. The tower stands over 100 ft high, and the splendid interior is glorified by a beautiful gilded chancel screen, a fine Tudor doorway and a strikingly painted roof. The church's 15th-century Flemish stained glass was brought from Belgium in 1855.

Nearby Banwell Abbey used to be the country residence of the Bishops of Wells, but it has been extensively changed since Bishop Bekynton built it in the 15th century. Above the village, on private land, Banwell Hill is crowned by an Iron Age earthwork, Banwell Camp, constructed more than 2000 years ago. Within the earthwork there is a great cross constructed out of turf. No one knows who built it, or when or why, but local legend says that the Devil kept raising gales to blow down each upright cross that the villagers erected so they finally foiled the Evil One by laying the cross on the ground.

Banwell lies at the tip of one of the westernmost headlands which the Mendip Hills throw out towards the Bristol Channel, and the steep hills above the village afford magnificent views to the west and north. Beneath the hills, in the early 19th century, the pioneer archaeologist William Beard discovered Banwell Cave, containing vast quantities of ancient bones, among them those of cave bears, cave lions and wolves, creatures that roamed the area in prehistoric times. Beard used many of them to build a curious bone wall in the cave, but visitors who wish to see it will be disappointed because the cave is no longer open.

BARBURY CASTLE
Wiltshire
5 miles south of Swindon

This Iron Age fort is one of the best known in southern England. Perched on the 850 ft high northern rim of the Marlborough Downs, the fort overlooks the Ridgeway long-distance route and gives sweeping views of the surrounding countryside. To the west lies a vast sprawl of rolling chalkland, a patchwork of green fields and a sprinkling of trees with hills rising like smoke in the distance. Half a mile to the north lies the battlefield of Beranburh where the Saxon chief Cynric and his son Ceawlin defeated the Britons in a bloody massacre. It established the Saxons as overlords of southern England and later, in AD 560, Ceawlin became King of Wessex.

Barbury Castle is a well-defined oval of about 12 acres, with entrances at the eastern and western sides passing through the towering double ramparts. Finds from inside are now in Devizes Museum, and include fittings for chariots. Below the fort on the eastern side can be seen the angular outlines of ancient field systems, probably dating from the Iron Age. They stand out clearly against the softer contours of the surrounding landscape.

The path down from the castle's western entrance joins the Ridgeway, and there is a pleasant 30 minute walk along it eastwards to Burderop Down and back to the car park. The deeply rutted track winds downhill, with pink and white hawthorns lining the path and yellow honeysuckle scenting the air.

BATCOMBE
Dorset
4 miles northwest of Cerne Abbas

The village of Batcombe is backed by steep hills from which it is possible to look down on to the flat roof of the church tower. Possibly it was this view which gave rise to the story of Conjuror Mynterne, a 16th-century squire of the manor who was reputed to have dabbled in witchcraft.

One day, as Mynterne rode out along the top of Batcombe Hill, he suddenly remembered that he had left his book of spells open on his desk. Fearing that someone might read it and perhaps come to harm by trying out the spells, he hurried back home. Galloping

by the shortest route, he jumped his horse from the top of Batcombe Hill clean across the village. As he sailed over the rooftops, his horse's hoof caught one of the four pinnacles surrounding the church tower and knocked it off. Despite this, the horse made a safe landing on a field called Pitching Plot; but such was the power of the magic that grass would never grow there again.

The broken pinnacle was replaced by a new one about a hundred years later. However, it leans out of true, and is easily distinguished because it is not so stained by the weather as the other three.

Conjuror Mynterne lived for several years after the incident. When he died, he left instructions that he was to be buried 'neither within the church nor without it'. So the magician lies buried under the church wall, with half his tomb inside the building and half outside.

On the road across Batcombe Hill there is a stone pillar known as the Cross-and-Hand (or the Cross-in-Hand), which is thought to date from the 7th century. So far, antiquarians have failed to give an adequate account of its presence; but this lack is fully compensated by local legend.

One story tells of a priest who lost a holy relic while travelling along the road. When he discovered his loss, he hurried back and turned a corner to find hundreds of animals – sheep, oxen, rabbits and badgers – all kneeling in adoration. Suddenly, a shaft of fire from the sky illuminated the place where the lost relic lay, and the pillar was built to commemorate the miracle.

Another story, quoted by Thomas Hardy in *Tess of the D'Urbervilles*, is less pleasant. In this, the pillar marks the grave of a criminal who was tortured and hanged on the site. It is said that the man had sold his soul to the Devil, and sometimes, at night, his ghost is seen near the pillar.

BATH

Avon

11 miles southeast of Bristol

According to legend, the city's origins go back to 860 BC when Prince Bladud, father of 'the King Lear immortalised by Shakespeare, caught leprosy, was banished from the royal court and became a swineherd. His pigs also suffered from a skin disease, but they were cured after wallowing in pools of warm mud. The prince followed them in and he, too, was eventually cured. He returned to the court and, after becoming king, founded a settlement on the site of the pool.

The springs originate in the eastern Mendips, collecting mineral salts on the way and reaching the surface again in Bath. The therapeutic value of the spa waters was quickly recognised by the Romans after they invaded Britain in AD 43. Elaborate baths were built near a temple dedicated to Sulis Minerva; Sul was an ancient Celtic god, and Minerva was the Roman goddess of healing. Known as *Aquae Sulis* (Waters of Sul), the settlement flourished until the 5th century, when the legions were recalled to Rome.

The Roman remains vanished slowly beneath centuries of accumulated debris. But in 1727, long after the city had been re-established as a spa, workmen digging a sewer in Stall Street, at the western end of the baths, unearthed a gilded bronze head of Minerva. More discoveries were made in the 1750s, but it was not until the end of the last century that the Great

Bath of the Roman era was uncovered. Still lined with the lead put in place by Roman craftsmen almost 2000 years earlier, it is fed by springs from unknown sources far below the surface. Each day they produce 500,000 gallons of water at a constant 49°C (120°F).

With the exception of Hadrian's Wall, the bathing complex is Britain's greatest memorial to the Roman era. Many relics of Roman times, and others relating to Bath's history in general, are preserved in a museum adjoining the baths.

The exhibits include the bust of Minerva, astonishingly well-preserved despite its long burial, and the nightmarish head of a gorgon, discovered in 1790, that originally decorated the temple's pediment.

After AD 410, Bath declined and suffered greatly from Anglo-Saxon raids. Later it became an ecclesiastical centre and wool-manufacturing town. By the 10th century an abbey had been built by the Saxons and in AD 973 it witnessed the crowning of Edgar, the first king of all England. The ritual followed then became the basis for all future coronations.

In 1088, the See of Wells was transferred to Bath and the monastic church was rebuilt by John De Villula of Tours. However, the present abbey was created by Oliver King, Bishop of Bath and Wells between 1495 and 1503. He had a dream, later immortalised in stone at the western end of the abbey, in which angels climbed up and down ladders to Heaven and a voice urged 'a king to restore the church'. He took this to mean that he should restore the abbey.

This was the last great abbey church in England, the Benedictine 'Lantern of the West', but its completion was interrupted by the Dissolution of the Monasteries in the 1530s. During the next 40 years, the stained-glass windows and lead were plundered, and the abbey left to decay. Restoration work started in the 16th century, following a public subscription by Elizabeth I, and the abbey was finished by the 17th century.

The interior of the abbey is notable for its soaring traceries of fan-vaulting and for hundreds of memorial tablets. In addition to the many monuments, the abbey has a rare, portable wooden font and four 17th-century alms boxes.

Bath began to regain fame as a spa in the early 17th century when Anne of Denmark, wife of James I, took the waters in the hope of curing dropsy. She was followed by other royal visitors, but despite the benefit of royal patronage, 17th-century Bath left many things to be desired. It became notorious for pickpockets, duels, crooked gamblers and quack doctors.

Early in the 1700s, Dr William Oliver built a bath here for the treatment of gout, and his name is preserved in Bath Oliver biscuits. However, the development of Bath as a place for high society owed much to Richard 'Beau' Nash, a talented dandy who brought the *élite* of London to the baths, balls and assemblies that made the city a byword for elegance and fashion.

The 18th-century novelists Smollett and Fielding described Bath in their works, and it was still a favoured resort in the 19th century, when it appeared in the novels of Jane Austen and in Dickens's *Pickwick Papers*. The original Pump Room, the social centre of the spa, was built during Nash's long reign, but the present building dates from 1796.

ROMAN SPRINGS *The Great Bath was uncovered in the 1880s, and measures 83 ft by 40 ft at its surface.*

Today sedan chairs stand in the room where soft, sedate music is still played while visitors sip their tea, eat Bath buns and fill their glasses from a fountain that spouts the health-giving waters – waters which Dickens's character Sam Weller described as tasting 'like warm flat-irons'. Above the Pump Room's entrance the motto 'Water is best' is carved in Greek.

Nash made Bath synonymous with high fashion, good taste, order and discipline – an outlook that was shared by other men who left more tangible memorials of the city's golden age. One was Ralph Allen, who revolutionised the nation's postal services, making a huge fortune in the process. He bought the Combe Down quarries 2 miles south of the city to provide the architects and builders with the raw materials that they used to create a city of classical beauty. Allen's own house, Prior Park, was built in the Palladian style – named after the 16th-century Italian architect Andrea Palladio – and was intended to proclaim the beauties of Bath stone and its use throughout the city. Prior Park is about 1 mile southeast of Bath and, although the house is occupied by a school, a chapel in the house and the park, with its celebrated Palladian bridge, are open to visitors.

Many artists in stone have left their mark on Bath, but the most prolific was John Wood, a Yorkshireman devoted to the Palladian style. When Wood arrived in Bath in 1727, the city was still essentially medieval. His first great project, Queen Square, was started in 1729, but work on his masterpiece, The Circus, did not begin until 1754, the year of his death. Its circumference is divided into three equal arcs, each containing 11 houses. The frontages are ennobled by Doric, Ionic and Corinthian columns, and more than 365 motifs symbolising the arts and sciences from a frieze above the ground-floor windows.

Many old houses were demolished under Wood's rebuilding scheme, but some were saved, including the house in Lilliput Alley where Sally Lunn lived. She is said to have sold buns in the streets of Bath, and a type of bun is named after her.

Wood's son, John Wood the Younger, was born in 1717 and carried on his father's work. His greatest contribution to Bath's heritage was the Royal Crescent, a majestic sweep of 30 houses faced with 114 huge Ionic columns. The first house in the crescent is now the property of the Bath Preservation Trust. It has been restored, redecorated and filled with Georgian furnishings, so that visitors can see something of the comfortable lifestyle of upper-class Bath at the end of the 18th century.

John Wood the Younger also built the Assembly Rooms between 1769 and 1771. Housed in two elegant blocks, on Bennet Street and Alfred Street, are the magnificent rooms where fashionable society mingled with men and women of letters and music, danced in the 100 ft ballroom, or gambled in the adjoining card room. The Museum of Costume, one of the largest of its kind in the world, is housed in the restored Assembly Rooms. Its extensive collections include clothing and haberdashery of many periods, from Tudor times to the latest fashions.

Many houses throughout the city bear plaques recording famous residents of the past. These included characters as diverse as John Wesley, the founder of Methodism, Lord Nelson, Thomas Gainsborough and the Emperor Napoleon III of France. Until the end of the last century, Bath's streets echoed to the clatter of horses, and more than 30 relics of those days are preserved by the Carriage Museum, tucked away in Circus Mews. The Holburne of Menstrie Museum contains fine silver, porcelain and paintings of the 18th century (Gainsborough, J. M. W. Turner and George Stubbs), and also 20th-century craftwork belonging to the Crafts Study Centre.

The Octagon, in Milsom Street, built as a chapel in 1767, now houses the Royal Photographical Society's National Centre of Photography. Burrows Toy Museum is now in York Street.

Pulteney Bridge across the River Avon was designed in 1771 by Robert Adam, and is the only example of his work in Bath. Inspired by the Ponte Vecchio in Venice, Adam lined it with shops.

A walk down Great Pulteney Street to Sydney Gardens leads to the Kennet and Avon Canal with its elegant 19th-century bridges designed by the engineer John Rennie. The canal towpath leads past the locks and the old pumping-engine house at Widcombe to the junction with the Avon. The Victoria Suspension Bridge spanning the river was built in 1836. The suspension rods incline towards the piers – an unusual method of construction patented by the designer J. Dredge.

Further along the River Avon at Bathampton, a toll bridge was constructed in 1863. As it formed a vital link in the old turnpike system, special tolls were collected to recoup the cost of construction. The old toll house still stands and tolls are still payable.

At Claverton, just outside Bath, the American Museum is well worth a visit – its furniture and exhibits show the development of American craftsmanship and taste from the early settlers through to the turn of the 20th century.

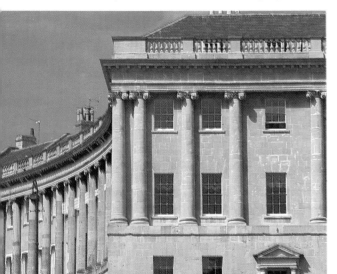

THE ROYAL CRESCENT *Designed by John Wood and begun in 1769, Bath's premier residences form a 600 ft long ellipse.*

BEACON HILL
Somerset
1 mile southeast of West Quantoxhead

Just about every range of hills in England has its Beacon Hill – sometimes more than one – where fires were lit to warn of the approaching Spanish Armada in 1588. They all have one thing in common – they can be seen for miles and are within view of other beacons. For the men who stood watch on the Quantocks Beacon Hill, the red glow on Crowcombe Fire Beacon and Hurley Beacon to the southeast would have been the signal to set ablaze their fiery warning. That warning would have been seen as far away as Dunkery Beacon on Exmoor and the Brecon Beacons across the Bristol Channel.

It was in the summer that the Spaniards came, and on any clear summer's day those far-off beacon hills can still be seen from the 1018 ft summit in the Quantocks – and in between lie sweeping panoramas of patchwork fields, wooded combes, gorse and heather-covered slopes and silver-grey sea.

To reach Beacon Hill, take the road from West Quantoxhead to Bicknoller. The first turn on the left at Staple Farm (opposite the road to Williton and Mine-head) leads to a parking place on the hills. From here there is a fine walk to the summit of the hill.

Beacon Hill is the last point in the Quantocks higher than 1000 ft before the hills drop away to the shores of Bridgwater Bay. The summit is crossed by the prehistoric track coming up from the southeast, and marks the end of the Ridgeway, or Pack Way, for walkers setting out from Lydeard Hill, 6 miles southeast.

BEAMINSTER

Dorset
5 miles north of Bridport

This small town, set among steep farmland hills, was much loved by Dorset's early 19th-century poet William Barnes, who wrote in the dialect of the county, and by the novelist Thomas Hardy, who made the town the 'Emminster' of his *Tess of the D'Urbervilles*. Its pinnacled market cross and prosperous 18th-century houses, built in the golden Ham Hill stone of the region or painted in attractive regional greens and blues, give the square an illusion of size; and the sparkling little River Brit, running along the side of the main street, adds charm.

Vivid green wooded hills descend close to the town on both sides, and there are rewarding walks in almost any direction. An enjoyable drive leads over Hackthorn Hill up the 800 ft rise of Toller Down, where there are secluded picnic spots with grand views over the surrounding countryside.

BERE REGIS

Dorset
7 miles northwest of Wareham

The Saxon parish church was largely rebuilt by Cardinal Morton, Henry VII's Chancellor, and is noted for the painted timber roof of the nave. Its arches, supported by figures of the 12 apostles in 15th-century dress, bear the arms of the Cardinal's various offices. The church has become a place of pilgrimage for admirers of Hardy's novel *Tess of the D'Urbervilles*. Its heroine, Tess, was buried here, and a 15th-century window bears the lion rampant crest of the old Dorset family of Turberville, on whom Hardy based his novel. On Woodbury Hill, just east of the village, stand the remains of an Iron Age fortification from which there are views across heath and river valleys stretching eastwards towards Poole. One of the most famous fairs in Wessex took place here until the First World War.

MURDER MOST FOUL *It was in Berkeley's fastness that the unfortunate Edward II was done to death.*

BERKELEY

Gloucestershire
5 miles west of Dursley

Berkeley Castle, built in the 12th century, stands in lovely grounds in a tranquil town where the liveliest noise comes from the hounds of the Berkeley Hunt in the kennels close by. The grounds have a terraced garden with an Elizabethan bowling alley and in the park there are red and fallow deer and wild geese. The Berkeley family have occupied the castle continuously since the 12th century. The massive Norman keep, dungeon, and curtain wall date from that time, and the great hall and kitchen were added in 1340. The state apartments contain paintings, tapestries and fine furniture and silver.

It was in the castle that Edward II was murdered in 1327, allegedly 'with a hoot brooche put into the secret place posteriale' – a gruesome end for the homosexual monarch. The king, ousted from the throne by his wife and her lover – and confined for months at Berkeley – paid a terrible price for his ineffective rule and injudicious choice of friends.

The parish church has a superb east window of nine lights, filled with pictures of Christ healing the sick – a memorial to Edward Jenner, discoverer of vaccination, who was born in Berkeley and returned there before his death in 1823. He is buried in the chancel.

Berkeley is the centre of the Vale of Berkeley – thousands of acres of flat land stretching for 15 miles on the east bank of the Severn. Little water-courses form crisscross patterns, with lanes crossing them on

stone humpbacked bridges beside meadows of grazing cows. A canal passes through the Vale from Gloucester to Sharpness – a vital 17 mile waterway which links Gloucester with the sea.

Five miles from Berkeley Castle and on the Berkeley Estate is the Wildfowl Trust, founded by Peter Scott. This has the world's largest and most varied collection of wildfowl, in beautiful surroundings. There are more than 2500 swans, geese and ducks of around 180 species, and there are six flocks of flamingos. The most spectacular sight is in winter, when thousands of wild geese find sanctuary in the Severn Estuary. From towers on the Trust land, geese can be seen feeding.

BIBURY
Gloucestershire
7 miles northeast of Cirencester

William Morris, the 19th-century artist and poet, thought Bibury the most beautiful village in England. Another Victorian, J. Arthur Gibbs, wrote of it eloquently in *A Cotswold Village*, published in 1898.

The slow-moving River Coln snakes between wooded banks, and is spanned by a road bridge dated 1770. On the bank of the mill stream, which flows into the river, stands a terrace of gabled and stone-tiled cottages called Arlington Row. The cottages were converted from a 14th-century sheephouse in the early 17th century to house weavers supplying cloth for the nearby Arlington Mill. This water-driven mill was built in the 17th century, but was restored and enlarged in 1859. Although originally a corn-mill it was also used for fulling – cleaning and thickening the weave of newly woven cloth by beating it under water with wheel-operated hammers. It is now a folk museum and contains a collection of furniture from the Cotswolds Arts and Crafts movement. Some of the mill's machinery can be seen in operation. Next door is a trout hatchery, open to the public every day during the summer.

The centre of Bibury is the square, overlooked by the Saxon Church of St Mary and dignified stone-built houses. St Mary's has many later additions, mostly Norman and medieval, but much of its Saxon work is still visible, particularly in the chancel. The churchyard contains carved chest tombs and headstones of the 17th and 18th century, whose rococo motifs are now coloured by lichen.

BICKNOLLER HILL
Somerset
4 miles southeast of Watchet

A pathway climbing up through a beech-lined combe leads to Bicknoller Hill, one of the most impressive points in the Quantocks. The route, particularly on a crisp autumn morning, provides a fusion of pastel colours, with the beeches, oaks and limes in the combe giving way to brambles and bracken as the hill is climbed. Red deer may be seen here, or may be heard in November when the throaty bellow of the stag's rutting call echoes through the woods.

PICTUREBOOK PRETTINESS *Beloved by tourists, Bibury's Arlington Row presents a classic Cotswold scene. The central cottages are medieval, with many carved stone features.*

Iron Age man settled on Bicknoller Hill, not on the top but on the southwestern slope, and the remains of the encampment – Trendle Ring – are still visible. Its builders obviously chose the site for its wide views – it is one of the best vantage spots in the Quantocks. About 4 miles to the west are the Brendon Hills and, beyond them, the dark shape of Exmoor; 8 miles to the south lies the wide Vale of Taunton Deane and the town of Wellington, with the Blackdown Hills rising behind the town. On a clear day Wellington's Monument can be seen 14 miles away on the northern edge of the hills, its narrow finger prodding the fluffy clouds above Wellington Hill. The obelisk commemorates the victor of Waterloo.

BIRDLIP HILL AND CRICKLEY HILL
Gloucestershire
6 miles southeast of Gloucester

The commanding and ancient peaks of Birdlip and Crickley Hills overlook the whole of the Vale of Gloucester to the Welsh hills.

Birdlip Hill has cool beechwoods and a windy, bare turf peak with views southwest to the enfolding Witcombe Wood, curving round the escarpment to Buckholt Wood and Cooper's Hill. The woods are private, and visitors should keep to the public footpaths that give access to the wealth of mixed woodland, birds and forest plants. The Roman Ermin Way runs east from the village of Birdlip, perched above its precipitous hill, and from the Iron Age burial mound at Barrow Wake – just north of the village – came the bronze Birdlip Mirror now in Gloucester City Museum.

Crickley Hill, a Country Park, has traces of both a New Stone Age settlement and an Iron Age promontory fort. The site was abandoned early in the Iron Age, but reoccupied during the 6th century AD. The sides of the promontory are steep and rugged, and modern quarrying has exaggerated them. Traces of quarrying can be found all over the hill, which has resulted in fascinating exposed geological formations. There is a nature trail on Crickley, together with geological and archaeological trails, and there are superb views to the Malverns and Cheltenham.

Both hills can be reached by road off the A417, and there are good footpaths. Not far from the road, a monument in memory of the young geologist Peter Hopkins clearly shows the geological formation so vividly characterised here by the twin escarpments of the Malverns and Cotswolds. Describing 'over 500 million years of Britain's history', the monument is made from sandstone, blue lias limestone, and Malvern gneiss found on the twin escarpments, and the 150-million-year-old pea grit and oolite limestone to be seen virtually underfoot.

BISHOPS CANNINGS
Wiltshire
3 miles northeast of Devizes

All Wiltshiremen are Moonrakers, and if anyone should be credited with earning them the nickname, it is the villagers of Bishops Cannings. Not those who live here today, of course, but the smugglers of the 16th to 18th centuries, who ran a profitable and illicit black market in Hollands gin and other forms of liquor, slaking the thirst of the Dutch and Flemish wool merchants whose headquarters was Swindon.

The story goes that one moonlit night, a patrol of Excisemen discovered two villagers from Bishops Cannings raking the surface of a local pond. When asked what they were doing, the men pointed to the reflection of the moon in the water, and said they were trying to fish out 'thik yaller cheese'. The Excisemen took them for idiots and rode off laughing. But the Moonrakers had the last laugh. In fact they were collecting kegs of liquor hidden in the pond.

Bishops Cannings is one of the oldest villages in Wiltshire, much older than the town of Devizes. Throughout the Middle Ages it belonged to the Bishops of Salisbury (hence the name), and the dean and canons of Salisbury Cathedral had a manor here; these high ecclesiastical connections are still reflected by the splendour of the church.

Built in the 12th century, and added to later, the church bears a certain similarity in design to Salisbury Cathedral, not least in its elegant tapering spire, perched on a two-storey tower. The entire building is larger and more imposing than you would expect in such a small parish, and both inside and out it is rich in carvings of birds, dragons, human faces, grotesques and animals. The organ, constructed in 1809, was given to the church by William Bayley, a local man

who sailed round the world as Captain Cook's navigator. A rare item in the church is a meditation seat, on which are painted a large hand and Latin inscriptions about sin and death.

The village is a dignified place of thatch, half-timbering, box hedges and neat farms, set among elms (though not as many as formerly, since Dutch elm disease took its toll) on the level plain of the Pewsey Vale. The great rounded mass of Roundway Down, where Royalists won a bloody victory over Cromwell's forces on July 13, 1643, stands about 1 mile to the west. Along a ridge just to the north extends a section of the Wansdyke, the impressive but still largely unexplained earthwork which stretches from the Berkshire boundary through Wiltshire to northern Somerset.

BISLEY
Gloucestershire
4 miles east of Stroud

Local people call the village 'Bisley-God-Help-Us', because of the winter winds which sweep across this remote, hilltop community. Its remoteness also contributed to its decline as a textile village at the time of the Industrial Revolution, and an old rhyme tells of 'Beggarly Bisley'. But neither local cynicism nor unkind verse can detract from Bisley's unarguable charm.

When entered from the southwest, the village appears as an amphitheatre of gabled, greystone houses climbing in terraces on either side of the main street. In George Street the Bear Inn, once the court

BISLEY *At the top of George Street stands the 17th-century Bear Inn, with its distinctive supporting columns.*

house, has detached 17th-century columns supporting the upper floor. Close by is a lock-up of 1824.

Church Hill climbs steeply to All Saints, with its lych gate at the entrance to the churchyard. A crumbling stone edifice in the churchyard is a 13th-century 'poor soul's light'. It was used to hold candles for Masses said for the souls in purgatory, and is believed to be the only outdoor example in England.

The Church of All Saints dates from the 13th century, and was restored during the 19th century. Its rector at that time was Thomas Keble, brother of John Keble, the poet and divine, after whom Keble College, Oxford was named. Thomas Keble was also responsible for the restoration of Bisley's seven wells, which now gush from spouts set in a gabled semicircle below the church. The wells are dressed on Ascension Day.

BLACK DOWN
Dorset
5 miles west of Dorchester

Gorse and heather cover the summit of Black Down, 777 ft above the sea and surmounted by a monument to Vice-Admiral Sir Thomas Masterman Hardy, Nelson's flag-captain at Trafalgar. The monument was erected by public subscription in 1846, and quickly became a familiar part of the Dorset landscape. The 70 ft high, octagonal stone stack captures the eye from far and wide, and from its base there are magnificent sea views across to the Isle of Wight, to Golden Cap and to Start Point almost 60 miles south-

west in Devon. A bridle-path winds down from the summit of Black Down to Portesham where Hardy lived as a boy, in a modest Georgian stone house which still stands.

The Downs in this area are rich in prehistoric burial mounds and standing stones. About a quarter of a mile west of the path, on the hill above Portesham, there is a partly reconstructed New Stone Age chambered tomb called the Hell Stone. At the end of the Valley of Stones, in a field $1\frac{1}{2}$ miles northwest of Portesham, lie the remains of another New Stone Age tomb known as The Grey Mare and her Colts. A bronze Age stone circle stands 1 mile to the southeast of the Grey Mare near the footpath to Portesham Hill. To the north of Black Down, the outline of ancient fields can be traced in the grass.

BLACK DOWN
Somerset
$1\frac{1}{4}$ miles south of Burrington

The highest peak on the Mendip Hills is also, without doubt, the loneliest. This long, seemingly unending hill rises above the limestone plateau like a giant tortoise, gaunt and forbidding against the soft countryside which surrounds it.

It is not surprising that Black Down presents a different appearance to the rest of the Mendip range, for the 1067 ft peak is sandstone, not limestone. The different rock structure is apparent in the vegetation: the thin, peaty soil is covered with whortle-berries, rough grass, ling and heath which, in the depth of winter, take on a black appearance, believed to be the reason for its name.

The best way up Black Down is to take the footpath that leads from beside Ellick House, which is at the top of Burrington Combe on the B3134, just a few yards beyond the Burrington Ham parking area. A series of tracks leads to the summit, which can be reached comfortably in less than 30 minutes.

The hill is crowned by the Beacon Batch Bronze Age barrows, and a line of what appear to be molehills – these were wartime decoys to simulate a town. On a clear day the views from the top are truly memorable: north over the soft folds of the hills to Bristol and beyond; west to Flat Holm and Steep Holm out in the Bristol Channel; south over the Somerset Levels to Glastonbury Tor.

BLACK ROCK
Somerset
2 miles east of Cheddar

Less than 2 miles from Cheddar lies the National Trust property Black Rock, a place so quiet, so unspoilt, that it could be miles from any tourist spot. Black Rock was once part of the medieval Mendip Forest, a royal hunting preserve, and is at the northeastern end of Cheddar Gorge. Here the gorge opens out into two valleys, one of which runs northeastwards and then north to Long Wood. Just south of Long Wood, the path splits again, and heads northeast along another valley. This is a historic trail; almost 2000 years ago it was a track leading to the Roman lead and silver mines at Charterhouse, 2 miles away through Velvet Bottom. In the valley itself were limestone quarries.

Even on the roughest days, Black Rock is a sheltered

spot. It has a wide range of trees and plants that are typical of those found in limestone areas – mostly ashes and yews – but on the hillside above the valley, larches and Scots pines also grow. In spring, before the trees are in full leaf, dog's mercury and bluebells flower, and along the dry-stone walls there are many lime-loving plants, notably spleenworts and liverworts.

BLAISE HAMLET
Avon
Located in northwest Bristol

Built for a Quaker banker, John Scandrett Harford, in 1796, Blaise Castle is appropriately plain and sober. Now used as a museum of social history, it looks across a deep gorge, landscaped by Humphry Repton, towards a mock castle on the opposite crest. An 18th-century cornmill and a dairy designed by John Nash – George IV's favourite architect – stand in Blaise Castle's grounds.

John Nash also designed the ten detached cottages which are dotted haphazardly around a village green in Blaise Hamlet. Each cottage is of a different design and they were originally built in 1809 to house pensioners of the Blaise estate.

BLANDFORD FORUM
Dorset
16 miles northwest of Bournemouth

The elegant Georgian appearance of Blandford Forum is the result of a fire which devastated the centre of the town in the summer of 1731. The fire started in a tallow-chandler's house in the middle of Blandford, and quickly spread from one thatched building to another. The primitive, wooden fire engines were destroyed by the flames, and a strong, high wind carried pieces of blazing thatch to the neighbouring villages of Bryanston and Blandford St Mary – parts of which also burnt down. Only 40 or 50 houses escaped out of a total of 500 in the town at the time, and nothing of its Norman origins remains.

A nationwide appeal to rebuild the town was then launched. George II gave £1000 to the fund, and two local builders, William Bastard and his brother John, were commissioned to supervise the work. They began immediately and by 1760 the 'new' Blandford had risen from the ashes of the old, distinguished by buildings of grey and green stone and shades of brick and mauve.

The brothers cleared many old buildings from the Market Place, and rebuilt the Town Hall and the large and handsome parish church of St Peter and St Paul – one of the finest of the period, faced with stone and with a fine square tower crowned by a cupola – whose churchyard now contains the Bastard family tomb. Working mainly in red brick, they also rebuilt the almshouses, the grammar school and many dignified town houses.

In 1760, to commemorate the completion of the work, John Bastard designed and built the Portland stone Fire Monument – complete with Grecian columns and a triangular gable-end – which stands on its own in the Market Place. Known in the town as 'Bastard's Pump', it was meant to supply water for fire hoses in the event of a future blaze.

Part of an inscription on the back of the monument

reads, 'in grateful Acknowledgement of the DIVINE MERCY, that has raised this Town, like the PHAENIX from it's ashes, to it's present beautiful and flourishing State ...'

Not all of Blandford dates from Georgian times, however. Among the few buildings which survived the Great Fire are the mid-17th-century Old House, in The Close; Dale House, dating from 1689, in Salisbury Street; and the Ryves Almshouses, built in 1682 with money left by George Ryves, Sheriff of Dorset. East of the town are the remains of Blandford's only medieval building, St Leonard's Chapel. It was built in the 13th century as a leper hospital and rebuilt in the 15th century to house the old and infirm. A museum of local history in East Street is open daily, except Mondays, from Easter until the end of September.

Damory Street and Damory Court Street owe their names to the French nuns of Ste Marie. In the 13th century, the nuns were given this part of Blandford, which came to be known as Dame Marie's Manor. Bryanston, with its famous public school, takes its name from Brian de Insula, a wealthy Dorset landowner in the reign of Henry III (1216–72).

Blandford Forum is set at an important crossing of the River Stour and was listed in the Domesday Survey of 1086 as Blaneford, meaning 'the place by the ford'. In the 13th century it was called Cheping Blaneford until its name was changed by Latin-speaking tax officials, who translated *cheping* – the Saxon word for 'market' – into forum, or public meeting-place. The town appears in the Wessex novels of Thomas Hardy (1840–1928) as Shottsford Forum, and Edmund Spenser mentioned the town in *The Faerie Queen*, published in 1590. Signposts on the road from Blandford to Salisbury point the way 'To 6d Handley' – the Saxon-named village of Sixpenny Handley.

BLEADON
Somerset
4 miles southeast of Weston-super-Mare

It is said that this place was originally called 'Bleed Down' in commemoration of a bloody skirmish between local people and Danish raiders in longboats. Leaving their boats unguarded turned out to be a fatal error for the Danes – the boats were cut adrift and with no means of escape, not one of the pirates survived.

A few miles to the east of Bleadon lies Loxton. The pathway which leads up from the centre of the village to the top of Bleadon Hill offers magnificent views in all directions. To the south is the solitary stack of Brent Knoll, an island of limestone rising over 450 ft above the marshes of the Somerset plain; east is the main bulk of the Mendips. Walking along the ridge of the hill opens up a marvellous vista of the Bristol Channel, Brean Down, the islands of Steep Holm and Flat Holm and, on clear days, the hills of South Wales.

In its early stages the path, the West Mendip Way, climbs steeply. Clumps of oak and beech line the pathway before the upper reaches of the hill are reached, where the vegetation becomes more sparse, and bracken and brambles predominate. Beyond Christon Plantation, the scenery becomes well wooded again and here you are likely to startle a pheasant into laborious flight. In wet weather the path at this point is very sticky, so sturdy footwear is recommended.

BOCKHAMPTON, HIGHER AND LOWER

Dorset
2 miles east of Dorchester

> *'It faces west, and round the back and sides*
> *High beeches, bending, hang a veil of boughs,*
> *And sweep against the roof.'*

This was Thomas Hardy's own description of the small, thatched cottage at Higher Bockhampton in which he was born in 1840. The cottage belongs to the National Trust and is open by appointment.

Hardy died in Dorchester – which he renamed 'Casterbridge' in his novels – in 1928. The centrepiece of his writing was the partly imagined 'South Wessex' – Dorset – whose rich farmlands, woods, hills, heaths, coasts, villages and towns he incorporated in his books and poems. For example, *Tess of the D'Urbervilles* draws on many Dorset locations, including Bere Regis and the valleys of the Frome and Piddle. The village of 'Weatherbury' in *Far from the Madding Crowd* is Puddletown, and Woodbury Hill nearby becomes 'Greenhill'. Hardy's wild 'Egdon Heath' in *The Return of the Native* is a mixture of areas around Puddletown Heath.

Although Hardy's ashes are interred at Westminster Abbey, his heart lies buried in Stinsford churchyard, not far from the swift-flowing River Frome. From the footbridge across a stream, a path leads westwards through old water-meadows of Grey's Bridge and Dorchester. Eastwards it runs alongside the stream, starred with the white flowers of river crowfoot and alive with strands of water weed, to the stone-and-thatch village of Lower Bockhampton, where Hardy went to school.

About 1 mile's walk or drive northwards across the downs is Higher Bockhampton, and the wildlife sanctuary of Thorncombe Wood. From here a nature trail about 1½ miles long leads through a magnificent collection of sweet chestnuts, beeches and oaks, and on the eastern side of the wood through 20 acres of black heath, a tangle of furze, birch saplings, holly, heather and rhododendrons.

A side track from the trail leads up the hillside to Hardy's cottage. Where the Great Heath once swept down to the little barred back window there are now the dark conifers of the Forestry Commission's Puddletown Forest. Along the 2¼ mile Forest Walk you may glimpse sika deer and see badger tracks.

BOURNEMOUTH

Dorset
24 miles southwest of Southampton

The Victorian love-affair with the seaside changed Bournemouth from a desolate heath to a bustling resort in less than 50 years. Rich men built their villas on the pine-clad slopes of the Bourne valley, speculators erected hotels on the high cliff tops, and by 1900 the town's population had risen from 695 (in 1851) to 59,000. Bournemouth has a mild climate, sandy beaches and fine coastal views, and the town's planners have landscaped the natural beauty of the valley and the Bourne stream to make spacious parks and gardens. Behind the gardens spreads a modern town of shops, hotels, theatres and cinemas, giving way to shaded streets where Victorian villas still stand among scented pines. Bournemouth was the 'Sandbourne' of Hardy's *Tess of the D'Urbervilles*.

A Dorset squire named Lewis Tregonwell founded Bournemouth in 1811, when he built a summer home on the site of what is now the Royal Exeter Hotel. It was the only building, apart from an inn, on the wild stretch of heathland that followed the sweeping curve of Poole Bay from Hengistbury Head in the east to Durlston Head in the west. The coastline could have been made for the holidaymaker: rugged and split by deep ravines, called chines, it opens out to the sea.

In 1837 Sir George Tapps-Gervis, a local landowner, conceived the idea of establishing a resort on the land to the east of Tregonwell's estate, and in that year Westover Villas, Westover Gardens and the Bath Hotel were all built.

A jetty was built in 1856, but was replaced in 1859. This second structure was itself replaced by an iron pier in 1880 which forms part of the present pier. In 1866 The Arcade was built on the site of a rustic bridge crossing the Bourne stream.

The railway came to Bournemouth in 1870, bringing more visitors, but the town had little to offer in the way of entertainment until the first Winter Gardens were built in 1875.

This building was used as a concert hall until 1935, when it was dismantled and replaced by an indoor bowling green – the first in the country. The building was taken over by the Royal Air Force during the Second World War, and after the war it was discovered that the hall had good acoustic properties. The Winter Gardens then became the permanent home of the Bournemouth Symphony Orchestra.

Fifty years passed before Bournemouth had another major centre of entertainment – the Pavilion. This was opened in 1929 and includes a 1600-seat theatre, ballroom and restaurant with terraces overlooking the Lower Gardens through which flows the Bourne stream.

The Lower Gardens are the hub of Bournemouth's seafront. They lie in a valley, bordered on one side by footpaths winding among pine trees where squirrels live. The gardens follow the Bourne, to form the Central Gardens and Upper Gardens, from which a short walk leads to Meyrick Park – pine-clad estate of 154 acres.

Five of Bournemouth's churches are listed as being of architectural or historical interest, the only one of great antiquity being St Andrew's, at Kinson, which has a 12th-century tower and 14th-century chancel.

St Peter's, in Hinton Road, was completed in 1879 in the Gothic style and has a square tower and a spire. In the churchyard is the Shelley Tomb, burial place of Mary Shelley (1797–1851) author of the novel *Frankenstein* and wife of poet Percy Bysshe Shelley.

The Russell-Cotes Art Gallery and Museum specialises in Victoriana. The building is an interesting example of Victorian architecture with a large conservatory, bowfronted upper windows and pinnacled roof.

The Rothesay Museum has Italian paintings and pottery, English furniture, African objects, and arms and armour. The Big Four Railway Museum has a large collection of locomotive nameplates and other railway relics. The British Typewriter Museum has nearly 400 machines on display.

SEASIDE BEAUTY *Bournemouth's garden paths climb steeply down to the promenade below* (overleaf).

BOURTON-ON-THE-WATER
Gloucestershire
4 miles southwest of Stow-on-the-Wold

The 'water' in the name is the River Windrush, flowing gently through the village beneath low stone bridges – two of them 18th century – and alongside a tree-shaded green. A riverside path leads to quiet corners where willows dip their branches in the water, and beyond the green are secluded lanes with cottages and houses of golden Cotswold stone.

But the village can also be explored in miniature, by visiting the model built in the gardens of the Old New Inn. It was the work of the present landlord's father and a small team of craftsmen in the 1930s, and is a one-ninth scale replica of Bourton complete in almost every detail – including a model of the model itself.

Fascinating though this Bourton-in-miniature is, however, it is a place where nothing moves, which cannot be said of the village's other major attraction, Birdland. There, in the grounds of a Tudor manor, brightly plumaged parrots and macaws fly among the trees, and penguins swim in a glass-sided pool. There are flamingos and toucans in the aviary, and hummingbirds and sunbirds in the tropical houses.

In Sherborne Street, by the bridge, a corn-mill – now a motor museum – and its adjacent cottages date from the 18th century or earlier. The Old Manse, close by, was built in 1784 and is now a hotel. Across the bridge in the High Street stands the Church of St Lawrence, with a 14th-century chancel and Georgian tower.

BRADFORD-ON-AVON
Wiltshire
3 miles northwest of Trowbridge

One day in 1856 workmen making repairs to some cottages in Bradford uncovered two carved angels. The vicar of Holy Trinity Church, Canon William Jones, had long suspected that there was a Saxon church hidden in the town and had noticed the cruciform shape of the cottages being repaired. So, seeing the two angels, he realised that they must be Saxon and that this was probably the church he had been looking for. But he had to wait some 14 years for final confirmation. Then at last a cluster of surrounding buildings was cleared away and a pure Saxon church was spectacularly revealed.

The Church of St Laurence had been built about AD 700 by St Aldhelm, the Abbot of Malmesbury, Frome and Bradford. The church belonged to a monastery which was destroyed by the Danes. St Laurence's then 'vanished' for 11 centuries. A plain and simple building, made of rough-hewn stone, it is only 38 ft long. During its 'lost' years it had been used as a school, a charnel house where the bodies of the dead were left, and finally as a house. At the same time it had also been gradually hemmed in by other buildings. St Laurence's was fully restored during the 1870s and today it is one of the town's chief treasures.

Set in the green Avon valley, Bradford rises above the river on a steep limestone slope. Its terraces of houses and cottages seem to grow out of the hillside, and the buildings are mostly made of the local Bath stone. This gives Bradford a unity which has developed over the last 300 to 400 years.

The highest of its three main terraces is Tory, from

the word 'tor' meaning 'high place'. It originally consisted of more than 30 weavers' homes; some have been restored or replaced, especially at the eastern end. Until the 1950s, the 18th-century houses at the western end had kitchens hewn out of caves in the rocky hillside. Nearby, the Chapel of St Mary was originally a hospice for Glastonbury-bound pilgrims.

Lower down is the second main terrace, Middle Rank, whose late 17th-century weavers' cottages have also been rebuilt or renovated. And farther down

again is Newtown, linked to the higher terraces by a steep road called Conigre Hill. 'Conigre' is an old word which means 'rabbit warren'.

Newtown can be reached by climbing up Barton Steps, which leads from Barton Orchard, another terrace of weavers' houses. Built in the 18th century as a unit, these were recently saved from falling into ruin and renovated. Just behind the terrace is Lady Well, a spring which bubbles from beneath a house built in the 17th century.

TOWN BRIDGE *Spanning the River Avon at Bradford is this nine-arched bridge, dating from the 13th and 17th centuries. The small building was the local gaol.*

A walk across the nearby meadow takes you to the early 14th-century Barton Bridge, and to Barton Farm Country Park beyond. The farm originally provided food for Shaftesbury Abbey and, after the Dissolution of the Monasteries in the 1530s, it continued to be worked until 1971, when the farmland was made into a country park.

Close by is Bradford's other main stone-walled treasure – the 14th-century tithe barn. It also belonged to the abbey and housed farm produce and the tithe (one-tenth) of its yearly output which went to the nuns. Almost 170 ft long and 33 ft wide, it is one of the largest tithe barns in England. Its steeply pitched roof is supported by massive timbers.

Bradford's centre lies to the northeast. There, the name of Barton, meaning farm, is found in Dutch Barton, a block of houses in Church Street which were the homes of 17th-century Dutch weavers who brought great prosperity to the town.

Gloucester, Somerset and Wiltshire were the great sheep farming counties of the west of England and by the 1630s Bradford was a thriving centre of the woollen cloth trade. In the early 1700s Daniel Defoe – author of *Robinson Crusoe* – observed: 'Clothiers in this county were worth ten thousand to forty thousand pounds a man'. The merchants handed out wool to be spun and woven by workers in the town and outlying districts – spinners and weavers working in their own homes. In 1791 the workers rioted when machines were first introduced but their action was in vain. Soon after 1800 there were 30 water-powered cloth factories in Bradford-on-Avon. By 1905, however, the last of these had closed down as the centre of the trade began to shift to Yorkshire.

The chief shopping areas are Market Street and Silver Street, which are joined by The Shambles – a narrow lane for pedestrians. It contains two fine timber-framed buildings and its post office has a rare Edward VIII monogram.

Spanning the River Avon, the Town Bridge connects the north side of Bradford to the south. The bridge has nine short arches and dates mostly from the 17th century, though two of the arches are 13th century. A small, dome-shaped building at the south end of the bridge is called the Chapel, but despite its name it was, in fact, a lock-up. Since it was often occupied by drunks, it became known locally as the Blind House.

Bradford's only 'country house', The Hall – also known as Kingston House – is an Elizabethan-style building near the river in the east of the town. Built in the early 17th century by a clothier named John Hall, it was restored in about 1850. The gardens are open all year. There, the main attractions include the Tudor-style stables, two temples – one probably Georgian, the other probably Victorian – and an eight-sided dovecote.

Southwest of the town is a small stone house of great charm, Westwood Manor. Founded in about 1400, it was enlarged in 1480 and again after 1515, when wealthy clothier Thomas Horton bought the house. The inside porches of the manor are panelled in oak – a decorative draught-excluding device. The hedges in the modern gardens have been trimmed into various topiary designs.

BRENT KNOLL
Somerset
2 miles northeast of Burnham-on-Sea

Iron Age people who lived in the 4 acre fort on top of Brent Knoll enjoyed a sweeping view from its 499 ft eminence over what is now lowland Somerset and its enclosing hills.

The earthwork on the Knoll is thought to have been re-fortified during the Danish invasions of the 9th century. The *Anglo-Saxon Chronicle* records a battle in which men of Somerset and Dorset banded together to defeat the Danes in AD 845 – perhaps near Battleborough Farm under the southern flank of the Knoll, thought to have been a farm since the 9th century.

Brent Knoll village, sometimes known as South Brent, has some fine old stone houses, set in orchards and well-maintained gardens. But the village's great pride is the Church of St Michael, with its Norman doorway, carved oak roof and three remarkable carved bench-ends. The apocryphal story goes that some time in the Middle Ages the Abbot of Glastonbury tried to seize revenues from the parish priest, who succeeded in foiling him – and the bench-ends were carved to celebrate the village's victory.

The first shows a fox dressed in the abbot's robes rounding up a group of animals and a flock of geese; in the second, the victims are shown in revolt, stripping the abbot of his robes and putting him in the stocks; and, finally, he is hanged, with the geese pulling on the rope. To add to the insult, the abbot's monks are carved with pigs' heads.

THE FOX OUTFOXED *The final bench-end at Brent Knoll shows the execution of the abbot/fox by rebellious animals.*

BRIANTSPUDDLE
Dorset
2 miles southwest of Bere Regis

Narrow lanes hemmed in by tall hedges crisscross the mid-Dorset countryside. They skirt the sides of grassy combes and trace a splattering way through muddy farmyards, leading the visitor suddenly to a series of hidden villages. Briantspuddle is one of these. It has no church and no inn, and consists solely of a string of whitewashed cottages with thatched roofs.

Between the two world wars Briantspuddle was part of a remarkable agricultural experiment. Sir Ernest Debenham, head of the large London store at the time, tried to bring scientific methods and factory-style efficiency to agriculture in the area, with intensive pig, poultry and dairy farming. The experiment was ahead of its time, but Sir Ernest's legacy lives on in the cottages – some of which were restored and others newly built. The Ring, for example, a group of cottages with two turrets capped with thatch, was built in 1919 as a dairy farm.

A few hundred yards west of the main street lies Bladen Valley, a hamlet purpose-built for estate workers during the First World War. Broad green verges, studded with clumps of daffodils in spring, sweep up past colour-washed cottages with thatched roofs. At one end of the hamlet is a war memorial sculpted in Portland stone by the artist-craftsman Eric Gill. Although it was modelled on a medieval market cross, it is entirely modern in feel. Around the base run the comforting words of the 15th-century mystic Juliana of Norwich: 'It is sooth that sin is cause of all this pain, But all shall be well and all shall be well and all manner of thing shall be well.'

BRIDGWATER

Somerset
19 miles northeast of Taunton

A quiet quay on the River Parrett serves as a reminder that this town was a busy port until it became overshadowed by the port of Bristol. Modern shops now line the quay, but it is still used by small coastal vessels. A tidal bore still sweeps up the river when the tide is flowing.

On the waterfront the Water Gate and a length of wall are all that remain of a 13th-century castle. Bridgwater gave Cromwell his great admiral Robert Blake (1599–1657). Blake's reputed birthplace is now a museum.

The 14th-century Church of St Mary survived the Civil War, and from its tower the rebel Duke of Monmouth surveyed Sedgemoor in 1685 before his defeat by the Royalists. The church has a 175 ft spire and a fine Jacobean wooden screen.

Castle Street, built by the Duke of Chandos in about 1720, has some good Georgian architecture, and The Lions on West Quay is an outstanding house of that period.

The four-day St Matthew's Fair in September and the Guy Fawkes Carnival are big events in Bridgwater.

BRIDPORT

Dorset
14 miles west of Dorchester

Rope and nets of all kinds have been made at Bridport for nearly 1000 years. In the past the bulk of the rope output was for the rigging of sailing ships. But ropes for gallows were also made here, and the hangman's noose was nicknamed the 'Bridport dagger'. The town is still the biggest net-making centre in Europe and the Bridport Museum – housed in a building dating from the early 16th century – has displays of rope-making apparatus.

The long gardens at the rear of Bridport houses were originally used as rope-walks, places where the flax strands were laid out and twisted into shape.

South of Bridport on the water, is the small port town of West Bay, popular with tourists for its fishing and sailing, as well as its dramatic sandstone cliffs. It is quite unspoilt and has two good bathing beaches, one of shingle and one of pebble. Old cottages and a slate-hung early 19th-century customs house, now a café, fringe the beach.

BRISTOL

Avon
106 miles west of London

In Bristol – city of contrasts – old docks, almshouses and inns steeped in history stand side by side with modern shopping and entertainment complexes and multi-storey car parks; it is a city of flowers, too, and colourful, massed displays beautify many of Bristol's aspects. Originally known as *Bricgstoc* (the place of the bridge), permanent settlement probably began in Bristol in Anglo-Saxon times. Unearthed coins show that by the reign of Ethelred the Unready (978–1013), Bristol had its own mint.

The settlement grew up around its harbour on the River Avon, and its importance as a port increased after the Norman Conquest. A castle was built on the narrow neck of land east of the town, between the rivers Avon and Frome, and it became the Key to the West. The trade of Bristowe (as it became known in the Middle Ages) increased rapidly during the 12th and 13th centuries, and as a result its area doubled and its wharfage increased. During the 14th century it became a major wool-exporting port, sending cargoes to Ireland and the Baltic countries.

Stimulated by sailors' tales of new lands and driven by the economic need for fresh markets and fishing grounds, Bristol's merchants dispatched ships in search of them. The most renowned, John Cabot, set sail in 1497 with his son Sebastian in the *Mathew*. He landed on the North American coast near modern Newfoundland, believing it at first to be Asia. His achievement is commemorated by the 150 ft Cabot Tower on Brandon Hill, erected 400 years later.

In 1552 the Society of Merchant Venturers was founded, to exploit Cabot's discovery and extend trade to other parts of the world. The port flourished, shipping wool and leather and importing wines, tobacco and chocolate – commodities that led to three of Bristol's major manufacturing industries.

Less happily, during the 17th century, the city also prospered on the slave trade; the abolition of this in the 19th century was a serious setback to the port, particularly as Liverpool was beginning to offer strong trading competition.

An opportunity for Bristol to develop as a transatlantic port came with the launching of Isambard Kingdom Brunel's steamships *Great Western* in 1837 and *Great Britain* in 1843.

In 1970 the *Great Britain* was brought back to Bristol from the Falklands where she had been abandoned, and is now being restored to her original condition in the dock where she was built.

CLIFTON SUSPENSION BRIDGE *Spanning the River Avon, the 245 ft high bridge is a feat of Victorian engineering (overleaf).*

The Bristol Avon is a more attractive river than the Severn, and the Avon Gorge, where the river flows between steep limestone cliffs, is spanned 245 ft above high water by the Clifton Suspension Bridge. In 1836 Brunel was commissioned to build a bridge, but only the abutments were built before work stopped through lack of funds. In 1864, however, five years after Brunel's death, the Institute of Civil Engineers finished the bridge as a tribute to their former colleague. Another example of Brunel's design work can be seen at Temple Meads Station, whose Gothic-style frontage still stands.

Close to the suspension bridge, on the Clifton side, is The Observatory. Once a snuff-mill, it now contains a camera obscura which gives panoramic views of the city. A passageway beneath the observatory leads to the Giant's Cave, which opens out on to a ledge on the side of the gorge high above the river.

Bristol Zoo, on Clifton Down, has a notable collection of rare animals, including the only white tigers in Europe.

Clifton is a residential suburb of Bristol, spreading across the downs above the city and known for its Regency crescents and Georgian terraces. Royal York Crescent, overlooking the gorge, is claimed to be the longest in Europe.

During the Second World War, Bristol suffered extensive bomb damage and lost many old churches and historic buildings. From these ruins soaring new structures of glass and concrete rose to mingle with the old buildings that had survived the war.

Bristol's churches range from the graceful St Mary Redcliffe to the humble Wesley's Chapel. St Mary's was built in the 13th to 15th centuries and has a 285 ft spire. The interior contains magnificent roof bosses and much stained glass. Wesley's Chapel, dating from 1739, was built by John Wesley (1703–91), the founder of Methodism. It is the oldest Methodist chapel in the world. St Mark's Church — also known as the Lord Mayor's Chapel — is the only church in England owned by a corporation. At the Dissolution it became the property of the civic corporation and has been the mayor's official place of worship since 1721. The church is renowned for its monuments — many of them chain mail-clad effigies of the Berkeley family.

Bristol Cathedral, which stands on College Green, was founded in the 1140s as the church of an Augustinian abbey, and became a cathedral in 1542. The Norman chapter house, the finest in England, the great gatehouse, the entrance to the abbot's lodging, the walls of the south transept and the east walk of the cloister all survive from the 12th-century building.

The carving of the Elder Lady Chapel is comparable to that in Wells Cathedral, and the 14th-century choir with its aisles of equal height and lack of flying buttresses is unique in this country. A nave to match this choir was built in the 19th century.

The cathedral contains fine 16th-century misericords (the hinged seats in the choir stalls) and many fascinating tombs and monuments. Some candlesticks which merchants completed their money transactions – which gave rise to the saying 'to pay on the nail'. The nearby Guildhall was erected in 1843 and stands on the site of the original medieval building.

One of Bristol's oldest streets is King Street, a cobbled thoroughfare with many old houses and Britain's oldest working theatre, the Theatre Royal, opened in 1766. It is the home of the Bristol Old Vic and now incorporates the adjacent Cooper's Hall.

Another old thoroughfare, Christmas Steps, rebuilt in 1669, is where antique dealers and booksellers trade.

The Llandoger Trow (1664), an old inn in King Street, was once the drinking den of pirates and is believed to be the original of Long John Silver's haunt 'The Spy Glass' in Robert Louis Stevenson's *Treasure Island*.

Several old houses in Bristol are open to the public: the 16th-century Red Lodge, which was altered in the 18th century and has carvings and furnishings from both periods; Chatterton House, the birthplace of the boy poet Thomas Chatterton (1752–70); and the Georgian House, which contains 18th-century furniture and fittings.

The village of Abbots Leigh is located 3 miles west of Bristol and was once the property of the Abbey of St Augustine, now Bristol Cathedral. It is set deep in the shelter of Leigh Woods, with a track leading past Leigh Court to the banks of the River Avon. From Nightingale Valley there is a good view of the spectacular Clifton Suspension Bridge. Leigh Court, where Charles II sheltered from his enemies, was rebuilt in 1814 in classical Greek style.

BROADWINDSOR *Buildings from the 12th to 17th centuries give character to this terraced village.*

of 1712 are thanksgiving gifts from the privateers who rescued Alexander Selkirk from a desert island in 1709. Selkirk was the man on whom Daniel Defoe based the character of Robinson Crusoe.

Other churches of note are Christ Church, with its wooden figures that strike bells at each quarter of the hour; the 14th-century St John the Baptist, built above a medieval vaulted gateway; the ruined Perpendicular Temple Church, which has a leaning tower, and the Norman Church of St Nicholas, now a museum containing church vestments, plate, and an altarpiece by Hogarth.

The City Museum and Art Gallery stand next to Bristol University. The museum has local archaeological and geological relics, and the art gallery displays paintings by Sir Thomas Lawrence – a Bristol man – and collections of ceramics and glass.

On display at Kings Weston Roman Villa, in Long Cross, are the mosaics, bath suite and foundations of a Roman house of the 3rd and 4th centuries AD.

Bristol University was opened in 1925. Its 215 ft tower, an almost exact replica of the 'Boston Stump' at Boston, Lincolnshire, is a city landmark.

In the old part of Bristol stands the Exchange, built by John Wood of Bath in the 18th century. Outside, on the pavement, are the 'nails', four bronze pillars on

BROADWINDSOR
Dorset
3 miles west of Beaminster

Some 40 cottages and houses, most of them dating from the 17th century, are the pride of Broadwindsor. They are listed as of historic interest by the Royal Commission on Historical Monuments, and perhaps the most notable of them stands in the centre of the village, at the crossroads near the church. It is a plain, tiled, cream-washed cottage in a terrace, and it bears a plaque stating that Charles II slept there on the night of September 23, 1651, when fleeing to France after his defeat by Cromwell's forces at the Battle of Worcester. The cottage, now a private house, was then part of the old Castle Inn. The king's stay is also commemorated by a plaque in the church.

Broadwindsor is large and compact, and is built up of terraces amid the west Dorset hills. Houses at one level look down on the chimneys of those below. All around are the fertile fields on which sheep grazed and flax was raised for the mills of nearby Beaminster. The 19th-century brownstone Church of St John the Baptist stands on a plateau overlooking the village. It has a 15th-century tower, a seven-sided Jacobean pulpit, and an 18th-century picture, on boards, of Moses and Aaron.

A prehistoric ridgeway cuts across the parish, which contains two 19th-century turnpike toll-houses. Among visitors to Broadwindsor were the poet William Wordsworth and his sister Dorothy, who lived at Racedown House, on the western outskirts, from 1795 to 1797. They both wrote about the village, and Dorothy described it as: 'The place dearest to my recollection upon the whole surface of the Island.'

BROMPTON REGIS

Somerset
3 miles northeast of Dulverton

Ghida, mother of King Harold, is said to have refused to surrender Brompton Regis – then called *Brunan tun*, 'the enclosure by the Brendon Hills' – to William the Conqueror's forces after she escaped from the siege of Exeter in 1068. She was allowed to live on there in her manor, under a form of house arrest, until her death when she was buried in the Saxon church there. Both the manor and its little wooden church were razed after her death.

Then nothing much of interest to the outside world happened in this tiny, remote village for about 900 years – until the winter of 1978–9, when a new 161 ft high dam on the Haddeo River came into operation and water began to flow into the 4500 million gallon Wimbleball Reservoir, 1½ miles to the east. The main purpose of the 370 acre man-made lake is to supply water to the Taunton, Yeovil and Bridgwater districts of Somerset, and the Exeter and Tiverton areas in Devon, but it has already been stocked with brown and rainbow trout, and the reservoir now forms part of the Exmoor National Park.

The village, which has several cottages dating back to the 16th century, is penned in by steep hills. From the porch of St Mary's Church there is a splendid view of 1163 ft Haddon Hill, 1½ miles to the south. The church was rebuilt in the 15th century, but the tower and some other features are 200 years older. Inside, is this touching poem on a 17th-century brass memorial to a girl of 19:

> *Reader, Tis worth thy Paines to know*
> *Who was interred here belowe.*
> *Here Lyes good nature, Piettie, Witt,*
> *Though small in volume yet most fairly writ.*
> *She died young, and so oft times Tis seene*
> *The fruit God loves He's pleased to pick it greene.*

BROOMFIELD

Somerset
4 miles west of North Petherton

Beech trees line the lane through Broomfield; the Vale of Taunton Deane glows red and green throughout the year. All Saints Church is delightfully situated amid a cluster of trees. The village was the birthplace of Andrew Crosse (1784–1855), who pioneered experiments with electricity. The prehistoric Ruborough Camp, 1 mile to the north, was used by the Romans as a fort; the site is now overgrown by trees.

Just outside Broomfield, Five Ponds Wood forms part of a nature reserve with a trail laid out by the Somerset Trust for Nature Conservation. The five ponds from which this wood takes its name were dug in the 19th century, probably to enhance the grounds of nearby Fyne Court, but have long since disappeared.

The woodland is only 600 yds long and 70 yds wide. The trail follows the course of a stream that runs through the valley, where native trees mingle with introduced species, planted about the same time as the ponds were dug. Most prominent of the planted trees are beeches, in a line topping a bank along the wood's southern edge, which were originally part of a hedge. Some have now grown to an enormous size; one particularly fine tree stands where the trail enters the wood – a perfect sentinel for the leafy walk among

elder, ash, hawthorn, hazel and holly. Sycamores and poplars have been added to the wood in the more recent years, to join the laurels, snowberries and rhododendrons so favoured by the Victorians.

In spring and summer the woods come alive with the colours of bluebells, red campions, snowdrops and primroses, and beside the stream the banks are speckled with the gold of kingcups and saxifrages.

BROWNSEA ISLAND

Dorset
The largest island in Poole Harbour

Brownsea Island, owned by the National Trust, can be reached by boat from Sandbanks or Poole Quay.

A castle overlooking the landing stage, fields ablaze with daffodils in spring, rhododendrons forming a quarter-mile-long tunnel, and a woodland path descending to a gently shelving beach, all give Brownsea the air of a paradise island. Herring gulls nest in scores along the cliff paths, rising in shrieking protest as visitors approach. Canada geese marshal their young to grassy feeding spots, red squirrels can be seen in the pinewoods, and the island echoes with the sharp cries of peacocks in the trees.

From the southern cliffs there are wide views across the shimmering waters of Poole Harbour to Old Harry rock and Corfe Castle tucked into its cleft in the Purbeck Hills. Nearby, a chunk of Portland stone commemorates the first, experimental Boy Scouts' camp, arranged here by Baden-Powell in 1907 – only scouts and guides can camp on the island.

From a lookout hut at the start of the island nature trail you can see cormorants resting on the shingle strip, and common terns nesting on the islands built for them. A 200 acre nature reserve occupies the north side of the island, and includes one of the largest heronries in England.

BRUTON

Somerset
7 miles southeast of Shepton Mallet

The small town of Bruton, in the valley of the River Brue, is crossed by a narrow packhorse bridge, known locally as Bruton Bow. R. D. Blackmore, author of *Lorna Doone*, was a pupil at King's School, which stands on the site of an earlier school founded in 1520 by Richard Fitz James, Bishop of London. A Bruton stable boy, Hugh Sexey, who became the King's Auditor, founded Sexey Hospital in 1638; the carved wood and the triple windows are worth seeing. A three-storeyed dovecote, on a hill above the town, is owned by the National Trust. Together with a precinct wall, it is all that survives of a 12th-century priory.

On a small road west of Bruton is the peaceful little hamlet of Wyke Champflower – its small green flanked by beeches, elms and oaks. Its name may derive from Champfleury in Normandy. The manor, Wyke House, stands near a church whose box pews have their own hat-pegs; on one wall are the armorial bearings of Henry Southworth, who built the church in 1623.

BIRDS LONG FLOWN *On a hill outside Bruton are the remains of a magnificent 12th-century dovecote.*

BURNHAM-ON-SEA

Somerset
8 miles north of Bridgwater

The story of modern Burnham began in the early 19th century when its curate built a lighthouse, exacted a toll from passing ships and used the money to sink two wells on the foreshore to make Burnham a spa. Although the spa was never prosperous, it laid the foundations of the resort. Burnham's appeal now rests on its 7 miles of sandy beach with its wooden 'lighthouse on legs' and sweeping views of Bridgwater Bay.

The church should be visited for the 14th-century tower, 78 ft high and leaning some 3 ft out of the vertical, and for the reredos of the so-called 'Whitehall Altar'. The superb carvings were commissioned by James II from Arnold Quellin and Grinling Gibbons for the chapel of Whitehall Palace. The altar went from Whitehall to Hampton Court and then to Westminster Abbey; it was bought by Bishop King of Rochester, vicar of Burnham, in 1820.

BURRINGTON

Avon
10 miles east of Weston-super-Mare

The village of Burrington lies at the northern end of Burrington Combe and clusters around the late-15th-century Church of Holy Trinity, with its tower and spirelet. In the churchyard stands a huge hollow yew tree, 24 ft in circumference. The gardens of the cottages are bright with flowers in spring and summer. Two miles west of the village stand the ramparts of the Iron Age fort called Dolebury, which later formed part of the medieval Dolebury Warren.

One of the largest lakes in the West Country, Blagdon Lake is 2 miles to the east of Burrington. Many species of wildfowl can be seen here.

The Holman Clavel Inn near Blagdon, west of Burrington, is said to contain a hearth spirit called Chimbley Charlie. His seat was the clavey – the beam above the fireplace – which is made of 'holman', the local word for holly. One story tells of an occasion when a dinner party was being prepared for a local farmer, who was known to have scoffed at Charlie.

The table was laid and the room made ready. But, when one of the maids came to check it before the party, the table was bare, the silver had been put away, and the tablecloths were neatly folded – a sure sign that Charlie did not like the farmer. The dinner was cancelled.

More than 200 years ago, the Reverend Augustus Toplady took shelter from a storm beneath overhanging rocks in Burrington Combe. The experience inspired him to write the hymn *Rock of Ages*. Burrington Combe clefts deep into the Mendip Hills for 2 miles and is flanked by towering cliffs with caves that provided shelter for prehistoric man. One of the caves, called Aveline's Hole, is known to have been used as a burial place around 10,000 BC.

In summer and at weekends, the combe attracts many visitors, but a short drive to the top of this miniature Cheddar Gorge leaves the crowds behind and leads to Burrington Ham, one of the great delights of the Mendips.

From the ridge, only a few yards from the car park, there is a view over much of the county of Avon, providing an inspiring panorama. The view is northeast over Blagdon Lake and Chew Valley Lake to the point where, 7 miles from the Bristol Channel, Bristol nestles comfortably in and around the Avon Gorge. On a clear day, the unmistakable outline of the Welsh hills looms on the northeastern horizon, on the other side of the murky waters of the Bristol Channel.

Burrington Ham represents the softer face of the Mendips. A broad bridleway drops gently down between brambles and bracken, a marvellous sea of brown, orange and gold in the soft light of autumn, to the village of Burrington.

BURTON BRADSTOCK

Dorset
3 miles southeast of Bridport

Each spring, migrating birds arrive in Burton Bradstock to take advantage of its situation in the warm and sheltered Bride Valley. Early spring flowers bloom throughout the area, which is filled with water-meadows; and the River Bride passes through a narrow gap in the hills on its way to the sea. The centre of the village is largely made up of stone or rubble-walled houses and cottages with thatched, stone, or slate-tiled roofs. They are mostly some 300 years old and are packed together in the narrow, curving streets, and in the lanes which lead to the north off the main road.

The 14th-century parish church of St Mary, which contains some handsome medieval panelling, stands beside the village school in a quiet cul-de-sac in the heart of Burton. Not far away is the triangular village green, bordered by White House bearing the date 1635, and a Wesleyan chapel of 1825, now the village library. Two other houses, the Rookery and Ingram House, in Church Street, are also 17th century – although they have been greatly changed and renovated.

Several of the surrounding hills are topped by prehistoric hill-forts, and they have magnificent views across the English Channel. Below Burton Cliffs, which shelter the village from the sea, is a beach with a car park. Three miles northeast of Burton is the hamlet of Chilcombe, which has a tiny Norman church in the farmyard of the manor.

ROCK OF AGES *Windswept Burrington Combe was the source of inspiration for a popular hymn.*

C

THE CADBURYS
Somerset
7 miles north of Sherborne

On a morning when haze engulfs the low-lying Somerset Levels, the view from Cadbury Castle shows Glastonbury Tor and other hills rising like islands from the swirling mist. This is how the Levels must have looked in the Dark Ages when the sea covered much of the land farther west, between the sweep of the Quantocks and the Mendip Hills. It is easy, then, to understand what a strategic position the massive earthworks occupied; and why it is thought that Cadbury Castle may be the site of King Arthur's legendary Camelot.

Here, it is said, Arthur held his meetings of the Round Table, and from here, too, came the inspiration for the medieval romances of Lancelot and Guinevere, Galahad and the Holy Grail. According to legend, the hill of Cadbury Castle is hollow, and there Arthur and his knights lie sleeping until such time as England will call on their services again. Every seven years, on Midsummer Eve, a great door in the hillside opens, and the gallant band rides down to water its horses at a spring near Sutton Montis church. This tradition has been kept alive for centuries. Even in the 16th century, when the antiquarian John Leland visited the sleepy little village of South Cadbury, he was told that the villagers had 'hard say that Arture much resortid to Camalat'.

Until the 1960s there was no evidence to support this theory, but then archaeologists began to excavate the flat-topped hill. Their work showed that in the 5th and 6th centuries – the time when King Arthur was said to be fighting the Saxons – Cadbury Castle housed a community wealthy enough to trade. It was not conclusive proof of Camelot, but it has certainly allowed the legend to live on.

Cadbury Castle is reached by a footpath from South Cadbury. In the village purple aubrietia spills over honey-coloured stone walls, and straw storks perch on the thatched roof of a cottage. There is an 18th-century former rectory, and a house with a bell on its roof which used to be the school. Castle Farm House, with its mullioned windows and thatched roof, dates from 1687.

The Church of St Thomas à Becket was built in the 14th century; in a niche in the south wall there is a faded wall-painting of a bishop in a cope and mitre which may represent the saint himself.

North Cadbury lies a mile or so away. Its cottages, with roofs of tile, slate or thatch, are mostly built of a grey stone which has weathered over the centuries to a mellow sandy colour. An avenue of beech trees leads to North Cadbury Court, an Elizabethan mansion, and to the churchyard which is flanked on one side by the house's stable block. This dates from 1715.

The large Church of St Michael was built in about 1417 by Lady Elizabeth Botreaux, whose tomb lies inside. Among the most remarkable features of the church are its 16th-century bench ends, which are thought to have been carved by continental craftsmen. Many bear heraldic devices, such as the Tudor Rose, or religious emblems, such as that of St Joseph of Arimathea – a ragged cross and two cruets with drops of blood. But others are simply fun: a flute player, a couple kissing and a cat catching a mouse which has escaped the mousetrap below. The letters of the alphabet are painted on the vestry wall, which was probably once the village school.

CALNE
Wiltshire
5 miles east of Chippenham

Although at the centre of busy crossroads, Calne manages to retain the aura of an old market town, sheltered comfortably in the valley. Like so many north Wiltshire towns, it derived its original prosperity from weaving. When the Industrial Revolution killed its livelihood, it turned to bacon-curing and the making of sausages and pies.

The Lansdowne Arms, reconstructed in the 18th century, is on the site of an old inn dating back to the Middle Ages, and the original brew-house is still in the yard. The old almshouses in Kingsbury Street look across to the impressive parish church; its soaring nave arcades date from 1160, and much of the later 15th-century building was an offering by wealthy wool merchants of the time. Bowood House, 2 miles southwest, seat of the Marquess of Lansdowne, was partly designed by Robert Adam. The park of more than 1000 acres has a splendidly landscaped lake, with an Italianate cascade and shady walks.

CASTLE CARY
Somerset
3 miles southwest of Bruton

The modern outskirts of Castle Cary have little of interest, but the centre of this old town is worth exploring. The main street contains pleasant old shops and houses; behind the market hall stands a little circular lock-up, built in 1779 like a stone beehive, with gratings instead of windows. Nearby Ansford was the home of Parson Woodforde, whose *Diary of a Country Parson* is a classic of 18th-century country life.

CASTLE COMBE
Wiltshire
5 miles northwest of Chippenham

Chosen in 1962 as the prettiest village in England, Castle Combe survived a Hollywood invasion four years later. Although it lies about 17 miles from the nearest coast, the village was transformed to look like a seaport for the film version of *Dr Doolittle*. A harbour wall and jetty were built on the cheerful little Bybrook, which sparkles along beside a row of 17th-century cottages. But the upheaval soon receded, and Castle Combe reverted to the slumber it enjoys between regular influxes of tourists.

Once a centre for cloth-weaving, the village lies in a hollow and is approached through a deep valley, shaded by tall trees. The valley leads down from the road between Chipping Sodbury and Chippenham. Visitors are expected to leave their cars at the top and walk down to the village, where parking is restricted.

The houses and cottages, church and 15th-century market cross are all of mellow, honey-coloured Cotswold stone. The roofs are pitched steeply to allow rain and snow to drain off the porous stone tiles.

Stone steps lead up to the covered cross, where a wool market used to be held. Below it is a three-arched bridge of rough-hewn stone which crosses the Bybrook. The manor house, which largely dates from the early 19th century, is now a hotel and stands behind a screen of trees.

St Andrew's Church, with its tower built in 1434 'at the expense of the clothiers of the district', is rich with decoration in wood and stone. Although it was restored in 1851, the church still has a chancel wall from the 13th century. In the north aisle is the 13th-century tomb of Sir Walter de Dunstanville, who built the now-vanished castle which gave the village its name.

Richard Scrope, Lord Chancellor of England, built the castle as a fortified manor in the 14th century. Mary, Queen of Scots was imprisoned there for six unhappy months in 1568, and a local legend tells that while trying to escape she dropped her shawl. This is said to be the origin of the name of Leyburn Shawl, a limestone hill behind the nearby market town of Leyburn.

Bolton Castle is remarkably intact, and the dining-room is now a restaurant. Close by the castle walls is St Oswald's Church, also 14th century and built of pale local stone.

CASTLE OF COMFORT
Somerset
2 miles northeast of Priddy

An isolated inn, at the meeting of the road from Priddy, Harptree and Chewton Mendip. It was patronised by the men who worked in the nearby lead mines, which are now disused. A mile to the north, on the lane to Compton Martin, a footpath leads east, past Spring Farm, within a few hundred yards of the Devil's Punchbowl, a notable 'swallet'. Swallet holes are small fissures in the limestone which temporarily 'swallow up' streams. In a field near the inn are traces of a Roman road from Uphill to Old Sarum; it is now a footpath, running southeast from Hill Grange to join the road half a mile east of Rookery Farm. The Priddy Circles, four earthwork rings, are near the inn.

CERNE ABBAS
Dorset
7 miles north of Dorchester

Giant's Hill, with its 180 ft tall outline of a naked man cut in the chalky turf, overlooks the entrance to the village. The Cerne Giant, as the figure is called, holds a 120 ft knobbly club in one hand and has been there for more than 1500 years. He is a pagan fertility figure, and is said to be an early British version of the hero-god Hercules, whose cult may have been brought to Britain by the Romans. A path from the village leads to the sheep-grazed slopes of the hill, and the stiff climb

CLOTH AND PROSPERITY *Castle Combe's fine cottages reflect the success of its weaving trade.*

to the top yields glimpses of the 2 ft deep by 2 ft wide trench that is the giant's outline, maintained by the National Trust. From the hillside there are fine views of Cerne Abbas in its bowl of green hills.

As late as the early 19th century, local women believed that sleeping on the hill at night would cure infertility, and so ensure that the village population grew and flourished. Higher up the hill is a rectangular earthwork called the Trendle, or Frying Pan, which until 1635 was the scene of maypole dancing.

At the foot of Giant's Hill is the site of a 10th-century Benedictine abbey. It forms the heart of the village, with its thatched, orange-stone and colour-washed cottages lining Long Street. There are half-timbered Tudor houses in nearby Abbey Street. Facing down Abbey Street is Abbey Farm, an impressive gabled Tudor building in flint and stone. The largest and most intact feature of the abbey, the three-storey Abbot's Porch, stands in the courtyard. Originally, this was the porch to the abbot's hall. Also still standing are the Guest House and a small barn.

The abbey church stood in what is now the village burial ground. St Mary's in Abbey Street, has a 15th-century tower and a fine east window which probably came from Cerne Abbey. A well-preserved pre-Reformation Madonna stands in a weathered niche in the west face of the tower. In the burial ground is a wishing-well named after St Augustine – the first Archbishop of Canterbury – who, in the 6th century, is said to have blessed it. Water from the well flows into a flower-fringed pool, the home of ducks, moorhens and wagtails, by the green just below Abbey Farm.

From Dogbury Gate, 2 miles north of Cerne Abbas, the road westwards to Evershot climbs over Gore Hill, with incomparable views down to the prehistoric Cross and Hand, a weather-worn monolith, eerie and mysterious in its isolated setting. In Thomas Hardy's novel *Tess of the D'Urbervilles*, Tess is made to swear an oath of fidelity on the stone.

JOLLY GREEN GIANT *A pagan fertility symbol, the great figure on the hillock outside Cerne Abbas still extends a powerful aura of ancient magic.*

CHARD
Somerset
12 miles southeast of Taunton

The highest town in Somerset, Chard stands nearly 400 ft above sea level. There are superb views from nearby Windwhistle Hill (733 ft) and Snowdon Hill (709 ft). Two streams flow along the High Street, one going northwards to the Bristol Channel and the other south to the English Channel.

The town was first granted a charter in 1234, becoming a borough in 1285, and for nearly 600 years had a thriving wool industry. Then, in the 19th century, local people turned to making the netting from which machine-made lace is produced. One local man, John Stringfellow, had even more progressive ideas. In 1849 he made a steam-powered model aircraft which flew for 120 ft before it crashed. It is now in the Victoria and Albert Museum, London.

The Choughs Hotel in High Street is one of several interesting buildings, including the 15th-century church, the 16th-century Court House (which is really a group of several Elizabethan houses) and a 17th-century grammar school. The town was the birthplace of Miss Margaret Bondfield (1873–1953), the first woman Cabinet Minister. She became Minister of Labour in the Labour Government of 1929–31.

Forde Abbey, 4 miles away in Dorset, stands in an 18th-century setting of lawns, ponds and fine trees, but in fact it was a Cistercian monastery for 400 years before the Reformation. It was dissolved in 1539, but its last abbot, Thomas Charde, made additions that demonstrate some of the finest Tudor stonework in England. In the 1550s it became a private house.

CHARTERHOUSE

Somerset
3 miles northeast of Cheddar

The lonely village of Charterhouse sits high on a hill in a flat, windswept landscape – but it is assured forever of its place in history. It was here, some 2000 years ago, that the Romans launched Britain's earliest lead-mining industry. Although there were many people living in the area in those times, today Charterhouse's population can be counted almost on the fingers of one hand. A track adjoining Manor Farm leads to the heart of the old mineworkings, 1023 ft above sea level. Some 2 miles west of Manor Farm, a footpath leads north from Tyning's Farm across the summit of Black Down, from which the Welsh hills can be seen across the Severn Estuary.

Little evidence of the Roman occupation remains at the site, but wildlife thrives. A nature reserve has been established in the 'gruffy ground' – patches of furrowed land containing the overgrown remains of the filled-in mine-shafts and other lead workings. Here alpine penny-cress and spring sandwort are found beside sheep's fescue, sea campions and other wild flowers. There are also many butterflies, such as marbled whites and dark green fritillaries.

There is an almost eerie stillness about Charterhouse, with few sounds apart from the gentle rustle of the wind in the leaves of the trees. Beeches, sycamores, alders, oaks and ash trees grow in isolated stands, alongside the scrub layer of hawthorns, elders and dogwood, just as they must have done before the Romans came. Blackmore Educational Nature Reserve is open to the general public and visitors may leave their cars in the car park.

CHEDDAR

Somerset
8 miles northwest of Wells

England's Grand Canyon, the Cheddar Gorge, carved by a river that now runs underground, slices through the Mendip Hills for more than 1 mile. Sheer limestone cliffs tower 450 ft above the road that leads down to Cheddar Village, where there are entrances to vast underground caverns. The finest views of the gorge are obtained by approaching from the north.

In the larger of the 400 or so caves and holes, visitors can see stalactites and stalagmites rich in colour and fantastic of shape. Underground rivers splash and gurgle. Gough's Cave Museum has a collection of Old Stone Age tools and weapons and the skeleton, discovered in 1903, of a man who lived in the gorge some 12,000 years ago. Roman coins of bronze, silver and gold have also been discovered in the caves.

Cheddar cheese originated here more than 300 years ago. Today it is made in more places throughout the world than any other cheese.

Gorsey Bigbury, a mile or two to the north, is marked by a circular bank some 200 ft in diameter, with an internal ditch cut into the underlying rock. This Neolithic henge is one of the few to have been fully excavated, and showed occupation by some Beaker People, perhaps as an itinerant camp site.

One and a half miles northeast of Cheddar is Long Wood, where the subterranean Mendip meets the surface beneath a glorious canopy of green. Shortly after the end of the Second World War a network of water holes – called swallets – was unearthed in the middle of this delightfully unspoilt stretch of woodland, leading to a complicated labyrinth of underground passages and caves. Today the entrances to the swallets are closed because of the dangers they present to inexperienced explorers.

The wood contains much wildlife, which can be seen from the $2\frac{1}{4}$ mile nature trail established by the Somerset Trust for Nature Conservation. Here you can find ancient stands of beech, some of which were planted 140 years ago, along with other trees associated with limestone – such as yews, elders and ashes. Blackberries grow profusely and, in the clearings between the trees, there are rosebay willowherb, hemp agrimony and the rarer herb paris. In the moister areas, fungi such as the uncommon amethyst agaric and the deadly yellow deathcap toadstool may be found.

At one point along the trail a blowhole can be seen. This was formed in 1968 when the underground stream burst through to the surface. The thickets are the home of thrushes, wrens and the green and lesser spotted woodpeckers. In spring, the air is filled with the sound of migrant birds – the willow warblers, blackcaps and redstarts – all competing for territory. Roe deer, badgers, foxes, squirrels, shrews and weasels are common, and adders and grass snakes can also be seen occasionally. Care should be taken when wandering along the paths, particularly during warm weather, so as not to disturb the poisonous adder, recognisable by its zigzag markings.

CHEDWORTH

Gloucestershire
4 miles southwest of Northleach

West of the Foss Way, where it plunges steeply to cross the River Coln at Fossebridge, the houses of Chedworth stand along the lower slopes of a shallow valley between Pancake Hill and Chedworth Beacon. Here the pale grey limestone of the Cotswolds can be seen at its best, not in grand houses and a soaring 'wool' church, but in simple homesteads and farms, and a Norman church that sits prettily and at ease among its sturdy neighbours.

St Andrew's Church retains its original plan of west tower, nave and chancel, but its plain Norman lines are enhanced by tall windows in the south wall that rise almost from ground level to the battlemented roof parapet. Below the church, in Church Row and Ballingers Row, there are 18th-century cottages, and a little farther to the east, Cromwell House and The Old Farm, both with gables and mullioned windows and dating from the 16th or 17th centuries.

A thousand years before the Normans came to the Cotswolds, however, the Romans were here, and using that same limestone to build Chedworth Villa. It was discovered in 1864, about 1 mile to the north of the present village.

The villa's mosaic floors were the first to come to light, and further excavations organised by Lord Eldon, who owned the land, revealed an elaborate range of baths with rooms designed for both humid and dry heat and a cold plunge. Another wing contained a number of living rooms.

The villa's floors are richly patterned and depict the seasons in the forms of figures, such as Cupid carrying

CHEDWORTH *Ancient versions of the sauna and steam bath, complete with underfloor heating, were uncovered in the Roman villa north of the village.*

a garland for summer. A museum, built in 1866, contains objects found in the villa, including pottery, iron tools and small altars.

By road the villa is most easily reached via Yanworth. Since 1924 the site has been owned by the National Trust who have built a visitors' centre. Above the villa, public footpaths cross mixed woodland, alive with colour in autumn, where edible Roman snails are said to live. There is a large herd of deer in Chedworth Woods, to the west.

About 1½ miles southeast of the village is Denfurlong Farm, a working dairy and arable farm which welcomes visitors from daylight to dusk throughout the year. There is an exhibition explaining different aspects of the working of a farm, and two trails, one round the fields and the other round the buildings. At afternoon milking time the automated milking parlour can be seen in operation from a viewing platform in the cowshed.

CHELTENHAM
Gloucestershire
8 miles east of Gloucester

The inland resort of Cheltenham lies in the heart of the Cotswolds and is a beautifully planned town graced by Regency architecture and wide, tree-lined avenues. As well as the attraction of its spa, Cheltenham has always offered a wide range of entertainments. Its festivals of music and literature are renowned throughout the world, and its many sporting events include the Cheltenham Gold Cup steeplechase and a Cricket Festival.

The original medicinal spring from which Cheltenham grew was discovered by accident in a field early in the 18th century. One of its owners, Captain Henry Skillicorne, a retired privateer, deepened and enclosed the well in 1738, built an assembly room and laid out walks and rides, thus founding the spa. His epitaph in St Mary's parish church is one of the longest in Britain.

Throughout the 18th century many more springs were found, and other pump rooms built. In 1788 the town suddenly became fashionable when George III and his family took the waters there. However, it was the Duke of Wellington who finally made the spa's reputation; he had a liver disorder which the waters relieved. He took the waters in 1816, and it is from around that time that the large-scale development of the town took place.

The Pittville Pump Room, the finest gem of the spa's Regency architecture, was built for Joseph Pitt, MP, in 1825–30. Set in a spacious park, it consists of a great hall surmounted by a gallery and dome, with a colonnade of Ionic columns based on the Temple on the Ilissus at Athens. Waters are still dispensed from a restored fountain surrounded by columns. The beautiful grounds contain sweeping lawns and tree-surrounded lakes.

The waters, which today can be taken at the Town Hall as well as Pittville, are the only natural, drinkable alkaline waters in Britain. Their medicinal properties are attributed to the magnesium and sodium sulphates and the sodium bicarbonate that they contain.

After the Pittville Pump Room, the town's best known examples of Regency building are Montpellier Walk and the Rotunda. The Rotunda was built behind an existing pump room to provide a bigger drinking hall. It is now the hall of a bank. The Walk is lined with female figures, modelled on those of the Erechtheion Temple at Athens.

Lining the broad, tree-lined Promenade is a fine terrace incorporating Ionic columns and a pediment at the entrance. The building is now the town's municipal offices.

The town is rich in examples of the beautiful ironwork that marked the Regency period. Some is so delicately cast that it resembles fine lacework. Outstanding examples can be seen on the verandahs and balconies opposite the Imperial Gardens of The Promenade, and also in London Road.

The only medieval building still standing is St Mary's parish church. This retains traces of early-12th-century Norman work, but is best known for its 14th-century window tracery, including that of an uncommon rose window in the north transept. The church also contains some fine Victorian stained glass.

The Art Gallery and Museum contains major collections of paintings, chiefly by 17th-century Dutch artists, porcelain, pottery, furniture, costume, and archaeological collections.

Staverton Airport, 4 miles west, is the home of the Skyfame Aircraft Museum which preserves British aircraft of the Second World War. It also houses a collection of aero engines and model aircraft.

Cheltenham holds more festivals than any other town in Britain. The Cheltenham International Festival of Music gives first performances of new works by British composers, and since 1945, when the festival began, more than 350 such works, by Benjamin Britten, Malcolm Arnold, Sir Arthur Bliss and many others, have been presented. Contemporary music from abroad is also played. The larger concerts are held in the Town Hall, which has a concert hall seating more than 1000. Competitors from all over Europe attend the Festival of Literature in autumn, and the town's oldest festival, that of Music, Speech, Drama and Dancing, held every spring.

The composer Gustav Holst (1874–1934) was born in Cheltenham. Holst, who is best known for his orchestral suite *The Planets*, was descended from a Swedish family, long settled in England. His birthplace at 4 Clarence Road, is a museum devoted to his life and work.

The town is well known as a centre of education. There are two public schools for boys, Cheltenham College and Dean Close, and also one for girls – Cheltenham Ladies' College.

The Cricket Festival, first held in 1877 in honour of W. G. Grace, takes place each August on Cheltenham College's fine ground.

CHESIL BEACH
Dorset
Shingle bank stretching from Abbotsbury to the Isle of Portland

Seen from high above Fortuneswell, on the Isle of Portland, Chesil Beach curves away into the distance like a gigantic hawser mooring the island to the mainland. On one side lies the sea, white with surf; on the other the placid waters of the Fleet, a lagoon bordering the great bank of pebbles for half of the 16 miles to its anchorage in the tawny cliffs near Burton Bradstock. And all along the beach there is a deep and continuous hiss and roar as the waves suck back then hurl forward the millions of pebbles.

About 200 yds wide and 40 ft high at the Portland end, the beach changes shape with the sea's moods. Fishermen judge their position along the beach by the colour and size of the pebbles, which the tide has graded from west to east; at Portland they are the size of a man's fist and greyish in colour, while at Burton Bradstock they are no bigger than raisins and various shades of brown-yellow.

Chesil Beach was the scourge of sailing ships when strong southwesterly winds swept across Lyme Bay. Many a good ship has been battered to pieces on the seething pebbles. Casualties include seven ships of the line in November 1795, with the loss of more than 200 men and women. They were part of a fleet commanded by Rear-Admiral Sir Hugh Christian, on his way to the West Indies to be Commander-in-Chief. In 1824 two West-Indiamen, *Carvalho* and *Colville*, met their fate here with all hands drowned, and the sloop *Ebenezer* was flung almost into the Fleet, in which it was later re-floated.

The gales of 1824 claimed not only ships but also the village of Fleet near the eastern end of the lagoon, swept away when a freak tide roared over the bank. Only the chancel of the old village church survives.

The shingle is a good hunting ground for beach-combers – in the course of time the sea has cast up everything from whales to Spanish galleons – but swimming is hazardous because of treacherous currents. The simple pleasure of net fishing for mackerel, which come close to the shore, can be safely enjoyed.

CHEW MAGNA
Avon
6 miles south of Bristol

John Leland, antiquary to Henry VIII, wrote of Chew Magna in 1545: 'It is a praty clothing towne, and hath a faire chirch.' 'Praty' it still is and its 'faire chirch' still stands in this red limestone village close to the Mendip Hills, surrounded by streams and rolling pastures.

Recorded for posterity in the Domesday Book, in medieval times Chew Magna was a thriving centre of the wool trade, and on every hand there are reminders of that prosperous era.

Outside the churchyard's main gate is the 16th-century Church House, which has a tiled roof. Feast days were often marked by a parish party – the church ale was so named because the ale consumed was frequently brewed by the church – and proceeds went to parish funds. Initially, the church itself was the scene of these festivities, but gradually other premises were bought for the purpose, which became known as the Church House. At one time it served as a manorial court and even later was used as a refuge for the poor. It was a school from 1842 until 1894. From the Church House, also known as the Old School Room, the High Street climbs gently westwards and is flanked for part of its length by pavements several feet above road level. South Parade, the highest section, has white railings and includes a range of whitewashed stone buildings and a pink-painted bank. Opposite are two inns, the 18th-century Pelican and the 19th-century Bear and Swan. Between the two inns is the Old Bakehouse. It is now a shop, but a long-handled baker's shovel still hangs outside.

Until the mid-18th century a maypole stood outside the Pelican, and the street was the scene of village fairs. Further along High Street, stone cottages rub shoulders with big houses of charm and character. Acacia House, set back from the road, dates from the 18th century and has an elegant facade and an astonishing array of chimneys. The Beeches is another Georgian house, built in 1762 by Ephraim Chancellor, a schoolmaster, whose earlier home was the Dutch-gabled Portugal House on the corner of Battle Lane.

Harford Square, tucked away behind High Street, is overlooked by the impressive frontage of Harford House. It was built in the 19th century by James Harford, an ironmaster who was lord of the manor. There was once a blacksmith's forge in the square, though it had no connection with Harford whose ironworks were in South Wales.

Silver Street runs down from Harford Square towards the north side of the churchyard and passes Church House. The Queen's Arms pub forms an attractive cluster with whitewashed cottages by a stream at the foot of Silver Street. A private house next to St Andrew's Church is known as Chew Court, and hides behind a high, sandstone wall. The house was once part of the 'Palace of Chew', the property of the Bishop of Bath and Wells in the 14th century. Much of the palace was demolished by a 16th-century bishop.

St Andrew's stands in spacious grounds, and is Chew Magna's strongest link with medieval times. Parts of the church are Norman, including the south doorway which is sheltered by a 14th-century porch.

GOTHIC FLIGHT OF FANCY *The 19th-century bridge at Chew Magna's manor house recalls a more leisured time.*

On the exterior right-hand side of the porch, and on the nave wall, are scratch dials – a series of carved lines radiating from a central point. They are thought to have indicated the time of Mass. Gargoyles glare down from the 100 ft high tower that was added some time between 1440 and 1550. It contains a peal of eight bells, while the chancel has fine beams and painted bosses.

Inside the church a tablet commemorates Alexander Whyte, a naval surgeon aboard HMS *Bellerophon* at Nelson's victories at the Nile and Trafalgar. Ten years after Trafalgar, in 1815, Napoleon was taken into exile on St Helena on the same ship, following his defeat at Waterloo. Whyte died at Chew Magna in 1838.

A carved oak effigy of a knight in the south aisle is believed to be of Sir John de Hauteville. According to legend, Sir John was a man of great strength who threw the Hauteville Quoit, an ancient standing stone, from the top of Maes Knoll to its present resting place between Chew Magna and the road between Bristol and Shepton Mallet. The effigy came from the chapel at Norton Hawkfield, which was destroyed in the 16th century. It has a Victorian inscription.

CHIPPENHAM

Wiltshire
12 miles northeast of Bath

A stone-built town on the Avon, with an ancient market place at its heart. The twin-gabled 15th-century town hall, with an unusual wooden turret, is probably the town's oldest building. The Hungerford Chapel of the parish church has many monuments of the 15th century, and some going back to the 13th century. The Grove was once the site of an early 18th-century spa, and Ivy House dates from about 1730. At Hardenhuish (pronounced Harnish), just outside Chippenham, John Wood the Younger, of Bath, built the elegant Georgian church with its Venetian windows.

Lacock Abbey, in the National Trust village of Lacock, 3 miles south of Chippenham, was the home of William Fox-Talbot, the father of modern photography. In 1833 he made the first photographic prints there. There is a museum of photography in the grounds.

CHIPPING CAMPDEN

Gloucestershire
8 miles southeast of Evesham

The name Chipping, also found in other Cotswold towns, is Old English for market or trading centre. The Market Hall, with its mellow arches, was built in 1627 and looks out onto a street little changed since medieval times. In the 14th and 15th centuries, Chipping Campden was a prosperous wool town, where merchants bought fleeces in the 14th-century Woolstaplers Hall, now a museum of photographic and medical equipment.

The mainly 15th-century Church of St James is one of the finest 'wool' churches in the Cotswolds and contains many fine monumental brasses, including the largest in the county – 8 ft by 4 ft. It is in memory of William Grevel, who is described in Latin as 'the flower of the wool merchants of all England'.

Old Campden House was burned down during the

Civil War by Royalists to prevent it falling into the hands of Cromwell, and only a fragment remains. The stable block was converted into the Dower House after the Civil War.

Dover's Games, held annually, are a re-creation of the classical Olympic Games. They were founded in the 17th century, and include the rare and rural sport of shin-kicking.

Northeast of the town, the magnificent gardens of Hidcote Manor and Kiftsgate Court are open to the public in the spring and summer. The gardens at Hidcote have been called the most beautiful gardens of the 20th century. In 1907 an American officer, Lawrence Johnston, began to transform what was virtually a wilderness into a series of superb gardens. A cedar of Lebanon, a clump of fine beech trees, barren fields and a stream trickling through a small valley were the raw materials. First, the windswept Cotswold scarp was converted into broad terraces. Along these Johnston planted protective hedges in unorthodox combinations. Red-leaved beech grows with ordinary beech, and golden-leaved yew with ordinary yew. The hedges form a series of compartments with plants from all over the world, and each compartment has a particular quality, such as the garden all with red foliage and flowers. The stream part of the garden is quite different. A path rambles downhill along it,

MELLOW ARCHES *Chipping Campden's market hall was built in 1627. The rest of the village seems little changed.*

roughly parallel to the formal axis. It is overhung by fine trees, while beside the banks are choice shrubs and alongside the water primulas and other moisture-loving plants grow in profusion. By the house, a large kitchen garden has its paths lined with old-fashioned roses and many kinds of clematis.

CHRISTCHURCH
Dorset
5 miles east of Bournemouth

An old settlement on the estuaries of the Rivers Avon and Stour, Christchurch was a walled town in Saxon times – one of Alfred the Great's strongholds against the Danes. Today it is a holiday resort, but the town centre still retains the Saxon street plan.

Behind Christchurch Quay stands the splendid priory church, its structure a blend of styles from Saxon times to the Renaissance. Its choir stalls are older than those in Westminster Abbey, and there is a monument to the poet Shelley.

A belief that Christ in person helped to build this church gave the town, originally called Twynham, its name. The church, started in the 11th century, was to have been built at the top of St Catherine's Hill, but building materials were mysteriously removed each

night. Taking this as a divine sign, workmen built the church where it now stands. As work progressed a carpenter arrived who would accept neither food nor drink. When a vital roof beam was cut too short, work was abandoned for the day, but next morning the beam was miraculously in place. It can still be seen above the ambulatory. The men believed that their mysterious workmate had been Christ himself and in his honour named the building Christ's Church.

The town has the remains of a Norman house, Place Mill, built in the 12th century for the resident steward of the nearby castle. The castle itself stands on a well-preserved motte or artificial mound.

CHURCHILL
Avon
3 miles south of Congresbury

This village of stone houses, just off the Bristol Road, is dominated by privately owned Churchill Court, seat of some of the ancestors of the first Duke of Marlborough and of Sir Winston Churchill.

A legend is attached to the effigy of a knight that lies in the village church. It was said that the crusader returned to Churchill after years in the Holy Land. The only gift he could afford to bring home to his beloved wife were two carefully cherished bulbs of a rare spring flower called Primrose Peerless. When the knight reached the village, he discovered that his wife was dead. Broken-hearted, he flung the precious bulbs over the churchyard wall and died of despair on his lady's grave. The bulbs took root and still grew there within living memory. A 17th-century memorial to Thomas Latch and his wife shows the husband looking in horror upon the face of his spouse, whose shroud he has raised.

Southeast of the village, just beyond some traffic lights, a track 1 mile long leads to Dolebury Camp. The Camp is a large and magnificent Iron Age earthwork, with a stone-walled enclosure.

The Red House Museum in Churchill was built in about 1760 as a workhouse, but now houses an art gallery – in the former stables and coach house, built in 1887. The museum concentrates mainly on displays of the geology, natural history, archaeology and history of the region. The archaeological section includes material from the Bronze Age, from a late Palaeolithic 'Reindeer Hunters' camp site at Hengistbury, and from the port and settlement which existed there from the Early Iron Age to Roman times. Special displays include the Kimmeridge Shale industry – a prehistoric luxury trade making personal adornments – the Kimmeridge ritual 'beheaded burial', and pottery from Roman kilns in the New Forest. An example of local industry is seen in the making of minute Fusee chains – used in the mechanism of watch movements and widely exported – confined almost solely to this district throughout the 19th century. Smuggling relics and 19th-century local domestic and dairy equipment can also be seen, including an original open hearth fireplace and equipment. Other Victorian items include lighting, smoking, letter-writing and needlework materials. Children's toys and games are on display, and dolls are shown in a Victorian setting which includes a selection from the extensive Druitt Collection of 18th- and 19th-century fashion plates. Some 19th-century costumes and accessories are also shown. The natural history section concentrates on the richness of the surrounding district, and there is an aquarium and herb garden.

THE CHURN VALLEY
Gloucestershire
4 miles south of Cheltenham

The River Churn is one of the most westerly tributaries of the Thames, and lays disputed claim to be its source. The Churn rises at the village of Seven Springs, near the junction of the A435 and A436, and its springs have never been known to run dry.

Narrow, wooded and winding, the Churn Valley is spanned by several interesting villages and fine houses, so that although the main A435 from Cheltenham to Cirencester follows it south, it has a secret and peaceful air. Turn west off the A435 towards Cowley, with its 17th-century manor and chain of lilied lakes, and cross the Churn at Marsden Manor. Look for dippers here, strange little birds that plunge into the shallow river and run along the bottom searching for food among the pebbles. There are pied and grey

wagtails, too, and sometimes herons. Further downstream is North Cerney, with a fine church incorporating Norman and medieval work. Incised on the outside south wall of the transept and on the southwest tower buttress is the grotesque figure of manticore – a mythical beast with the body of a lion and the head of a man, said to be a man-eater.

To the southwest of North Cerney is the village of Bagendon, where the British tribe of the Dobunni had an important settlement associated with metalworking. Bagendon may have been the forerunner of the Roman town of Cirencester (Corinium), which became the new tribal capital – a new market and administration centre for the Dobunni. Excavations at Bagendon have yielded precious objects such as jewellery, pottery, glass and coins, establishing these pre-Roman people as prosperous and unexpectedly civilised farmers, merchants and manufacturers. Nor is there any evidence of fighting here: Romans and local people seem to have lived together peaceably.

Up on high and windy North Cerney Downs the ancient track called the White Way, an extension of the old Salt Way, runs south to Cirencester and the Foss Way. There is a long but lonely walk east from North Cerney up to these downlands and woods. The lane crosses the White Way to the perfect little hamlet of Calmsden with its row of tiny stone cottages with long, narrow gardens.

Just beyond North Cerney to the northeast is Rendcomb, and its late Perpendicular Church of St Peter. Built at the beginning of the 16th century, it has contemporary roofs and a 16th-century screen across the whole church, some glass in the Renaissance manner and 19th-century glass in the east window. The Norman font has carvings of 11 Apostles – the space for Judas was left blank.

CIRENCESTER
Gloucestershire
14 miles northwest of Swindon

Beneath the streets of this ancient market town are the remains of the Roman town of Corinium Dobunnorum, founded about AD75. Next to Londinium (London) it was the largest and one of the most important Roman towns in England – and excavations have shown it was built to their classic grid plan of straight streets. It was destroyed by Saxons in the 6th century, but reborn in the Middle Ages as Cirencester (pronounced 'Syrensester'), when the grid pattern was abandoned and the streets turned and twisted in all directions. Even the Market Place, which replaced the old Roman forum, was given a distinct curve.

Set at the junction of three of the great Roman roads, Foss Way, Akeman Street and Ermin Street, Corinium was also planned as an administrative centre for the area inhabited by the Dobunni – a conquered British tribe who lived in the southern part of the Cotswold Hills.

Cirencester's huge 15th- to 16th-century parish church of St John the Baptist, in the Market Place, is built of pale yellow stone, and was largely paid for by wealthy wool merchants – it is one of the numerous Cotswold 'wool churches'. Its outstanding features include the soaring west tower and the fan tracery of the unique three-storey south porch. The peal of its 12 bells is the oldest in the country. The money for its pinnacled tower came unwittingly from the Earls of

CIRENCESTER *Interesting old streets radiate off the Market Place, in which stands the Church of St John the Baptist.*

Salisbury and Kent. They rebelled against Henry IV in 1399, but while passing through Cirencester they were arrested by zealous townsfolk and executed for treason. Grateful Henry allowed the townsfolk to keep the earls' treasure chests – which paid the builders.

Inside the church, the impressive pulpit is shaped like a vast wineglass, and on the wall beside it is a 17th-century hourglass which was used by the preacher to time his sermons. By the door of the south aisle is a coloured statue of a blue-coated boy, used in the 18th century to 'beg' funds for the church's primary school. The school was founded in 1714 by Rebecca Powell, and is still flourishing today.

On display in the south aisle is the silver-gilt Boleyn Cup made in 1535 for Anne Boleyn, second wife of Henry VIII, the year before she was executed for alleged adultery. Perched on the lid are a falcon holding a sceptre, and a rose tree – Anne's personal emblem. After her death the cup went to her daughter, Elizabeth I, who in turn passed it on to her physician, Dr Richard Master, who later gave it to St John's.

Also in the Market Place are the Corn Hall, a Victorian building with finely detailed decoration, and next to it the King's Head, an inn with an 18th-century facade.

Surrounding the Market Place is a network of fascinating old streets. Among them are Spitalgate, with the remains of a 12th-century almshouse, the Hospital of St John; Coxwell Street, an unspoiled row of wool-merchants' houses and workmen's cottages; Thomas Street, which contains the Weaver's Hall, continuously occupied since it was founded in 1425 for poor weavers; and Dollar Street, containing bow-windowed shops with dim interiors, some dating back to the 17th century.

North of the parish church are the grounds of the now-vanished abbey, through which the River Churn winds into a lake graced by swans.

Little visible evidence of the Roman occupation survives in the town, but the Cornium Museum houses one of the country's most impressive collections of Roman remains, including some beautiful mosaic floors, sculpture and domestic objects. Some of the highlights are a reconstruction of a town-house dining room, built around a mosaic of the four seasons, and a cut-away view of a central-heating system.

At the top of Cecily Hill, to the southwest, is Cirencester Park, home of the Earl Bathurst. His mansion, hidden behind a 40 ft high yew hedge planted in 1818, is not open to the public. But the park is; you can walk along its 5 mile tree-lined Broad Avenue or ride horseback along part of it.

The 3000 acres of wooded parkland were laid out in the 18th century by the 1st Earl Bathurst and his friend the poet Alexander Pope (1688–1744). At a point where ten rides meet is a summerhouse named Pope's Seat, which was a favourite retreat of the poet.

CLAVERTON

Avon
3 miles east of Bath

At the age of 23, Winston Churchill delivered his first political speech at a fête at Claverton Manor on July 26, 1897. He spoke in support of the Primrose League, which had been formed by his father, Lord Randolph, to infuse new life into the Conservative party. The manor, standing close to the River Avon, was designed in 1820 by Sir Jeffry Wyatville, architect to George IV, and is built of Bath stone. It is now occupied by the American Museum, which was founded in 1961 by two Americans, Dallas Pratt and John Judkyn, to increase Anglo-American understanding. The museum has 18 rooms set out with American furniture dating from the late 17th- to mid-19th centuries. There are especially interesting items dealing with the religious sect called the 'Shakers', and with many aspects of American folk art.

In addition there are galleries of silver, glass and pewter, and a collection of American quilts. One section of the museum is devoted to the arts and customs of the American Indians. Another depicts the opening up of the American West.

In the grounds, a prairie wagon and the observation platform from an American train show two methods of transport that helped to open up the West.

Ralph Allen, one of the creators of Georgian Bath, lies buried in Claverton churchyard.

CLEARWELL

Gloucestershire
2 miles south of Coleford

Clearwell's castle has a fairy tale all to itself – a modern one with a happy ending. Built around 1727 by landowner Thomas Wyndham, it was England's first neo-Gothic mansion. But it burnt down in 1929 and, despite renovation, went into decline until 1953, when an unlikely saviour appeared – Mr Frank Yeates, son of the castle gardener.

He spent his boyhood at Clearwell, then went on to become a successful baker in Blackpool. However,

he returned finally to his roots, bought the derelict shell of the great house where his father had worked, and spent the last 20 years of his life restoring it to its former glory. It is now a hotel.

The castle and grounds are open to the public Easter to October, on Sundays only. The house has an elegant main hall of Elizabethan origin and, upstairs, rooms with merman motifs, incorporated from an earlier building on the site. It was used by the infamous Judge Jeffreys when he toured the countryside, hanging and transporting followers of the Duke of Monmouth after the unsuccessful 1685 rebellion.

The village itself, on the fringes of the Forest of Dean, was a mining community for 3000 years, until the 1940s. Iron ore was dug in prehistoric times; Roman quarrymen left oak shovels behind in caves – or 'churns' as they are known locally. In Puzzle Wood, to the north, is a 2000-year-old open-cast iron pit and, beneath it, the Clearwell Caves, a 600 ft deep labyrinthine mining complex which is being developed as a museum.

Relics of this eventful past are the large, white-painted Wyndham Arms, an inn which has a sign proclaiming it as 'c. 1340'; and a 14th-century sandstone cross where wandering friars would preach. Tudor Farm is said to have been occupied at one time by Oliver Cromwell. On the outskirts is the oddly named Stank Farm. The name means fishpond, and this was probably where the lord of the manor kept his carp.

The Church of St Peter was built by Caroline Wyndham, Countess of Dunraven, who lived in the castle during the 19th century – the last in her family line to do so. The church is large and exuberantly decorated, and some locals describe it as 'a fancy layer cake'. The countess was also responsible for building the village school and the cemetery chapel on the site of the original St Peter's, at the other end of the village.

CLEEVE HILL AND CLEEVE CLOUD
Gloucestershire
4 miles northeast of Cheltenham

At 1083 ft above sea-level, the ridge $1\frac{1}{4}$ miles southeast of Cleeve Hill is the highest point of the Cotswolds, with Cheltenham spread below. This airy upland remains one of the most breathtaking viewpoints anywhere in England. Herefordshire Beacon is 16 miles northwest, marking the spine of the Malvern Hills. Tewkesbury Abbey, in the same direction, seems close enough to reach out and touch, and the Sugar Loaf Mountain, 45 miles to the west in the Brecon Beacons, is clearly silhouetted against the distant horizon.

Wild flowers carpet the high limestone heath of Cleeve Common: yellow rock-roses, hawkweed and lady's bedstraw gild the turf, while the wild thyme adds a touch of purple.

CLEVEDON COURT *The 14th-century manor house lies outside the small town associated with Coleridge and Thackeray.*

Just over 2 miles east of Cleeve Cloud, the west-facing ridge below Cleeve Common, is one of the finest of the 30 or more long barrows of the Cotswolds – Belas Knap, a green-turfed hump on the wooded escarpment above the vale of Sudeley. The barrow was built by New Stone Age men about 5000 years ago, and is some 180 ft long and 60 ft wide. It contains four burial chambers in which the remains of more than 30 people have been found. A man and five children were buried – possibly sacrificially – behind an impressive false entrance at the broad end of the mound; this may have been to mislead tomb-robbers or evil spirits. The barrow is superbly built, in the same manner as Cotswold masons still construct dry-stone walls today. Its name comes from the Anglo-Saxon words for a beacon on a hill. Brooding, mysterious, Belas Knap symbolises the ancient past of the Cotswolds.

Belas Knap can be reached on foot from Cleeve Hill by following the path southeast over Cleeve Common, past the radio mast, and east to Wontley Farm. From there turn northeast along a track and footpath to the barrow.

The walk from Cleeve Hill to Belas Knap and back takes about three hours. Alternatively, to reach the barrow, drive north on the A46 and just before Winchcombe turn south on to a minor road to Charlton Abbots. A mile beyond the junction a steep lane branches southwest, signposted to Corndean. Either take this lane and join the path from Cleeve Cloud just past a small farmyard, or drive on half a mile to a lay-by and walk up a steep, signposted path through woodland on the west side of the road to Belas Knap above.

CLEVEDON
Avon
8 miles northeast of Weston-super-Mare

The Victorian influence can be seen everywhere in Clevedon; in its houses, hotels and gardens, and the pier – now partly collapsed – which is claimed to be the finest Victorian pier in England.

There are two good medieval buildings, the parish church and Clevedon Court. St Andrew's Church is partly Norman, and stands on a headland. Tennyson wrote *In Memoriam* after a visit to the tomb of his friend Arthur Hallam in the church in 1856.

Clevedon Court was built about 1320, and is one of the few surviving manor houses of the period. In 1709 the house was bought by Abraham Elton, a wealthy Bristol merchant. It contains the Elton Ware pottery collection and a display of Nailsea glass. The novelist Thackeray wrote much of *Vanity Fair* while staying here and used the house as a background to his novel *Henry Esmond*. Sir Arthur Elton transferred the house to the National Trust in 1961.

Clevedon is a good centre for walkers, standing as it does where two ranges of hills meet. One range runs northwards to Portishead, sloping to steep cliffs by the sea; the other, the larger of the two, runs inland towards Bristol, where it comes to an end at Leigh Woods, and the Avon Gorge, a good viewpoint.

On a hill 3 miles east of the town is Cadbury Camp, an Iron Age fortification (not to be confused with the more famous Cadbury Castle west of South Cadbury, in south Somerset).

CODFORD ST MARY
Wiltshire
4 miles south of Heytesbury

A typical small village of the Wylye Valley, on the edge of Salisbury Plain, Codford St Mary is joined by a single street to the even smaller village of Codford St Peter. The plain sweeps up behind the two villages towards the 617 ft prehistoric Codford Circle. Inside Codford St Peter's church is an unusually beautiful piece of stone carving, in the form of part of a 9th-century cross, showing the figure of a man dressed in a short, draped tunic and performing a ritual dance.

COLEFORD
Gloucestershire
4 miles southeast of Monmouth

A town of special interest to metallurgists and industrial archaeologists, Coleford was once a centre of the iron trade; some 5125 cubic feet of wood from the surrounding Forest of Dean would have been used to produce one iron bar. The iron trade declined during the first half of the century, when further deforestation on this scale was forbidden. A local 'free-miner' named Robert Forester Mushet (1811–91) discovered the value of speigeleisen – an alloy of iron, manganese and small quantities of carbon and silicon – for restoring the quality of 'burnt iron'. Applying this discovery to the Bessemer process for refining iron ore, he produced cast steel.

COMBE FLOREY
Somerset
6 miles northwest of Taunton

Combe Florey is a beautiful sandstone village in the foothills of the Quantocks. The manor house, chiefly 18th century but with a gateway built in 1593, was the home of novelist Evelyn Waugh. Another distinguished resident was Sydney Smith, described in his day as 'the wittiest man in England', who served as vicar (1829–45) and described country life as 'a kind of healthy grave'. At Cothelstone, 2 miles to the east, there is a fine 17th-century manor house.

COMBE HAY
Avon
3 miles south of Bath

The lane to Combe Hay plunges through woods, and between the trees there is a glimpse of a village of attractive cottages overlooking a brook, with a white-washed inn standing on a knoll. Adjoining the church, the lawns of the Georgian Combe Hay Manor House slope down to an ornamental lake. Behind the inn a steep track offers a circular walk, about 2 miles long, passing Fortnight Farm and then dropping south via Week Farm back to Combe Hay.

Further upstream, as the brook turns towards Bath at Midford, stands a long, high stone viaduct which carries the A36 over Midford Brook. Built in the 1800s, its designer is reputed to have been Thomas Telford.

COMPTON PAUNCEFOOT
Somerset
3 miles east of Sparkford

This was the 'compton', or narrow valley, belonging to a Norman knight called Pauncefote ('Fat-bellied'). Opposite the village church is the Old Rectory, a pleasant Georgian house. Compton Castle is a Gothic fantasy built about 1825, but the back part of the house is older, probably 17th century.

CONDICOTE
Gloucestershire
3 miles northwest of Stow-on-the-Wold

This is upland country where remote stone villages sit snugly in summer and doggedly in winter, following the ancient patterns of settlement that cover the area northwest of Stow-on-the-Wold. From the village of Condicote the Roman Ryknild Street runs southeast and straight across the top of the high downland. It forms a clear track from here to the A436. Northeast of Condicote is Eubury Camp, a wide, Iron Age fortification of high bank-and-ditch construction

studded with thorn and elder bushes. It is on the north side of the minor road that runs from the village to the A424, and is clearly visible from the road. A closer look at the massive bank can be taken from the path on private land that winds round the valley bottom past a water tower. The sight of a string of horses at exercise adds to the atmosphere of bygone days that pervades these uplands.

On the same minor road, almost in Condicote itself, a large triangle of grassland on the south side of the road marks the site of a prehistoric henge – an enclosure marked by stone or timber and built for some unknown purpose about 2500 BC.

Four miles southwest of Condicote is Cotswold Farm Park, a breeding farm for animals that were once widespread in Britain but now face extinction. The farm has more than 20 rare breeds, including the Cotswold sheep which created much of England's wealth in the Middle Ages and Tamworth pigs which most resemble the animals that foraged in the oak forests of ancient Britain.

The science of breeding new types of animals was first developed in Britain in the late 18th century, when Robert Bakewell of Leicestershire established selective mating as a means of fatstock improvement. However, as new breeds developed, old ones were discarded and sometimes became extinct.

The animals at Cotswold Farm Park include Longhorn cattle, which are probably the nearest direct descendants of the wild cattle tamed by Stone Age farmers. The breed was improved by Bakewell, whose Longhorns were unrivalled in their ability to fatten, but it declined when smaller joints and therefore smaller animals became popular. White Park cattle are believed to have been introduced by the Romans, possibly as sacrificial animals for a religious cult. When the Romans left Britain, the cattle became forest animals.

Sheep at the farm include the Soay, the last survivor of Europe's prehistoric domestic sheep. They shed their wool, so farmers could pluck them instead of using shears.

In the Middle Ages, Norfolk Horn sheep foraged on the heathlands of East Anglia. The last Norfolk Horn ram died in 1973, but by crossing surviving ewes with Suffolk sheep, which include a Norfolk strain, a 'New Norfolk Horn' has been created to continue a breed close to the original. Other sheep at the farm include the North Ronaldsay (or Orkney) sheep which grazes on seaweed in the Orkneys, and the St Kilda sheep, with a black fleece, yellow eyes and up to six goat-like horns, giving it an almost devilish look. The St Kilda is probably the last remnant of the Hebridean sheep which are thought to have been brought to the Hebrides by the Vikings.

Pigs at Cotswold Farm Park include the Gloucester Old Spot, which foraged on waste from cottages and small farms in the Vale of Berkeley. A breeding experiment at the farm has also produced a type of pig similar to those found on farms in the Iron Age.

CONGRESBURY
Avon
5 miles south of Clevedon

Tradition has it that St Congar built a wattle church at Congresbury and then, wanting shade, thrust a yew stick into the ground, where it sprouted like Joseph of Arimathea's staff at Glastonbury. The church which

CONGRESBURY *The fine old vicarage was built c. 1445.*

stands here today has one of the finest old vicarages in Britain, dating from the 15th century, with moulded beams. A Regency wing was added between 1824–27. Just south of the AA box a footpath leads through Ball Wood to Wrington Hill, a 500 ft high viewpoint.

COOPER'S HILL

Gloucestershire
6 miles southwest of Cheltenham

A celebrated and distinctly dangerous cheese-rolling ceremony is held each Whitsuntide on Cooper's Hill, when those prepared to risk life and limb chase a whole cheese down a precipitous slope below the cockerel-crowned maypole on its northern rim. But for the rest of the year the hill is a peaceful nature reserve of some 137 acres of common land. The reserve is now in the care of Gloucestershire County Council. Steep paths lead up the hill from a signposted car park below its western flank on the A46.

Cooper's Hill was once one of the largest Iron Age fortifications in the Cotswolds, probably also known to Bronze Age predecessors, but it has been common land since well before the 10th century. Local property owners still have commoners' rights such as pannage, the right to let pigs loose to feed on beechmast, or estovers, the right to gather wood for fuel.

The cheese-rolling ceremony is thought to have its origin in ancient prehistoric ceremonies concerning sun worship – it used to be held on Midsummer Day. The cheeses may have represented the sun.

Views from Cooper's Hill are very fine, looking out over the Vale of Gloucester with the Severn Bridge just visible to the southwest and Bredon Hill and the Malverns to the north. There are exposed limestone scarp slopes on the western edge, with some handsome beechwoods.

A mere half mile away is Great Witcombe Villa, a fine Cotswold Roman villa which nestles in a sheltered combe on the scarp of Cooper's Hill. When first excavated, some of the walling still stood to a height of about 6 ft. The site contains tessellated pavements and a bath wing. The fabric of the remains has been renovated.

Prinknash Abbey, nearby to the southwest, was built between the 14th and 16th centuries for monks from Gloucester Abbey. In 1928 it became a Benedictine abbey and is famous for its pottery.

CORFE CASTLE

Dorset
4 miles southeast of Wareham

In Anglo-Saxon, *Corfe* means 'a cutting' or 'pass', an apt term for the deep gully that slices through the main ridge of the Purbeck Hills. Two roads from the west and three from the east converge on Corfe, but none bypasses it, stressing the strategic importance of the castle, towering high above the village on the top of its steep little hill.

The village has grown up around the hill, which has been fortified since at least Saxon times. The present castle dates from the late 15th century, but stands on the site of a much earlier fortress possibly built or enlarged by King Edgar in the 970s. His son, the young King Edward, afterwards canonised as St Edward the Martyr, was stabbed to death there in 978 – according to legend on the orders of his ambitious stepmother, Aelfthryth – or Elfrida. In 1202 King John was said to have sent 22 captured French knights to Corfe and starved them to death in the castle dungeons.

The military role of Corfe Castle came to an abrupt end during the Civil War. For a time, it was the only Royalist stronghold between London and Exeter, but it fell at last when a member of the garrison turned traitor and admitted the Parliamentary besiegers who destroyed it with gunpowder. The ruin is now much as Cromwell's sappers left it in 1646.

Much of the attraction of Corfe lies in its uniformity. The entire village and the castle are made of grey Purbeck stone – not just the walls, but the roofing slates too. Much of the old village is built of stone taken from the ruined castle.

Many of the houses have neat little dormer windows and tall stone chimneys. The Company of Marblers and Stone-Cutters of the Isle of Purbeck, an ancient organisation of craftsmen, has its headquarters at Corfe. It meets every Shrove Tuesday at the Fox Inn, when church bells are rung and newcomers are initiated by having to carry a loaf and a mug of beer, harassed by the members, without spilling any. After the ceremony, a game of street football is played along the road from Corfe to Swanage and back to the castle. The purpose is to maintain the ancient right of way to Swanage Harbour, from which Purbeck marble was once shipped.

The Church of St Edward the Martyr was extensively restored in 1859, having fallen into ruin through centuries of neglect after Civil War damage. According to a contemporary report, the Parliamentarians found that 'the most advantageous part of their batteries was the church, which they, without fear of profanation, used not only as their rampart but as their rendezvous. Of the surplesse they made two shirts for two soldiers, they broke down the organs and made the pipes serve for cases to hold their powder and shot, and, not being furnished with muskett-bullets, they cut off the lead of the church and rolled it up and shot it without even casting it in a mould'.

From the church, the two main streets, West Street and East Street, lead away from the castle and village centre, slightly diverging. Between them lies meadowland, carefully preserved as Common Land.

CORFE CASTLE *The ruins of the Norman fortress brood on the hill overlooking the village of Corfe* (overleaf).

CORSHAM

Wiltshire
4 miles southwest of Chippenham

Warm, cream-coloured Bath stone characterises the small Cotswold town of Corsham. The Flemish-gabled cottages on the cobbled street and the baroque-pedimented Hungerford almshouses all derive from its wealthy past as a weaving village. The school adjoining the almshouses has its original seating arrangement with the master's pulpit desk and original seating of 1668 still in place.

St Bartholomew's Church was extensively restored in 1874, but still displays much work from Norman times.

Corsham Court is a splendid Elizabethan mansion which has an impressive pedimented gateway. Mr 'Customer' Smythe, so-called because of his office as Collector of the Customs of London, built the house. Georgian additions were made by Nash and a park was laid out by 'Capability' Brown, the famous 18th-century landscape gardener. The state rooms are filled with old masters and superb furniture.

The town lies at the eastern end of Box Tunnel, the 1.8 mile long railway tunnel built by Isambard Kingdom Brunel in 1836–41. It is said that the sun shines through the tunnel at sunrise on one day each year – April 9, Brunel's birthday.

The tunnel links Corsham to Box, a large, straggling village with quarries that are still worked to produce the fine Bath stone.

COTHELSTONE HILL

Somerset
6 miles northwest of Taunton

The road climbs steeply from Cothelstone village to the crossroads on the hill. To the right a clump of wind-ravaged beeches shares the summit, known locally as Cothelstone Beacon, with the ruins of a folly tower. Perhaps Lady Hillsborough, who built the tower about 1770, used it as a point from which to enjoy the view. It is said that several counties can be seen from here on a clear day, but at any time the view is captivating with ash and beech woods cladding the slopes, and the fields and meadows of the Vale of Taunton Deane spread out below.

The left turn at the crossroads leads to Lydeard Hill, where there is a car park, and passes through the mixed oak and beech woodlands with picturesque names, such as Paradise, Badger's Copse and Much Care Wood.

At the foot of Cothelstone Hill, near Cothelstone church, are the grounds and buildings of Cothelstone Manor, a skilfully restored Elizabethan/Jacobean house of pink sandstone with its original gatehouse. There are memories here of the infamous Judge Jeffreys, who hanged two of the Duke of Monmouth's followers in the gateway after the duke's defeat at Sedgemoor in 1685. The village itself is charming, with red-sandstone cottages and a holy well. The well, called St Agnes's Well, lies hidden in greenery in a field a little way up the hill.

CRANBORNE

Dorset
8 miles northwest of Ringwood

Red-brick and colour-washed cottages give Cranborne a bright and attractive appearance. The narrow streets and market place are flanked with handsome town houses – many of them Georgian and late Stuart – and there is a multitude of shining roof tiles from the kilns down the River Crane valley. The village is set on the edge of the rolling chalk uplands, Cranborne Chase, one of the great medieval forests. Several monarchs – including King John and James I – hunted there, and for centuries the woodland was governed by Cranborne Chase Court – the official body controlling hunting rights.

The outstanding building in Cranborne is the Church of St Mary, St Peter and St Bartholomew. The church was originally attached to a 10th-century Benedictine abbey, but the oldest part now remaining is the Norman doorway in the north porch, retained when the church was rebuilt in the 13th century. The church has a fine barrel roof, and its treasures include a finely carved medieval oak pulpit and fragments of 13th- or 14th-century wall-paintings. In the south wall there is a late-Victorian window to John Tregonwell, who died in 1885. He was the son of Lewis Tregonwell, a local squire who was the founder of the seaside resort of Bournemouth, some 14 miles to the south. Lewis visited the area, mostly heathland beside the Channel, in 1810, and because the climate suited him

well, he bought land and built there.

Near the church is the greystone Manor House, the former administrative centre of Cranborne Chase. It is mainly Jacobean, but its central block dates from the 13th century and was probably a hunting lodge built for King John. It has been in the family of the Cecils, Marquesses of Salisbury, since it was granted to them by James I. Its gardens feature Italian statuary and specialise in sweet geraniums, roses, herbs and silver foliage. They are open to the public on certain days from April to October. Another notable mansion is Cranborne Lodge, built of traditional red brick in the 1740s.

In the centre of the village is the gabled Fleur de Lys Hotel, where Rupert Brooke stayed and about which he wrote one of his nostalgic poems.

Half a mile southeast is Cranborne Castle, with a well-preserved medieval motte (mound) and crescent-shaped bailey (courtyard).

Three miles southwest are the Knowlton Circles, three Neolithic henge-circles in a row, over 4000 years old. The largest, some 800 ft in diameter, is roughly bisected by the Cranborne to Wimborne road, and the other two lie to the north. A ruined Norman church with later additions stands in the middle of the central circle. To the east of this circle is an enormous Bronze Age round barrow, and smaller barrows are grouped close by.

CREWKERNE

Somerset
8 miles southwest of Yeovil

The market town of Crewkerne stands on a sheltered site and has been a place of importance since before the Norman Conquest. There was a settlement here in Roman times and the Saxons had a royal mint in the town. Crewkerne was the market centre for surrounding farms and also once had an ancient industry, sailmaking – sailcloth for Nelson's ships was made here. The craft has recently been given new life through the modern interest in yachting.

The Church of St Bartholomew, mainly 15th century, has an enormous west window. In Abbey Road is a Jacobean building, formerly the ancient grammar school, founded in 1499. Nelson's flag captain in the *Victory*, Captain Hardy, was a pupil there.

On the 4th and 5th of September each year the market square is the scene of a street fair which dates back to Saxon times.

CRICKET ST THOMAS

Somerset
3 miles east of Chard

One of the most beautiful estates in the West Country, Cricket House is a Georgian mansion that belonged to the Bridport family who were connected by marriage with Lord Nelson – a frequent visitor. Today it is also known as the home of the series *To the Manor Born*. The extensive grounds contain a wildlife park, open to the public; and the parish church of St Thomas also stands in the grounds.

THE WARDEN'S HOUSE *The gabled Hungerford Almshouses at Corsham, c. 1668, have an elegant central building.*

CRICKLADE
Wiltshire
7 miles northwest of Swindon

Cricklade is the only town in Wiltshire on the River Thames, which at this point is merely a channel. The wide main street has good 17th- and 18th-century houses, and just beyond the town is the 13th-century priory, now divided into small houses.

The parish church of St Sampson has a cathedral-like turreted tower built by the Duke of Northumberland in 1553, some good Norman features and splendid carved heraldic work. A museum at the west end of the main street has a collection that illustrates the history of the town from the Roman occupation, through its Saxon period, when it had a mint, to the present day.

Nearby is the village of Ashton Keynes, set in the water-meadows of the upper reaches of the Thames. A stream runs beside the main street, and the houses are reached over separate small bridges.

At the end of Church Walk, the stream widens in front of two mellowed stone houses, Brook House and Ashton Mill, to become recognisable as the infant River Thames.

CROSCOMBE
Somerset
3 miles east of Wells

The small village of Croscombe has two medieval manor houses, the remains of a medieval cross at the foot of the church path, and a skyline of steep and thickly wooded hills. Just north of the village, a lane leads into Ham Woods (600 ft). On a hill 1½ miles north of Ham Woods stands Maesbury Castle.

For many people, Maesbury Castle is the most exhilarating spot on the whole of the Mendip Hills. This impressive Iron Age fort crowns a hill on the southern side of the plateau, and from it there are compelling views of the Somerset countryside, with the main ridge of the hills rising to the northwest.

Maesbury would have been a difficult place to conquer in those prehistoric days, situated as it was in such a commanding position. Today it is rather easier to tackle; by simply walking across a field from the road which runs along the hill. The outline of the original fortifications which encircle the top of the hill can still be seen in the oval-shaped mound, now covered with grass.

CROWCOMBE
Somerset
7 miles southeast of Watchet

The top of what was once Crowcombe's church spire lies half forgotten and gathering moss in the churchyard here – a relic of a dramatic December afternoon in 1725. Worshippers were just arriving for evensong amid a gathering storm when a great bolt of lightning struck the church. The top of the spire was brought crashing through the roof, causing much damage. But the worshippers, who had taken shelter in the porch, were unharmed. The Church of the Holy Ghost – duly repaired after the incident – has a splendidly carved late 14th- or early 15th-century font, and the now spireless red-sandstone tower is 14th century.

There are many who consider Crowcombe to be the fairest of the Quantock Hills villages. A delightful ribbon of stone and cob (a mixture of mud and straw) cottages, many with thatched roofs, it slumbers contentedly on the lower slopes, looking across rich farmland to the Brendon Hills. Most visitors reach the village from the Taunton to Williton road, which passes half a mile to the west. But the best approach is over the Quantocks from Nether Stowey, 5 miles to the northeast. As you descend into Crowcombe a canopy of trees frames a glorious view over the surrounding countryside.

In medieval times the village was an important junction on the hill crossing from Taunton to Bridgwater Bay. It had a market as long ago as 1226, and a stone market cross that still stands at the centre of the village served also as a focal point for the annual fair, which began in 1234. Sadly, there is neither market nor fair nowadays, but the steps of the cross bear the marks of wear from those who, all those centuries ago, traded and roistered here.

The village church has handsomely carved Tudor bench-ends symbolising fertility – one of which depicts two men struggling with a dragon. The contents also include an early 17th-century pulpit and a fragile Jacobean screen with fine tracery and, in the churchyard, a 14th-century cross with a preacher ensconced above a grinning head. Close by, opposite the church, is the 15th-century Church House, with mullioned windows and a Tudor door. It served originally as a sort of parish hall, where villagers could hold meetings and celebrations. Holy ale was brewed and holy bread baked for medieval church suppers; travelling tradesmen could sell their wares here and seek shelter for the night. For almost 200 years, up to 1871, the building was used as a school and almshouse, and, stout as ever, still serves the parish as a village hall.

Across the road, at the end of a long drive, is the huge, red-brick mansion, Crowcombe Court. The house was begun about 1725 by a Devon architect, Thomas Parker, who was later sacked for theft. Building was eventually completed ten years later by a Wincanton man, Nathaniel Ireson, for the lord of the manor, Thomas Carew.

On the lane leading east to Stogumber, stands an ancient tree, the Heddon oak, famed for its widespreading branches. Stogumber church is famous for a legend concerning Sir Francis Drake.

When he wooed Elizabeth Sydenham, her noble family, aware of the great sailor's humble origins, refused to permit the match. Sadly, Drake went back to sea, and Elizabeth, tired at last of waiting for her roving lover, became betrothed to a man of her parent's choice.

On the wedding day, the guests assembled in Stogumber church and, as the bridal party approached the door, there was a blinding flash and a thunderous roar in the sky. A huge cannonball fell at the feet of the bride, who was convinced that Drake had somehow known of her marriage and had fired a shot across the world to show his anger. She refused to allow the ceremony to continue and, in due course, Drake returned to claim her. The couple were married in 1585. A meteorite which is nearly as big as a football, and is kept in the hall at Coombe Sydenham House, is said to be the 'cannonball'.

DEERHURST

Gloucestershire
7 miles northwest of Cheltenham

Deerhurst was once an important settlement of Hwicce, the Anglo-Saxon sub-kingdom of the lower Severn valley. Here was the little kingdom's most important monastery, where, during its decline in the 10th century, the martyr St Alphege was a monk. Later, as Archbishop of Canterbury, Alphege was taken by the Danes and killed because he refused to allow himself to be ransomed, knowing that the poor would bear the burden of raising the ransom money.

Here also, some years later in 1016, on a nearby island in the Severn, the English king, Edmund Ironside, made a treaty of friendship with the Danish Canute.

Nowadays the village is a tiny group of largely timber-framed cottages and farmhouses clustering round the Priory Church of St Mary, which stands out from the flat surrounding countryside of the Severn valley. This fine Saxon church dates in part from the 7th century, when the monastery was near the height of its prosperity. High in the east wall of the tower is an elaborate double window with triangular heads. The window resembles nothing else surviving from Saxon England, but it is said to be similar to a window in the Ethiopian monastery of Debra Damo in Africa.

There are also some notable Saxon carvings: a haunting, probably 9th-century angel in the apse; some delightful animals on several arches; a plaque of the Madonna and Child in the porch; and what some consider to be the finest Saxon font in existence. Moving forward in time, there is the only animal to be named in any medieval memorial brass. This is Terri, the pet dog of Alice, Lady Cassey, who, with her husband Sir John – the Chief Baron of the Exchequer from 1389 to 1400 – is commemorated in the north aisle. The Casseys lived in a house on the site of the 16th-century Wightfield Manor, 1 mile south.

Adjoining the church is the stone, mostly 14th-century, Priory House and nearby stands the timber-framed Abbot's Court, with, at its northwest corner, the remarkable Odda's Chapel. This simple little stone chapel dates from 1056, and inside is a copy of the Odda Stone – a dedication stone found close by in 1675 and now in the Ashmolean Museum, Oxford.

Its inscription, translated from the Latin, opens: 'Earl Odda has this royal hall built and dedicated in honour of the Holy Trinity for the soul of his Brother Aelfric which left the body in this place.' Earl Odda was a friend and kinsman of the Saxon king of England, Edward the Confessor (1042–66).

DEVIZES

Wiltshire
10 miles southeast of Chippenham

A castle built in the 12th century by Roger, Bishop of Salisbury, and sited between two manors gave the town of Devizes its name. It comes from the Latin *ad divisas* (at the boundaries). Devizes is a pleasant old market town with timbered buildings dating from the early 16th century and several fine 18th-century houses. On the cross in the market place is an inscription telling the salutary story of the sudden death in 1753 of one Ruth Pierce, after cheating at the local market. The museum has collections of finds from Neolithic, Bronze Age and Iron Age sites in Wiltshire. The most important of which is the Stourhead Collection of Bronze Age urns, beakers and ornaments, which were excavated from barrows on Salisbury Plain in the early 19th century. Two of the town's several churches have Norman features.

West of Devizes the land falls away into a shallow valley, dropping more than 200 ft in 2 miles. But to the Georgian engineer John Rennie, whose Kennet and Avon Canal had to cross the valley, this was no problem. He built locks, 29 of them, and 170 years later they are still there for all but the unimaginative to wonder at.

Four steps down from the main road out of Devizes lead to the canal; wide at this point with deep, dark and still waters. Reeds and water-lilies fringe the banks; ducks, dabchicks and moorhens nibble at the weeds and patient anglers nibble at their sandwiches. To the northeast, the western escarpments of the Marlborough Downs edge the skyline like pale green clouds.

A walk westwards along the gravel towpath brings the first of the series of locks into view, its gates replaced by baulks of timber to dam back the water, and a white bridge a little further on makes a splendid vantage point for looking down into the valley. The locks descend like a giant staircase, with little more than a narrowboat's length between them, and although the locks are not fully functional, there is enough water and cleared canal for an annual canoe race to make its way from London to Bath.

When the Kennet and Avon Canal was a vital part of Victorian England's waterways, this tranquil scene bustled with activity as the bargees sweated and strained to work their laden craft through the 29 locks – each doublegated. No wonder it took half a day, and no doubt those eastward bound paused at the Black Horse, whose present landlord breeds the Aylesbury ducks which speckle the water where the painted narrowboats once plied.

DIDMARTON

Gloucestershire
6 miles southwest of Tetbury

Cotswold stone houses of the 18th and 19th centuries line the busy road winding through Didmarton. But the heart of the village is at the foot of a hill, where the Church of St Lawrence is shaded by a tall Wellingtonia tree with, set back behind it, a 17th-century manor house and its huge barns.

The church is disused but kept open, a rare example of a building that was originally medieval, and has remained unaltered since the 18th century. Instead of their usual restoration job, the Victorians built a whole

ST LAWRENCE'S *Though disused, this little medieval gem has been carefully preserved since the 18th century.*

new church, St Michael's, a few hundred yards up the road. Now the airy interior of St Lawrence's is disturbed only by the rhythmic tick of the church clock. Box pews, painted a subtle shade of Georgian green, are overlooked by a three-decker pulpit, set high between two windows. A row of hatpegs is set 16 ft above the floor at the back of the church: one might think that a race of giants worshipped here. The prosaic explanation is that there was once a gallery.

Across the road from the church, a semicircle of stones encloses St Lawrence's Well. Village legend tells that in the 6th century St Lawrence himself visited the place and blessed the well, promising at the same time that it should never run dry.

Halfway up the village street, near St Michael's, Chapel Walk leads past a terrace of tiny cottages to a pretty little Congregational chapel, set somewhat incongruously among the cabbages and cauliflowers of the village allotments. From here there is a view across fields, separated from one another by stone walls, to an isolated hamlet – Oldbury on the Hill with its little Church of St Arild and the ancient stone Manor Farm peeping out from behind it.

DINTON
Wiltshire
5 miles west of Winton

The delightful village of Dinton, built on a hillside, is bordered by three beautifully landscaped houses. Philipps House, in Dinton Park, has an early 19th-century neo-Grecian white facade.

Little Clarendon, just east of Dinton Church, is a handsome, early Tudor manor house. Lawes Cottage, also close to the church, dates from the 17th century. It was the home of William Lawes, a composer and friend of John Milton, and some of his music for Milton's *Masque of Comus*, written in 1634, is said to have been composed there.

DORCHESTER
Dorset
7 miles north of Weymouth

Dorset's county town was largely rebuilt after a series of fires in the 17th and 18th centuries destroyed most of its medieval buildings. The site has been occupied since prehistoric times, but it was the Romans who founded the town in AD 70, calling it Durnovaria.

Dorchester was a Saxon mint in the 10th century, a hunting centre under the Normans, and a Roundhead stronghold during the Civil War of 1642–9. In the early 17th century a group of local Puritans founded New Dorchester in Massachusetts.

Maumbury Rings, south of the town, were built by Stone Age men as a Sacred Circle, but the Romans turned it into a vast amphitheatre where 10,000 spectators could watch gladiatorial combats on the scale of the Colosseum in Rome.

In the Middle Ages it was used for bear-baiting, and

it did when its occupant was one of the busiest men in Dorchester. It is a private residence.

Several mosaic floors still survive in the Roman House, which is next to the Country Hall at Colliton Park. The foundations, which have lasted nearly 2000 years, can also be seen.

Dorset Military Museum, which is housed in The Keep – the entrance to the former Dorset Regiment barracks – records the history of all the Dorset regiments from 1661. The display includes pictures, uniforms, medals, and weapons, including the sword and saddle used by Cornet Glyn in the Heavy Brigade Charge at Balaclava. An unusual exhibit is a desk from Adolf Hitler's Berlin Chancellery. It was presented by the Russians to the Dorset Regiment in 1945.

Dorset's history, from the Stone Age to the 20th century, is traced in the Dorset County Museum. The museum's Thomas Hardy Memorial Collection includes some of the novelist's manuscripts and personal possessions, housed in a reconstruction of his study. The museum also has relics of William Barnes, and paintings by local artists. Geology, natural history, archaeology and local history are also covered, and there are important finds from Maiden Castle.

Nearby Charminster, about 1 mile to the north, has the 12th-century aisled Church of St Mary, with original Norman arcades and chancel arch. It has a 16th-century tower and late Gothic additions, including an attractive 19th-century chancel. A further couple of miles to the north lies Godmanston, which claims the smallest public house in England – the 600-year-old Smith's Arms. Its front is only 11 ft wide. Once the pub was a smithy, and the story goes that Charles II bestowed the licence on the smith who reshod his horse, so that the king could drink ale while he waited. The licence has been kept up ever since.

as late as 1767 'Hanging Fairs' – public executions – were held there.

The Old Crown Court, in High West Street, was in 1834 the scene of a noted trial, that of the six Tolpuddle Martyrs who were sentenced to seven years' transportation after forming the Friendly Society of Agricultural Labourers – the start of the trade union movement in Britain. The court is now a public memorial to the Martyrs, who were pardoned in 1836 after prolonged local agitation.

St Peter's was the only church in Dorchester to survive the fire of 1613, which destroyed 300 houses. It is mainly 15th century with a 13th-century doorway and a 14th-century Easter sepulchre. In the churchyard stands a statue to the poet William Barnes, who lived in Dorchester from 1847 until his death in 1886. Barnes, who was Rector of Came, just south of the town, wrote in the Dorset dialect.

In 1685, following the Monmouth Rebellion, Judge Jeffreys held a 'Bloody Assize' in Dorchester. Afterwards the heads of the men who were executed were impaled on the church railings. Jeffreys is believed to have held his court in a room which still exists at the rear of the Antelope Hotel. He lodged in a house in High West Street, and this is reputed to be haunted still by his ghost.

Napier's Almshouses, also known as Napper's Mite, were founded in 1610 by Sir Robert Napier, a Dorset judge who was elected MP for Dorchester in 1586. The building provided lodgings for 'ten poor men', but now consists of shops and a cafe.

The Hangman's Cottage is a 16th-century thatched building close to the River Frome. It still looks much as

DOWN AMPNEY
Gloucestershire
2 miles north of Cricklade

Visible for miles across the flat pastureland through which runs the infant Thames, the 14th-century spire of All Saints' Church, Down Ampney, beckons above the tall trees that surround it. Looking out over the meadows in front of the church, it is so peaceful that it is hard to imagine the whine and roar of Second World War planes taking off from these fields bound for the D-Day invasion and, later, the ill-fated airborne mission to Arnhem.

Every year in September the church, which dates from 1265, is filled for a service commemorating the Battle of Arnhem. A stained-glass window preserves the memory of Down Ampney's airmen, among them Flight Lieutenant David Lord who was posthumously awarded the Victoria Cross for bravery when flying in desperately needed supplies.

An earlier warrior, Sir Nicholas de Valers – sometimes spelt Villiers – reclines in effigy in the south transept, his feet crossed. Beside the church a tall yew hedge screens Down Ampney House, a fine stone Tudor building 'modernised' in 1799.

Set back from the road is the Old Vicarage, which has a tall pine beside its gate. Ralph Vaughan-Williams, the composer, was born here in 1872, when his father was vicar. Later he wrote the music of a tune to the hymn *Come down O Love Divine* and called it *Down Ampney*.

DOWNTON
Wiltshire
6 miles south of Salisbury

Two rows of houses, mostly brick and thatch, line a wide street with a broad strip of grass down its centre. This is The Borough, the medieval Downton built by the Bishop of Winchester about 1205.

The River Avon divides the village in two, and at its centre is a tannery, built in 1918 and still in use, with its frontage on the river bank. High Street is a continuation of The Borough on the eastern side of the river and has several 18th-century houses.

The Church of St Lawrence is large, with mixed architecture from 12th century to Victorian. It stands on the site of an earlier church, consecrated by St Birinus in 638. Inside are monuments by Peter Scheemaker, the 18th-century Dutch sculptor. South of the church is Moot House, an 18th-century building with a garden laid out on the foundations of a Norman castle. The small amphitheatre facing Moot House – which resembles a Saxon meeting place, or moot – is the result of 18th-century landscaping. A Roman villa with seven rooms and a bath house was excavated near Moot House in 1955. It dates from about AD 300.

Nowadays, Downton is renowned as an angling centre for the Wiltshire Avon and its neighbouring chalk streams, the Wylye, Nadder and Ebble. Lord Radnor's estate, on the northern edge of the village, has a trout farm with more than 100 breeding pools. The long, low, 300-year-old Bull Hotel, on the Salisbury to Bournemouth road where it turns into The Borough, has attracted anglers since pre-war days. Its walls are hung with superb stuffed specimens of trout and pike.

DUNSTER
Somerset
7 miles west of Watchet

Dunster is a dream of a West Country village, watched over by an ancient castle, full of old buildings with intriguing nooks and crannies, and possessed of a venerable church whose quirky history reflects the salty character of the local people. Add to these the Bristol Channel and Exmoor as backdrops, and you may understand why there is a story that the Victorian hymn-writer Mrs Cecil Alexander composed the words for *All Things Bright and Beautiful* while walking on nearby Grabbist Hill.

The Norman Mohun family built Dunster's first castle shortly after the Conquest, on the natural hill overlooking the High Street. They died out after 300 years and it was then bought by the Luttrell family, who in turn owned it for six centuries until 1976.

Sir James Luttrell died after the second Battle of St Albans in the Wars of the Roses, and his family lands were taken over by Yorkist enemies until Henry VII came to the throne in 1485 and restored them. The second time round, the family were even luckier. Thomas Luttrell held the castle for the Roundheads in the Civil War, then handed it over to the Cavaliers, who were eventually besieged. For 160 days the Royalists under Colonel Francis Wyndham fought off their enemies. The Roundhead general, Robert Blake, is said to have threatened to put Wyndham's mother between the firing lines to force a surrender, but backed down when the grand old lady urged her son to do his duty regardless. Eventually, in 1646, the defenders of the last Royalist stronghold in Somerset marched out battered and ill, but with drums beating and colours flying, in honourable surrender.

Cromwell had much of the castle pulled down, but the Luttrells returned at the Restoration of Charles II and turned what remained into a magnificent house. To this period belong the oak and elm staircase, carved with lively hunting scenes, and the splendid plaster ceiling of the dining room and its hanging leather panels embossed to show the story of Antony and Cleopatra. Later centuries, too, brought their additions – a chapel in the 18th, two new towers and living accommodation in the 19th. The 20th century brought death duties which finally led to the National Trust taking over the castle.

As lords of the manor, Luttrells were dispensing local justice in the 15th century – which may have been something of a headache if surviving records are true. It 1493 John Huyshe and Jerard Goldesmyth were ordered to stop their wives quarrelling and abusing neighbours, goings-on which cost them a fine of one pound. On another occasion, no fewer then 86 people were fined 6d (2½p) for brewing ale at home – a prerogative the lord liked to keep to himself.

The villagers' contentiousness led, ironically, to the finest feature in St George's parish church. The living had been given to Benedictine monks by 1100, and the villagers were eternally squabbling with them about which bit of the church belonged to whom. In 1498, after centuries of quarrels, a screen was built to divide the building. The screen, 54 ft long, fan-vaulted and with richly carved friezes, is one of the county's finest. Within 50 years the monks were swept away by the Dissolution, but remnants of their buildings include a circular dovecote with a revolving ladder. There is also the Old Priory, now a private house, and a tithe barn.

Among other fine buildings is the Luttrell Arms, which was altered between 1622 and 1629 by George Luttrell. It has a hall which has a hammer-beamed and vaulted ceiling and an ancient fireplace in which is carried out the venerable Christmas Eve custom of Burning the Ashen Faggot, accompanied by rounds of punch and the singing of the traditional Dunster Carol. There is also a porch with openings for arrows.

In Church Street is another venerable building misleadingly called The Nunnery – a name given to it in the 18th century. This three-storey, slate-hung house was built at the end of the 14th century. It served as a guesthouse for visitors to Dunster Priory and was owned by the Benedictine monks. In the market place the Yarn Market, an octagonal structure built about 1590, reflects the old industry of the village. Merchants would arrive here to buy the local cloth, called Dunsters, which was noted for quality and strength.

Old-world images are everywhere in Dunster – lattice windows, old chimneys, doors on medieval hinges, a churchyard yew tree said to be 1000 years old, a restored water mill. Only one place is not what it seems; Conygar Tower, the landmark facing the castle from the opposite end of the High Street. It is not medieval but that most English of buildings, a folly, built in 1775 as one of the improvements then being made to the castle and its estate.

THE OLD WATER MILL *Pale pink stucco faces the 17th-century mill on the River Avill outside Dunster.*

THE CROSSROADS AT DUNTISBOURNE ABBOTS *Sheep graze between dry-stone walls in the peaceful Duntbrook Valley.*

THE DUNTISBOURNES

Gloucestershire

4 and 5 miles northwest of Cirencester

This is one of the most enchanting and timelessly gentle valleys anywhere in England. The tiny, un-hurried stream of the Duntbrook meanders southeast through two exquisite little villages, two hamlets and four fords in the space of about 2 miles. Eastwards on the ridge above, the Roman Ermin Way takes the A417 arrow-straight to Cirencester: westwards, the valley rises gently to parkland and downs, then falls away steeply into the wooded valley of the River Frome.

At Duntisbourne Abbots, the larger of the two villages, the Duntbrook becomes part of the old cobbled road, with high walls and a raised pavement on either side. Carters washed their horses' feet and cleaned their wagons here, and villagers resist all attempts to culvert the sometimes swift-flowing stream. The village water supply still trickles into a stone pool here, though the pool is mossy now.

At Duntisbourne Leer and Middle Duntisbourne, barns and farms drowse in the sun by their fords. The tiny hamlet of Duntisbourne Leer was once owned by the abbey of Lire in France. Further down the open, green valley the tiny Saxon and Norman Church of St Michael at Duntisbourne Rouse perches on a slope above its own stretch of the Duntbrook. The 15th-century west tower has a saddle-back roof. Inside the church are a fine Norman font and crypt.

DYMOCK
Gloucestershire
5 miles south of Ledbury

Set on a small hill, Dymock rises serenely out of the delightful undulating countryside. In the few years before the First World War, the village and its surroundings were much loved by the Dymock poets, whose quarterly magazine *New Numbers* was sent throughout the world from Dymock post office. Rupert Brooke was one of their number, and many of his most famous poems were first published in *New Numbers*. So, too, were those of John Drinkwater, the American Robert Frost and his close friend Edward Thomas, who first contemplated writing poetry while staying in the village. Brooke and Drinkwater had been drawn to Dymock by their friend, the poet Lascelles

Abercrombie who, in 1911, took up residence in the tiny hamlet of Ryton, which is about $2\frac{1}{2}$ miles to the east.

Abercrombie's home was The Gallows, a timber-framed cottage below Ryton Woods. Here, a figure of local folk history, Jock of Dymock, was hanged for poaching the king's deer. Jock is famed for an alarming custom. On wild nights he used to jump out from a tunnel near Dymock church, with a stag's antlers on his shoulders, and scare passers-by. His tunnel has long since disappeared, but the fine early Norman Church of St Mary and the shady Wintour's Green in front still make a delightful centre of the village. Inside, the church has some interesting relics, including the last Dymock railway ticket, issued September 1959.

Beside the church is the 18th-century, red-brick Old Rectory and, farther down the main street, the Old Cottage still shows its A-shaped cruck beams at the side. The red-brick White House, opposite the church, was the birthplace in 1637 of John Kyrle, the Man of Ross, who was Ross-on-Wye's great benefactor.

Many of Dymock's most delightful houses lie scattered in the countryside round about. The red-brick Old Grange stands three-quarters of a mile northwest, off the Preston road. The core of the house, which once belonged to the Cistercian abbey of Flaxley, is probably medieval, although it was altered in the 18th and 19th centuries. The Welsh rebel leader Owain Glyndwr is believed to have sought refuge here in the early 15th century, and the house still has some secret chambers where he could have hidden.

Beyond The Old Grange, in the tiny hamlets of Greenway and Leddington, are the delightful timber-framed cottages named Little Iddens, home of Robert Frost from 1914 to 1915, and The Old Nail Shop, where his friend Wilfred Wilson Gibson, the sixth of the Dymock poets, lived. It was at Gibson's encouragement and suggestion that Frost came to live here.

The old Church of St Mary, Kempley, 2 miles west, has an almost complete set of 12th-century frescoes, and between Kempley and Dymock, the delightful Dymock Wood is rich in all kinds of wild flowers, including, in the spring, daffodils and bluebells.

DYRHAM
Avon
4 miles south of Chipping Sodbury

The pride of Dyrham village is the 17th-century house built by William Blathwayt, Secretary of State to William III. Dyrham Park is one of the National Trust's finest properties – a country mansion in a deer park – and worth a visit for its gardens and tapestries alone. There is an orangery, designed by William Talman, where oranges, grapefruit and mimosa grow. The interior expresses the Dutch-influenced taste of William's reign, with gilt leather hangings, delftware, paintings by minor Dutch Masters and paintings which have associations with the 17th-century diarists Pepys and Evelyn.

The village Church of St Peter is mainly Perpendicular in style, but a late Roman arcade survives in the nave. A tower stands over the west end. Inside the church is a fine Norman font and a brass of 1416, depicting the armoured figure of Sir Maurice Russell, and his wife. There is also a large monument to Sir George Wynter, with recumbent effigies, mourning children and gloriously flamboyant heraldry.

E

EAST COKER
Somerset
3 miles south of Yeovil

None of the golden-stone houses and cottages of East Coker is more interesting than the thatched home of the village's most renowned son, the great navigator William Dampier. He explored the west coast of Australia, and was navigator of the ship that rescued Alexander Selkirk – the real-life Robinson Crusoe.

Dampier was renowned in the 17th century as a pirate. A journal he kept of his buccaneering days is in the British Museum, and he is still remembered for his book about natural phenomena, *Discourse of the Winds*. He was brought up in Hymerford House, which still stands by the mill-stream.

He was baptised at the Norman font of the village Church of St Michael, which houses a brass memorial to him. Another memorial commemorates the poet T. S. Eliot, whose ashes are buried there. His ancestors emigrated from the village to America. In his poem, *East Coker – 1940*, Eliot wrote:

> 'In my beginning is my end. Now the light falls
> Across the open field, leaving the deep lane
> Shuttered with branches, dark in the afternoon,
> Where you lean against a bank while a van passes,
> And the deep lane insists on the direction
> Into the village ...'

Coker Court, its hall built in the 15th century and the front and wings added 300 years later, shares a low hillside with the church. A path shaded by dark yews and giant cedars leads up to it, past a row of tall gabled almshouses founded around 1640 by the Helyar family, who lived in Coker Court for centuries. The local pub, cosy and whitewashed, is called the Helyar Arms.

EAST HARPTREE
Avon
7 miles north of Wells

The ruins of Richmont Castle are about $\frac{1}{4}$ mile south-east of the village church in East Harptree. The castle was besieged in 1138 when King Stephen captured it from Sir William de Harptree, a supporter of Queen Matilda's cause in the Civil War between the king and queen. The castle was demolished by its owner, Sir John Newton, in the reign of Henry VIII; Sir John's huge, canopied tomb stands in the Norman porch of the church, which also contains a display of Roman coins found at East Harptree in 1887.

EASTLEACH
Gloucestershire
4 miles north of Lechlade

Two hamlets, Eastleach Turville and Eastleach Martin, face each other across the River Leach and together make up the village of Eastleach. Turville rises in terraces up the steep western bank and is divided

EAST COKER *The green-doored Helyar Almshouses are greeted by a blaze of yellow daffodils in spring.*

from its neighbour by a road, the river and a meadow. A road bridge over the Leach links the two communities. Originally, the two villages were independent of one another and were ruled over in Norman times by different noblemen.

The Keble family held the manor of Eastleach Turville for five generations from the 16th century. John Keble, the divine and poet in whose memory Keble College, Oxford was founded, was made the non-resident curate of Eastleach's two churches in 1815. Both churches are Norman; St Andrew's at Turville has a 14th-century saddle-back tower with a gabled roof, St Michael and St Martin's was founded by Richard Fitzpons, a Norman follower of William the Conqueror. It contains later Early English work, a 14th-

century font and medieval carved benches.

There are a number of old cottages in the village, some 19th-century almshouses and several picturesque farms and farm buildings of Cotswold stone.

EASTON GREY
Wiltshire
3½ miles west of Malmesbury

The young River Avon sketches a curling silver line through the meadows of Easton Grey early on its journey to Bath and Bristol. Ponies come down to drink from the shallow river beside the 16th-century stone bridge, built with five low arches.

Set around the bridge and climbing a short, curving street is an intimate huddle of houses in mellow grey stone. Windows are mullioned; lichened roofs are steeply pitched to bear the weight of stone tiles; and gardens are bordered by dry-stone walls from which purple aubrietia cascades in early summer.

Since 1236 the lords of the manor have looked down on the little hamlet over which they held sway from a succession of manor houses set back on a rise above the river.

In the 14th century John De Greye held the manor in exchange for maintaining one of the king's falcons. The present Easton Grey House is a handsome early 18th-century mansion with a classical facade and portico, surrounded by elegant gardens. Just inside the iron gates of the house is a little church with a squat Norman tower; the interior, apart from the Norman font, was extensively restored in 1836. Herbert Asquith, later 1st Earl of Oxford and Asquith (1852–1928), spent his summers here when he was Prime Minister (1908–16). The house was occupied then by his sister-in-law, and he used it as a country retreat — rather as modern prime ministers use Chequers.

The late Duke of Windsor, when Prince of Wales, appreciated the fine stabling facilities at Easton Grey and its proximity to the Duke of Beaufort's hunt at Badminton. He spent the hunting season there in 1923.

EBBOR GORGE
Somerset
3 miles northwest of Wells

About 270 million years ago, enormous pressure from inside the earth's crust pushed down a strip of millstone grit beneath the limestone to form an impermeable floor, over which a river once ran. The result of this transformation of the landscape was Ebbor Gorge, a wooded chasm which is now part of a 116-acre nature reserve managed by the Nature Conservancy Council. It is claimed to be the loveliest and most unspoilt gorge in the Mendips, and is certainly far less trodden than its more famous neighbour, Cheddar Gorge. Here ashes, pedunculate oaks, wych elms and other trees grow in dense and glorious confusion, providing a greenery unmatched elsewhere in this area. After wandering through the woods, another path leads up to the lonely Mendip Plateau.

Caves and fissures worn by rainwater provided shelter for New Stone Age man, who lived in the gorge about 3000 BC, and his bones, tools and ornaments have been found there. In Bridged Pot Shelter, at the head of the gorge, a superb axe of highly polished greenstone was found; it is now in the museum at Wells. Remains of animals such as bears, reindeer and lemmings have also been uncovered.

EBRINGTON
Gloucestershire
2 miles east of Chipping Campden

There are few more appealing sights than the combination of golden Cotswold stone and neatly trimmed thatch, and it is never more attractive than at Ebrington. The village descends in irregular steps on the northern fringe of the hills, to a valley of cherry orchards and vegetable gardens.

There was a manor at Ebrington as far back as the 13th century, though most of the present house dates from the 17th century. The Church of St Eadburgha has a Norman nave, a Saxon stone coffin, benches, a canopied 17th-century pulpit and a medieval tower. A monument in the church depicts Sir John Fortescue, who died around 1476, in his legal robes of Lord Chief Justice.

About 3 miles north of the village is Hidcote Manor, a late-17th-century house with a Georgian frontage. The manor is notable for its gardens, now owned by the National Trust. They were laid out by Major Lawrence Johnston over a period of 40 years during this century, and are claimed to be among the finest in England. Each section is devoted to a particular type of

flower, and has a distinctive colour scheme, and the gardens are divided by hedges of many varieties.

EDINGTON
Wiltshire
4 miles east of Westbury

Few people visiting Edington can fail to be amazed at the sight of its great church, matching many a cathedral in size and beauty. The Church of St Mary, St Katharine and All Saints stands below the village, aloof and impressive.

The building was started in 1351 by William of Edington, Bishop of Winchester and treasurer to Edward III. In 1358 his college of priests was transferred to the Bonshommes, hermits who followed the Benedictine Order. A local tradition says that it was the Black Prince, Edward III's son, who encouraged him to bring them to Edington from their only other English house, at Ashridge in Hertfordshire. The church was consecrated in 1361.

This noble building, cruciform, with battlemented tower and parapets, has a perfect background in the sombre lines of the Downs rising behind it. A medieval clock, apparently blacksmith-made and one of the

EASTON GREY *Since 1236 the lords of the manor ruled the hamlet, but the present house dates from the 18th century.*

oldest in England, is in the tower. A yew tree, said to be nearly as old as the church, flourishes in the churchyard. Font cover, pulpit, altar rails and the plaster ceiling of the nave are all 17th century. There are also several interesting monuments, from the 15th century onwards.

In 1450, the sanctity of the church failed to save the life of William Ayscough, Bishop of Salisbury, who had sought refuge there during Jack Cade's rebellion. Supporters of Cade, who was rebelling against the corruption of Henry VI's government and officials, dragged him out to the top of Golden Ham Hill, above the village, where they pelted him to death with flint stones.

Modern Edington, with a population of 700, is a village of farms and meadows, with some orchards and arable land extending over the flat landscape to the north. Its houses lie on the lower slopes of the Downs, and are approached by undulating lanes.

EXFORD
Somerset
17 miles west of Watchet

Exford's glory is not the usual rich historic sense of continuity built up over the centuries but an instant treasure, acquired with the help of a tape measure and the collecting plate.

In 1857, the old Church of St Audrey at West Quantoxhead was pulled down for rebuilding and its superb 15th-century fan-vaulted rood screen packed away in pieces in a barn. It lay there for 40 years until Church authorities realised they had a masterpiece on their hands. It was unpacked with a view to putting it together again in Williton church, near Watchet. However, it would not fit, and so was sent to South Kensington, London, for possible display in the Victoria and Albert Museum. This proved impractical, so a search was started for a church of the right size that was willing to pay for the screen to be put up. St Mary Magdalene, Exford, proved inch-perfect, and the villagers collected £700. So the perfect match was made and the screen looks now as if it has been there for centuries, although it was only installed in 1929.

The church itself is half a mile outside the village, on the Wheddon Cross road. It is mid-14th century with clustered pillars and a quaint carved group of a demon and angels outside the west window. The village is on lower ground, with Georgian and Victorian cottages of brick and stone, many painted cream, grouped round a green.

Exford is in hunting and fishing country, and the Exe is a youthful river here, yet still making an impressive sight after heavy rains as it rushes under the stone bridge near the gabled White Horse inn. The village is the centre of the Devon and Somerset stag hunt and the kennels, stables and houses for the hunt servants are here. The blacksmith's forge is largely kept busy shoeing horses for the hunt. In the Auction Field by the river, sheep auctions are held three times a year. Although the village is set in pleasant fields, there is bleak moorland only 1 mile from the centre.

The churchyard gives a fine view over the moors and the Exe Valley, to the hills along which a prehistoric route ran from the Parrett at Combwich to Barnstaple. This route kept to the hilltops as the valleys were densely forested – the blackened trunks of ancient oaks are still found only a few feet beneath the soil.

FAIRFORD

Gloucestershire
8 miles east of Cirencester

The Church of St Mary the Blessed Virgin at Fairford is renowned for its 15th-century stained glass – among the best to have survived in England. The 28 windows illustrating biblical stories may have been made for St Mary's when it was rebuilt, about 1500, by a rich wool merchant, John Tame. The glass may have come from the school of Henry VII's Master Glass Painter, Barnard Flower – who glazed part of Westminster Abbey.

The chancel stalls have carved misericords – hinged bracket-seats – depicting grotesques and people in scenes from contemporary life.

Nearby Quenington has the Church of St Swithin, with two Norman doorways which include elaborate tympana. That on the south door depicts the Coronation of the Virgin, that on the north, The Harrowing of Hell.

A few miles to the south lies Kempsford, whose Church of St Mary is originally Norman. Its fine central tower was added by John of Gaunt, and has large Perpendicular north and south windows in the lower stage and weather-vanes on all the crocketed pinnacles. The vaulting within has carved and painted heraldic shields as bosses. Some of the Victorian stained glass is by Kempe; the chancel was enlarged by G. E. Street in 1858. On the walls of the nave are framed Puritan texts.

FARLEIGH HUNGERFORD

Somerset
5 miles southwest of Bradford-on-Avon

A mighty castle, owned by an ancient family who were as rich, dynamic and sometimes unscrupulous as any in an American television saga, once dominated Farleigh Hungerford.

The remains of Farleigh Castle appear almost intact as you approach the village from the Trowbridge road – an immense range of towers and curtain walls rearing from the green valley of the River Frome. But entering from the Radstock road, on the western side, opposite, all is seen to be a facade. Behind the imposing front are just a few low ruins and the foundations of walls carefully preserved amid noble trees and the greensward.

The castle was started by Sir Thomas Hungerford, first Speaker of the House of Commons, whose family boasted they could ride to Salisbury and back without leaving their own lands. Sir Thomas bought the old manor from the widowed daughter-in-law of a crony of his, Lord Burghersh. He then laid out a 180 ft courtyard and surrounded it with 6 ft thick walls topped with four 60 ft towers.

The Hungerfords survived here for 250 years, weathering the turmoil of the Wars of the Roses and the Tudors – although one Hungerford was beheaded by Henry VII on charges of treason and unnatural vice. The tower in which this wayward lord is believed to

have locked up his wife for four years is still standing. Another of Henry's many axe victims was Margaret, Countess of Salisbury, who was born in the castle. She had too much royal blood to be allowed to live as a possible rival.

The castle was held for King Charles in the Civil War, but fell to the Parliamentarians without a fight. From this time on, the family went into decline and the castle, though still intact, was 'very ruinous', until in the 1730s it was acquired by a Trowbridge family, the Houltons. They were interested in it more as a quarry than as a home, and they carted away hundreds of tons of stone to embellish and develop their Gothic-style house – now a school – on the other side of the village. Nor were they the only ones to use the castle in this way; many of the village houses are built with its stone.

In 1891 the Houltons sold the sadly battered castle to Lord Donington, whose wife was Baroness Hungerford in her own right. But the re-established family connection was destined not to last, and the castle was sold again. The place is now owned by the Department of the Environment.

But the Hungerfords still make their presence felt. The family Chapel of St Leonard, intact within the protecting wall, contains an awesome throng of tombs, beginning with the plain, solid one of old Sir Thomas and going on to the grandiose marble extravaganzas of the later Hungerfords.

In the crypt are the lead coffins of six adults and two children. The adults' coffins are in human form, four with portrait heads moulded on them, giving an eerie effect in the half light. Much else from the earliest period still survives in the chapel, including a magnificent 15th-century mural of St George and some fine stained glass. The priest's house also survives near the chapel, and is an excellent little museum.

To make up for the loss of the village church which they appropriated to create this chapel, the Hungerfords provided a new one in 1443 – another St Leonard's. It is simple, but with a splendid stained-glass glowering portrait of the great Sir Thomas in armour.

Though it is at least three centuries since a Hungerford ruled this part of Somerset, the church rather touchingly maintains a 'living' representation of their coats of arms – a real wheatsheaf and two practical-looking sickles in heraldic form.

Nearby is the local inn – popular in summer, for its garden gives a superb view across the valley – the village itself lying at the junction of two combes, the wooded ravines so typical of the county.

FLAX BOURTON

Avon
5 miles west of Bristol

Flaxley Abbey in Gloucestershire once owned the village of Flax Bourton, and this gave it half of its name. The church has some good Norman features and there is an attractive old pub, the Angel Inn.

A track leads south from the village to Bourton

FOSSE COTTAGE *All the charm of Fontmell Magna's village life is captured in this blooming country garden.*

Combe, a wood of great beauty, nearly 600 ft up. At the southern tip of the combe the track swings round to the north and narrows into a footpath which leads back to the village.

To the south of Flax Bourton lies Barrow Gurney. Flanked by Barrow Wood and three reservoirs, Barrow Gurney church incorporates part of a 13th-century Benedictine nunnery and is rich in stone and wood carving. Barrow Court is a Jacobean mansion, standing beside the church in a splendid garden. A footpath by the northern reservoir leads half a mile to a hilltop wood called The Wild Country.

FONTMELL MAGNA
Dorset
5 miles south of Shaftesbury

At the heart of the village of Fontmell Magna and its 17th-century cottages, the clear waters of a chalk stream, Fontmell Brook, dive down a mill-race and under the road. They pass Holbrook, a cottage built of grey stone and the alternating bands of flint and red brick that are so typical of Dorset. The area is rich in ash, beech and pine trees.

On a mound above towers the Church of St Andrew, which dates from the 14th century but was extensively rebuilt in 1863. Every three hours the church clock at Fontmell Magna chimes the time to the tune of the hymn *O Worship the King*. The large

cross in the churchyard commemorates a local hero –
Philip Salkeld, the son of a former rector of the parish.
As a lieutenant in the Bengal Engineers he was mortal-
ly wounded during the Indian Mutiny of 1857 while
blowing up the Cashmere Gate at Delhi.

An inscription explains how it was he 'who person-
ally fastened the powder bags to the gates, fixed the
hose, and although fearfully wounded continued to
hand to a non-commissioned officer the light to fire
the train'. For his heroism he was awarded the Victoria
Cross.

Until the 19th century, Fontmell Magna was a self-
supporting community of some 800 people. With the
arrival of modern farming methods and machinery,
the population declined; and by 1906 a guide book
described the village as 'one of those peaceful retreats
from the excitement of cities and great towns which
the wearied crave and the invalid rejoice in'.

This is now only partly true. For Fontmell Magna is
still at the heart of a prosperous farming community. It
has its own carriage-builder and, a mile away at
Bedchester, a maker of traditional harpsichords. Next
to the Crown Inn, a large red-brick building which now
houses the thriving Fontmell Potteries was once a
brewery belonging to the Flower family. It drew its
water from the stream whose spring gives the village
part of its name.

The name Fontmell comes from *funta*, Old English
for 'spring' and *mael*, Celtic for 'bare hill'. The stream
rises east of the village at Springhead. Here, at the foot
of a grassy chalk hill, there has been a mill ever since
the time of the Domesday Survey. Springhead consists
of a fine white-walled thatched house with a mill-
building at right angles to it. Behind it stretch splendid
gardens – weeping willows, herbaceous borders and a
Venetian rotunda on the edge of the millpond.

In 1933, Springhead was bought by Rolf Gardiner,
who promoted summer music schools at Springhead
until his death in 1973. The Springhead Trust continues
to develop his work. It runs courses for all ages in
subjects ranging from painting to prayer, and from
archaeology to environmental studies. The gardens
are open to the public twice a year.

Just to the north is Sutton Waldron, whose Church
of St Bartholomew is one of the prettiest in Dorset.
Built by Archdeacon Huxtable in 1847, its brightly
painted interior is by Owen Jones.

FOREST OF DEAN
Gloucestershire
Between the River Severn and the River Wye

A sense of life as it was hundreds of years ago
pervades the Forest of Dean. Secret and wild it seems,
stretching on and on whichever way you turn. But
then the green glade widens and you can see out over
undulating blue-green tree-tops to cultivated fields,
distant hills and shimmering curves of river.

In reality the forest is far from wild. Replanting has
gone on over the centuries and does today, making
the mixture of trees very different from what it was in
the forest the Normans knew. Now the oaks mingle
with beech, birch, ash and chestnut – and foreign
softwoods outnumber these. Spruce, larch and fir are
the fast-growing crop of the modern working forest.
All the 22,000 planted acres of trees are nursed and
thinned over the great triangular spread of forest that
lies between the Wye and Severn.

Ferns and mosses, lichens and liverworts carpet the
ground. You can glimpse shy deer and swift squirrels,
and hear the busy drilling of woodpeckers. Deer were
the quarry of the royal huntsmen who held this vast
domain as their preserve from the 11th century. King
Canute set up the Court of Verderers to be responsible for anything that grew or lived in the forest. The
court still meets at the 17th-century Speech House
deep in the heart of the woodlands. It was originally
built when iron-founders moved into the forest. The
courtroom was used to settle disputes between them
and the foresters who lived by woodcutting and
poaching. The courtroom is now a hotel dining room,
but is still used ten times a year for official sittings of
the Verderers' Court. The house stands in the centre of
the forest near Cannop Ponds, which were dug in 1820
to provide a water supply for iron smelters.

Except for the Forestry Commission workers, most
people come to the Forest of Dean now for leisure and
quiet enjoyment. It was very different in previous
centuries, for the forest, with its natural resources of
coal and iron ore as well as timber, played an important role in England's economy for hundreds of years.
The iron was mined from before Roman times until the
Industrial Revolution. In medieval times the forest
supplied timber for shipbuilding, and was so vital to
British naval power that its destruction was an ob-
jective of the Spanish would-be invaders in 1588.

During the Victorian era, the forest was a coalfield
producing a million tons of coal each year. After a
decline in the 1930s, open-cast mining has been
resumed in some areas. A few seams are exploited by
'free' miners. Their rights are a reward dating back to
1296, when the city of Berwick-upon-Tweed was
under siege. Miners from the Forest of Dean were
enlisted by Edward I, and won his gratitude by tunnel-
ling under the city walls.

There are numerous marked nature trails and forest
walks laid out by the Forestry Commission. The Forest
of Dean also has a maze of leafy lanes, and the
Forestry Commission has route-marked a scenic drive
starting near Coleford.

FORTHAMPTON
Gloucestershire
4 miles west of Tewkesbury

Forthampton is a tiny village of outstandingly fine
timber-framed cottages and farmhouses scattered in
the green and gently undulating countryside of the
Severn valley. At its centre is a high knoll topped by
the partly 13th-century Church of St Mary; at the foot
of the hill are stocks and a whipping post – which still
has the iron manacles that held its victims.

Near these relics stand some of the village's most
delightful buildings. Vine Farm, nearly opposite, is a
timber-framed and stone farmhouse of the 16th and
17th centuries. Down a lane, running northeast, is the
17th-century Alcock's Farm; and another lane, running southwest, leads past the timber-framed Hill Farm
House and The Sanctuary, which has a 15th-century
hall, to the large 18th-century Forthampton House.

Beyond the church, a road leads from the village
centre to the charming Lower Lode Inn, 1 mile south-

FOREST DRIVE *Foundry Wood in the Forest of Dean cloaks old
iron mines with the leafy canopy of oaks and beeches.*

east on the banks of the Severn. From the inn there are fine views over the river and across the flat meadows beyond to Tewkesbury and its abbey. On the way, the road passes the fine early 18th-century Southfield House, with a large elegant dovecote beside it, both built in warmly mellow red brick; and, set back in its park, the long, low Forthampton Court, whose grounds are occasionally open to the public. It was originally the country retreat of the abbots of Tewkesbury, and it still has a late 14th-century hall, a chapel with a 13th-century picture of Edward the Confessor, and a 14th-century tomb of a crusader. At the end of the 19th century, the court and the chapel were altered by the architect and designer Philip Webb.

FRAMPTON

Dorset
5 miles northwest of Dorchester

The tiny village of Frampton, Dorset, can claim two notable buildings: the Church of St Mary and the classical lines of Frampton Court. Later additions to the original 15th-century church include the 17th-century west tower, the 18th-century north aisle, and the south porch, added in 1820. Monuments include 17th-century recumbent effigies, and a large wall monument of *c.*1750 with a bust and flying cherub, probably by Sir Henry Cheere.

FRAMPTON ON SEVERN

Gloucestershire
7 miles west of Stroud

Many villages have a green, but few can beat the one at Frampton for size and splendour. Three ponds and a cricket ground lie within its 22 acres, and it is surrounded by Georgian houses and half-timbered buildings. The Bell Inn is conveniently sited for cricketers and their team supporters, and there is a 15th-century barn near the church.

The outstanding house on the green is Frampton Court, screened by trees and built in the Palladian style in the 1730s for Richard Clutterbuck, a Bristol customs official. A canal in the grounds is overlooked by an orangery built in Gothic style, and peacocks strut on the lawns.

Frampton is said to be the birthplace of Jane Clifford, Henry II's mistress, 'Fair Rosamund', reputedly poisoned by Queen Eleanor in 1177. She is remembered in the village by the green, which is named Rosamund's Green.

The 14th-century Church of St Mary is reached by a footpath across a water-meadow, and beside it is the Sharpness Canal which links Gloucester with the River Severn. The sight of sea-going vessels passing within a few feet of the church tower is an occasional attraction.

FROME

Somerset
11 miles south of Bath

The River Frome (pronounced Froom) meanders through the centre of Frome, below steep, narrow streets – which are best explored on foot – lined with medieval and Tudor buildings. Cheap Street, exceptionally quaint, is flagstoned, with a central watercourse.

Fine buildings in the town include the Blue Coat School almshouses of 1726, close to the bridge. St John's Church has Saxon carving, and in the churchyard lies Bishop Ken. Rook Lane Congregational Chapel in Bath Street was built in 1707, and is a fine example of an early Nonconformist church.

FROXFIELD

Wiltshire
3 miles west of Hungerford

On moonlit nights, the Hounds of Hell can be seen pursuing the ghost of Wild Darrell across the fields around Froxfield. That is the story villagers tell about the 16th-century owner of Littlecote House, who murdered a new-born baby by throwing it on to a blazing fire. Darrell escaped justice through the intervention of powerful friends, but later broke his neck when jumping over a stile.

The magnificent Tudor house, 2 miles north of the village, is open to the public at weekends and on Bank Holidays during the summer. Its Great Hall has a fine collection of Cromwellian arms and armour.

A magnificent Roman mosaic has been uncovered on the site of a Roman villa on the Littlecote estate.

Pleasant brick-and-flint cottages, some with thatch, make up most of the village, but its dominant group of buildings is the Somerset Hospital, or almshouses. On a high bank stands a quadrangle of 50 houses, built in 1694 by Sarah, Duchess Dowager of Somerset, for 20 widows of clergymen and the widows of 30 laymen. An imposing archway, added in 1813, leads to the quadrangle with its small chapel surrounded by immaculate lawns and colourful flower borders. In contrast, the parish church of All Saints is small and plain, with a bell-turret added during a 19th-century restoration.

FYFIELD DOWN

Wiltshire
2¼ miles east of Avebury

Fyfield Down can be reached by a diversion from the Ridgeway route, beginning about 2 miles from Overton Hill. This pleasant 30 minute walk leads to a stretch of natural downland which is believed to be the source of the sarsen stones used in the building of Stonehenge. The half-buried boulders of sandstone look, from a distance, like flocks of grazing sheep. For this reason they are known as 'grey wethers', the word 'wether' coming from the Old English for 'sheep'.

Fyfield Down is a nature reserve on which visitors should not wander. Only the paths across it are rights of way. But there is plenty to see without leaving the paths, such as heath bedstraw and sheep's sorrel growing in pockets of acid soil formed by the lichen-covered stones. In autumn a haze of gentians softens the cold grey of the wethers.

An alternative approach to Fyfield Down is to take the path from Avebury that climbs east over Avebury Down to meet the Ridgeway long-distance route, and join the diversion north of Overton Hill. On old maps it is called a 'herepath', a name that comes from the Old English *here* meaning an army or multitude. It suggests that this may have been a route taken by marauding Saxons as they invaded Wessex.

GILLINGHAM

Dorset
4 miles northwest of Shaftesbury

A good shopping centre for tourists caravanning or camping in the dairy vale of Dorset, Gillingham has some fine Georgian houses to recall the time when the town and the countryside around it was acclaimed a beauty spot by the painter John Constable. Unfortunately the 18th-century silk mill featured in one of his works in the Tate Gallery was recently destroyed by fire. A farmhouse beyond Wyke, on the main road north of town, still has a lovely octagonal dovecote and a little stream flowing past its mellow brick-and-stone frontage.

On the road to Mere is the old Gillingham Grammar School founded 450 years ago: the school itself has now been moved to the other side of Gillingham.

West Stour, an attractive village with a 13th-century church, lies 3 miles to the southwest. The village has associations with the novelist Henry Fielding, who modelled the character of Parson Adams in *Joseph Andrews* on the vicar.

GLASTONBURY

Somerset
13 miles east of Bridgwater

Two great English legends are linked with Glastonbury. Joseph of Arimathea, the man who gave his tomb to Christ, is said to have come from the Holy Land to convert the British, choosing Glastonbury as his base.

The legend says that he placed the Holy Grail – the cup used by Christ at the Last Supper – beneath a spring known as Chalice Well on Tor Hill, east of the town.

Joseph is said to have built a chapel at Glastonbury, and an abbey was later founded here which was to become one of the richest and most famous in England. It was rebuilt several times and constantly added to throughout the Middle Ages, and was barely complete when Henry VIII dissolved the monasteries in 1539. The last abbot was dragged to the Tor to be hung and quartered.

Extensive remains stand in 20 acres of parkland in the centre of the town, on the site of the cradle of Christianity in England. The thorn tree in the abbey grounds is said to have sprung from a cutting of the original staff of Joseph which took root on Wearyall Hill. That tree was destroyed during the Civil War.

The abbey and surroundings are also associated with King Arthur: The Holy Grail sought by his knights and found by Galahad – or Parsifal – is still said to rest on Glastonbury Tor. Glastonbury is also claimed to be the legendary Avalon, to which Arthur's body was taken after death.

Legend gives way to fact in Glastonbury's bustling streets. It is a market town with local industries in the sheepskin and leather trades. Notable buildings include The George and Pilgrim's Inn, one of the few English inns to survive from pre-Reformation times,

GLASTONBURY ABBEY *Legends claim that this is the site of the first Christian church in Britain and King Arthur's burial place.*

and St John's Church and St Mary's Almshouses. There is also a Rural Life Museum housed in the 600-year-old tithe barn of the Abbey. There is a fine collection of period tools and demonstrations of rural crafts.

A series of mounds in a marshy valley a mile from the Tor are the only remaining evidence of one of several lake villages which existed in this area prior to the Roman Conquest. Articles found here, now in Glastonbury's Tribunal in the High Street, include pottery, weapons and ornaments.

GLOUCESTER
Gloucestershire
32 miles northwest of Bristol

In Roman times Gloucester was a fortified port on the River Severn, called Glevum. It was built for the invasion of Wales during the 1st century AD. Glevum's gates lie roughly beneath Northgate, Southgate, Westgate and Eastgate Streets. The only visible remains of the Roman settlement are coins, pottery and other objects in the City Museum. This also contains one of the finest examples of Celtic bronze craftsmanship in Britain – the Birdlip Mirror, made about AD 25, just before the Roman Conquest. Medieval traces remain in the architecture of several buildings, particularly the New Inn, Fleece Inn and the 16th-century Greyfriar's ruin.

The glory of the city is its cathedral, one of the most beautiful buildings in Britain. Its Norman core, built between 1089 and 1260, has a massive nave lined with piers which support a triforium and clerestory in Romanesque style. The monument tomb to Robert, Duke of Normandy, is a marvellous relic of that period, carved in oak and painted to represent life. Robert was his father's, William the Conqueror's, obvious successor, but the son twice revolted against him, so that William's second son, Rufus, was designated his heir.

The transepts and choir, remodelled in the mid-14th century to house the tomb of Edward II, are among the earliest examples of Perpendicular architecture. The choir is dominated by the east window, which depicts the Coronation of the Virgin. It is a memorial to those who died at the Battle of Crécy in 1346, and is the largest stained-glass window in Britain, measuring 72 ft by 38 ft.

The 14th-century cloisters are perhaps the most perfect in Britain, mainly because of the exquisite fan tracery of the roof.

After the cathedral crypt, the oldest building in Gloucester is St Oswald's Priory. An arch incorporated in its north nave arcade may date from the 10th century.

The Church of St Mary de Crypt is Norman in origin, with 15th-century additions and several 17th- and 18th-century monuments, including one by Peter Scheemaker, who carved Shakespeare's bust in Westminster Abbey.

Bishop Hooper's lodging in Westgate Street is a 15th to 16th-century timber-framed house in which the Protestant bishop is supposed to have spent the night before his martyrdom in 1555.

Gloucester's port was overtaken by Bristol in the Middle Ages. To revive the city's fortunes, artificial docks and a canal connecting them with the mouth of the Severn were begun in the late 18th century and opened in 1827. Nine of the original warehouses are still in use, and the canal now accommodates ships of nearly 1000 tons, as well as smaller vessels.

Four and a half miles away lies Elmore Court, in a loop of the River Severn. Begun in 1564 by John Guise, it took 24 years to complete. The interior is still as it was then and offers a fine display of furniture, tapestries and historical manuscripts.

GOLDEN CAP ESTATE
Dorset
4 miles east of Lyme Regis

When Golden Cap hill glistens in the sun, it is one of those landmarks so unforgettable that whole regions revolve around them. A flat-topped band of orange sandstone, the hill crowns the highest cliff on England's south coast, overlooking Lyme Bay. The National Trust has made Golden Cap the focal point of a miniature national park, which spans 5 miles of colourful coastline from Eype Mouth westwards to The Spittles rocks near Lyme Regis, with beaches, woods, two rivermouths, two cliff peaks and miles of downland slopes and combes. The Dorset Coast Path runs right along the estate coastline.

A narrow lane winds down to Eype Mouth, southwest of Bridport. At Seatown the River Winniford twists down a long combe to end in a small pool on the inland side of the pebble shore; here, the cliffs to the east are a subtle blend of green and grey, merging above into a tawny yellow.

The coast path crosses Seatown beach after descending westwards over Doghouse Hill from the green, 507 ft high Thorncombe Beacon; then it climbs steeply westwards to the 626 ft high summit of Golden Cap. Another, easier route to the cliff-top starts from the Langdon Hill car park west of Chideock (the only car park on the east side of the estate), and leads south through woods and downs to the summit.

Out to sea the views from Golden Cap stretch from Start Point in Devon to the white cliffs of Bill of Portland, and inland to the west the long ridge of Stonebarrow Hill drops to the sea at the sombre cliffs called Cain's Folly. Beyond Charmouth are the tumbled landslips of Black Ven, a favourite haunt for fossil hunters.

GOLDEN VALLEY
Gloucestershire
Part of the River Frome valley southeast of Stroud

Steep, twisting Chalford and golden-stoned Sapperton are two ancient villages, each with a sturdy character of its own, which lie in the magnificent woods of the Golden Valley. Chalford, with its heritage of mills and fortunes made by the wealthy clothiers, terraces the precipitous hillside of the River Frome and has been nicknamed 'the Alpine village'. Its parish embraces hilltop villages and hamlets such as Bussage and Oakridge. The manufacture of woollen cloth, a Chalford industry since the Middle Ages, reached its peak there at the turn of the 18th century. The mills no longer work, but some of the buildings survive in private ownership. Chalford Mill, which straddles the river, is one of these.

Sapperton was first recorded in Anglo-Saxon times. Its name means 'soapmakers' farmstead' – soap, however, may have meant fullers' earth which was used for 'fulling', or cleaning wool, not for washing.

The two ancient backwater villages mark the hidden path of the old Thames and Severn Canal, now no longer navigable. At Daneway the canal is dry and has become a garden of willow, whitebeam and sedge. The old towpath rises to Sapperton Tunnel, the second longest canal tunnel in Britain. Almost $2\frac{1}{2}$ miles long, it was completed in 1789 with an entrance in the classical style – the Coates portal. Like most early canal tunnels it had no towpath and boats had to be 'legged' through – by men lying on their backs and pushing against the tunnel wall with their feet. The tunnel is still remembered in the name of the inn by its entrance – The Tunnel House Inn – even though the waterway has been closed and forlorn since 1911. Where the old canal runs beside the river, magnificent and solitary woods enfold the Frome in Golden Valley, gilded in autumn by the dying foliage of oak, beech and ash trees.

GREAT BEDWYN

Wiltshire
5 miles southwest of Hungerford

In a hollow near Savernake Forest the large village of Great Bedwyn climbs gently up from the banks of the River Dunn and the Kennet and Avon Canal. Brook Street crosses the canal, river and railway, and nearby is a square building which once was the village lock-up. At the top of Brook Street is the centre of the village, The Square, where a Victorian lamp standard stands on a traffic island.

In Farm Lane, running north from The Square, is Castle Cottage which has a cylindrical Norman chimney – thought to be all that remains of a small monastic building of the late 14th or early 15th centuries. The old Malt House, still with its kiln tower, has been converted into flats.

A walk southwards from The Square along Church Street takes in a stonemason's yard which has a collection of stonework of all types from the 18th century onwards. The Church of St Mary the Virgin dates from the 11th century and was enlarged in the 14th century. In the chancel is the tomb of Sir John Seymour, father of Jane who was Henry VIII's third wife and who died after giving birth to Henry's son, later Edward VI.

Above Great Bedwyn are the tall ramparts of Chisbury Camp, built by the Saxon leader Cissa to defend Wessex against the kingdom of Mercia. An indecisive battle between the two kingdoms was fought at Crofton, just south of the village, in 675.

At Crofton, by the canal, there is a pumping station with two beam engines, one dating from 1812. The station is owned by the Kennet and Avon Canal Trust, and the engines can be seen operating about seven times a year.

GREAT WISHFORD

Wiltshire
5 miles northwest of Salisbury

Crossing the River Wylye on the way to Great Wishford, wild ducks, lapwings, moorhens, snipe and even a heron or two may be seen. Many of the village houses are made of Chilmark stone, quarried over the hill in the next valley. Some are interlaced with flint, others are thatched, and many are steeply roofed.

One of the first things that strikes the eye is the churchyard wall, with its stone inscriptions recording the price of bread in the village in times past. In 1800 it was 3s 4d a gallon, in 1801 it was 3s 10d, in 1904 only 10d and by 1920 it had risen again to 2s 8d. The sign is a reminder that bread was sold by volume, not weight. The church itself, St Giles, was rebuilt in 1863–4. It has two 14th-century effigies, possibly of Nicholas de Bonham and his wife, and floor brasses of some of the children of Thomas de Bonham, who died in 1743. A local tradition says that when Thomas returned from the wars after a seven-year absence, his wife was delivered of seven babies all at once. The old village fire-engine, bought in 1728 for £35, is kept in the church. Opposite the church are the stone-built Grobham Almshouses, founded in 1628, and Great Wishford School, made of chequered brickwork and founded in 1722 for the instruction of the children of the poor.

Oak Apple Day, May 29, is the ideal time to visit Great Wishford, for on that day the villagers reaffirm their ancient right of collecting firewood from Grovely Wood on the summit of the hill along the southern horizon. Before daybreak the young people of the village awake every household by banging tin pans and shouting 'Grovely, Grovely, Grovely and All Grovely'. Then, armed with billhooks, they trudge up the sunken lane to Grovely Wood. There they cut green branches for their houses, and a larger bough for the church tower. Later in the morning a party of villagers, led by the rector, go to Salisbury Cathedral, where four women, dressed in 19th-century costume and carrying nitches – bundles of sticks – dance on the cathedral green. Afterwards, the villagers go into the cathedral and the rector reads from the charter of 1603, confirming their rights in Grovely Wood.

Another vestige of bygone days is the Midsummer Tithes auction just before sunset on the Monday of Rogation Week, in late April or May, when the grazing rights on two small pastures from Rogationtide to August 12 are sold. The auction is conducted by the churchwarden, who walks up and down the church path collecting the bids. The moment the sun vanishes below the horizon he knocks down the bargain to the last bidder, using the church key as a hammer.

GUITING POWER

Gloucestershire
6 miles west of Stow-on-the-Wold

In the 1970s, a Guiting Power landowner, Raymond Cochrane, set up a trust to ensure that his houses, about half of those in the village, would continue to be occupied by local people at uninflated rents. This action has helped to preserve the rural character of the village.

Houses and cottages of Cotswold stone cluster around a gently sloping triangular green. A cross on the green appears to be medieval, but is in fact a war memorial erected after the First World War. St Michael's Church, standing away from the green, has Norman origins but was heavily restored in 1903. In Well Lane, the old bakery dates partly from about 1600 and has a porch with a stone roof supported on columns.

The Cotswold Farm Park, about 2 miles north, has rare breeds of farm animals including Cotswold Lions – a heavily fleeced sheep.

H

HAILES

Gloucestershire
8½ miles northeast of Cheltenham

The Cistercian abbey at Hailes was founded in 1240 by Richard, Earl of Cornwall, the youngest brother of Henry III, in gratitude for an escape from shipwreck in the Scilly Isles. In the Middle Ages, its holy relics included what was said to be some of Christ's blood, an object of reverence for pilgrims which is mentioned by Chaucer in *The Canterbury Tales*. The abbey fell into ruin after the Dissolution of the Monasteries in 1539 and the only substantial building that remains above ground is the shell of the cloister. However, excavation has revealed the footings of other walls.

Nearby is the Norman parish church of Hailes. It was built *c.* 1130, before the nearby abbey, which later owned it. It is not known to whom the church was dedicated. Inside, there is medieval stained glass and a series of well-preserved wall paintings of *c.* 1300. Many of the tiles were brought to the church from the abbey. The canopied pulpit dates from the 17th century, as does much of the panelling and the choir stalls.

HAWKRIDGE RESERVOIR

Somerset
1 mile southwest of Spaxton

One of the reservoirs that serves Taunton and Bridgwater, Hawkridge Reservoir is little more than half a mile long and about 150 yds wide. Its small size, however, adds to its charm and there is little to suggest that this is a man-made lake. At the western end the neat, rounded hills of the eastern Quantocks reach down to the water. The road from the village of Spaxton, 1 mile to the northeast of the reservoir, follows the southern shore. There are plenty of parking spaces around the reservoir.

Hawkridge Reservoir was completed in 1962, and has become 'naturalised' with remarkable speed. Meadowsweet and cuckoo flowers grow in the damp ground, and at the water's edge the golden marsh-marigold can be seen in spring.

Water birds lost little time in taking advantage of the reservoir, particularly coots and moorhens; they are new to the Quantocks since there is no other stretch of inland water in the area apart from a reservoir on the outskirts of Bridgwater. In the dense vegetation away from the water's edge, the songs of reed warblers and sedge warblers can sometimes be heard during the summer months.

HENGISTBURY HEAD

Dorset
At west end of Christchurch Bay

Heath, woodland marsh and meadow are packed into the mile-long Hengistbury Head, a wild and windswept promontory curling like a bent finger around Christchurch Harbour. It is a tiny world in itself, with a

history of human activity spanning 11,000 years.

Paths run to Warren Hill, at the southern side of the Head, passing an Iron Age double dyke with a 12 ft high rampart on the way and then crossing short-grassed meadowland. At the foot of the hill the promontory is almost cut in two by a deep gully, which was an ironstone quarry in the 19th century. Ironstone boulders, called 'doggers', can be seen embedded in the gully sides and floor.

The 118 ft summit of Warren Hill forms a broad plateau ending in tawny sand-cliffs plunging sheer to the sea. A constant wind scything in from the sea keeps the clumps of ling, heather and gorse low-growing, and the turf is thin and patchy.

About 11,000 years ago, when Britain was still joined to the Continent, Stone Age men built a camp on Warren Hill, and behind the double dykes which defended the promontory, craftsmen plied their trades

HAWKRIDGE RESERVOIR *The waters of this man-made lake give the impression of having always filled this Quantock valley.*

and produced pottery and silver coinage for the tribal chieftain. Imported coins and pottery from Brittany and Normandy, and wine from Italy, are evidence of the site's significance as a focus for overseas trade. Flint tools from that period have also been found there. During the Iron Age, some 8500 years later, Hengistbury was a busy port. It remained so under the Romans but was abandoned when they left. It did not attract the invading Saxons, who built their village on the other side of the harbour, and Hengistbury reverted to desolate heathland – until the quarrymen came to dig for ironstone.

Hengistbury Head is one of the finest vantage points on the south coast. Christchurch Harbour, held in the crook of a sand-spit curving round from the Head, is almost a lake, its protected waters sequined with bright-coloured sails and flecked with the dazzling white hulls of motor cruisers. The harbour's outlet to

the sea is a 30 yd gap – the Avon Run – between the sand-spit and Mudeford Quay where local fishermen net the running salmon in the spring.

At the back of the harbour lies Christchurch, a greystone jewel set at the water's edge where the River Avon meets the Stour, and the green apron of Stanpit Marsh divides the harbour into muddy channels. The 312 ft church is the longest parish church in England. East of the harbour, across Christchurch Bay, are the bulky outlines of the Isle of Wight, with the gleaming Needles rocks and the coloured cliffs of Alum Bay easily visible on a clear day. Westward the land curves around Poole Bay and the misty Purbeck Hills loom above the chalk cliffs of Ballard Down.

HEYTESBURY

Wiltshire
4 miles southeast of Warminster

Heytesbury has two notable links with the ecclesiastical past. One is the large cruciform Church of St Peter and St Paul. Its origins are Norman, during which time it was a collegiate church, being presided over by a dean and having a chapter of canons. There is much 13th-century work and additions up to the 15th century. There is a fine stone screen to the north transept with fan-vaulting on both sides. The church was restored by William Butterfield in 1866–7.

The second link is the Hospital of St John, an almshouse founded in the 15th century by the Hungerford family. The present Georgian building dates from 1767, when it was rebuilt after a fire.

HIGH HAM

Somerset
4 miles west of Somerton

Before the Somerset marshes were drained – between the 2nd and 19th centuries – ships could sail as far inland as Glastonbury, and the hill on which High Ham stands was an island, looming large above the lagoons and swamplands of the region. It is still a notable landmark, rising some 280 ft above the surrounding flatlands and crowned by this delightful village, built with lavish use of the beautiful honey-coloured stone of the hill itself.

Although splendid vistas of the peat moors and distant hills can be enjoyed from the summit, the heart of the village is quiet and sheltered by tall trees, with ancient houses sitting around a small village green, on one side of which is the 14th- to 15th-century Church of St Andrew. The church has an excellent carved roof, a magnificent 500-year-old rood screen and benchends decorated with poppy heads. But perhaps its most striking feature is an amusing row of gargoyles, including a trumpeter, a fiddler and a piper, a man throwing stones and a monkey nursing a baby.

THATCHED WINDMILL *The straw hat of High Ham's 19th-century windmill is a well-maintained landmark.*

From the other side of the green, a lane leads to Windmill Road and, half a mile to the southeast, a thatch-topped windmill kept in meticulous repair by the National Trust and open to the public on summer Sunday afternoons, or by appointment. The mill dates from about 1820 and is a tower-mill with a reed-thatched cap.

HIGHWORTH

Wiltshire
6 miles northeast of Swindon

A charming old town built on the crest of a 400 ft hill, Highworth has some superb 17th- and 18th-century houses and fine views. Jesmond House Hotel and Highworth House are perhaps the best examples of this rich period in domestic architecture. The parish church has a monument to Lieutenant Warneford, V.C., who in 1915 destroyed the first German Zeppelin airship in the First World War.

HINTON CHARTERHOUSE

Avon
4 miles south of Bath

A hilly village among woods, Hinton Charterhouse is named after the 13th-century Carthusian priory 1 mile northeast of the village. This is the second-oldest Carthusian house in England, after Witham Friary, and the remains are more extensive than those at Witham.

Hinton Charterhouse is reached by a footpath north of Hinton House, an 18th-century mansion incorporating parts of the priory lodge and gatehouse.

HINTON ST GEORGE

Somerset
2 miles northwest of Crewkerne

Rich golden stone from Ham Hill, 5 miles to the northeast, was used to build the village of Hinton St George. Houses, cottages, barns and garden walls glow with it, and modern buildings blend pleasingly with the 17th- and 18th-century stone houses. The broad High Street has a late-medieval cross with a carving said to be of St John the Baptist.

Several dozen of the houses and cottages are thatched, some with roofs renewed with reed, others with thatch bright green with moss. There are more fine houses in West Street, and from there a stone-paved footpath leads up to the mainly 15th-century Church of St George. Its battlemented and gargoyled tower has some scratch dials on its buttresses, which indicated the service times.

Hinton St George was the seat of the Poulett family, and the church has many Poulett memorials. It is said that Sir Amyas Poulett had the future Cardinal Wolsey put in the stocks for being drunk and disorderly when he was a young parish priest. The village inn is the Poulett Arms, and Hinton House, now converted into several private homes, was the family residence, with parts dating from the 15th century.

On the last Thursday evening of October the children of the village celebrate Punkie Night, when they parade with lanterns – punkies – made from mangel-wurzels. The custom may date from the ancient fire rites of Celtic Samain; an alternative explanation links the custom to an event in the Middle Ages, when the men went to a nearby fair and failed to return by evening, so their wives went out with punkies to look for them in the dark.

HOLFORD
Somerset
3 miles northwest of Nether Stowey

A lane past the tiny church in Holford leads to Alfoxton House (now a hotel), which the poet William Wordsworth and his sister Dorothy rented in 1797. With Samuel Taylor Coleridge, they roamed the Quantocks, enjoying the incomparable countryside for a brief spell that produced some of Wordsworth's finest poetry – *Lyrical Ballads,* by Wordsworth and Coleridge, was published in 1798.

Leaving Alfoxton House on the right, a track leads past some cottages up through woods to the roof of the Quantocks, Longstone Hill. This was a favourite walk of Wordsworth's – 'Upon smooth Quantock's airy ridge we roved'. The climb is easy, a gentle stroll along a bridle-path that leads through a magnificent tunnel of windswept beeches and oaks arching across the broad path.

Higher up the hill the beeches and oaks give way to more open ground, with bracken and clumps of gorse. Now other and more distant views attract the eye. To the southeast is Hodder's Combe, lying invitingly among the trees with a stream rushing through. Beyond it lies Holford Combe, where Wordsworth composed his poem *Lines Written in Early Spring . . .* 'through primrose tufts in that green bower, the periwinkle trailed its wreaths . . .'

The summit of Longstone Hill is 1000 ft above sea-level, one of the highest points at the northern end of the Quantocks. To the southeast the hills and combes roll away into the distance; to the north the Bristol Channel is a glistening seascape, with the South Wales mountains making occasional hazy appearances.

HOLT
Wiltshire
2 miles north of Trowbridge

The pleasant village of Holt is composed largely of 17th- and 18th-century houses, surrounding a green. It was a well-known spa in the early 1700s. The well still exists, incorporated into a factory.

Here, set in beautifully laid-out gardens, is The Courts, where local weavers, until the end of the 18th century, came to settle their disputes. The elaborate facade dates from c. 1700, though the mansion itself is in the neo-Gothic style of a century later.

HORTON
Avon
3 miles northeast of Chipping Sodbury

The National Trust owns both Horton Court, a fine Cotswold stone manor house, and the small village of the same name. The house was much altered in the 19th century but has a 12th-century Norman great hall and early Renaissance features. In the garden is an unusual late Perpendicular ambulatory.

A mile or so to the northeast is Little Sodbury Manor, a 15th-century mansion built for Sir John Walsh. Its outstanding feature is the great hall. The northwest wing was destroyed by fire in 1702.

HINTON ST GEORGE *Mellow Ham stone, thatched roofs and roses spilling over the gate epitomise the ideal Somerset village.*

84

ILCHESTER

Somerset
5 miles northeast of Yeovil

Once a Roman town on the Foss Way, Ilchester later became a medieval town of some importance. It is now a busy road junction, but there are still many relics of its past around the village green.

There are several Georgian houses, one of which is the town hall; it contains a small local museum. At the top of the 18th-century market cross is a sun-dial.

Ilchester claims to be the birthplace of Roger Bacon, one of the greatest scholars of the 13th century, who predicted the invention of submarines, aircraft and the telescope.

Lytes Cary, a fine Tudor manor house 3 miles to the northeast, has a 14th-century chapel and a fine Elizabethan-style garden.

Seven miles to the northwest lies Langport, an ancient market town on a hill beside the River Parrett, part of which flows below the main street. East of the church, an archway spans the road, carrying a small chapel, the Hanging Chapel, built for a medieval craft guild. Having served as a grammar school, it is now a meeting place of Freemasons.

ILMINSTER

Somerset
10 miles southeast of Taunton

This is a busy market town at the foot of the Black Down Hills, whose highest slopes (800 ft) look down at Ilminster from across the River Isle. The minster itself is a splendid example of Perpendicular architecture, and the old grammar school (now a girls' school) dates from 1586. Where the High Street joins North Street, an old road climbs Beacon Hill, from which, it is said, 30 churches can be seen in fine weather.

Barrington Court, 3 miles northeast of the town, was built *c.* 1570 and has striking spiral chimneys.

IRON ACTON

Avon
3 miles west of Chipping Sodbury

The Church of St James the Less in Iron Acton is a handsome church, mainly of the 14th and 15th centuries; it has a pinnacled west tower and, in the churchyard, a rare 15th-century memorial cross. Interesting features inside include a canopied 17th-century pulpit, 19th-century mosaic floors, and attractive modern reredos and side chapel screen. Some of the stained glass and a series of effigies of the Poyntz family date from the Middle Ages.

Of several old buildings in the village, the Lamb Inn is particularly interesting. It is dated 1690 and has two large gables. Iron Acton Court is largely 16th century; it was the manor house of the Poyntz family and has been in disrepair for several years.

One and a half miles east is the village of Yate, whose Church of St Mary has an impressive Perpendicular west tower which dominates this low-built church. It is buttressed and pinnacled, and has a large stair-turret. Inside is a brass of 1590 to a man, two wives and 11 children, and several wall monuments.

IWERNE COURTNEY AND IWERNE MINSTER

Dorset
4 and 5 miles north of Blandford Forum

Sometimes known as Shroton, the charming village of Iwerne Courtney is well sheltered by hills, including Hambledon and Hod Hills. Nearby is Iwerne Minster, a prosperous-looking village with thatched cottages and an old timbered inn, The Talbot. Its church is mostly Norman, and the 15th-century spire is a rarity in Dorset. Outside the village is the site of a Roman villa.

Child Okeford, 2 miles west, is another prosperous farming settlement with thatched cottages, Georgian porticoed houses and an impressive manor. General Wolfe trained his troops here before the attack on Quebec in 1759.

The two Iron Age hill-forts of Hod and Hambledon Hills confront each other across the narrow valley where the road winds from Child Okeford to Stepleton House. On one side looms Hambledon Hill, grim and bare and over 600 ft high; on the other, slightly lower, stands Hod Hill. Both hills have been the scenes of local stands against invaders – both unsuccessful.

On Hod Hill in AD 43, a band of Dorset people – Durotriges Celts – tried to halt the Roman advance through southern Britain. The 2nd Augustan Legion under the Roman general Vespasian poured a deadly rain of ballista bolts on the defenders and quickly took the fort. The Romans used a corner of the 50 acre hill-fort – the largest in Dorset – to construct their own smaller fort, with barracks and a commander's house.

On Hambledon Hill in 1645, during the Civil War, some 2000 villagers made a stand against Cromwell. They belonged to a group known as the Clubmen, because of their primitive weapons; these men were sick of war and damage to their property and crops, and resisted both Royalists and Roundheads. But they were routed by 50 Roundhead dragoons, who locked some of them in Shroton Church.

Southeast from Hambledon's Iron Age hill-fort are remains of a much older causewayed camp enclosing about 20 acres. Excavations in the late 1970s showed that this was just part of a large Stone Age settlement on the hill where, some 4500 years ago, men lived and kept herds of milk cattle within a defensive timber-faced earthen rampart and ditch. That they were subject to attack is evident from the discovery of a skeleton with an arrowhead embedded in the chest, and signs of fire damage to the defences.

IRON ACTON *A 15th-century preaching cross lies outside the entrance to St James's Church.*

KEINTON MANDEVILLE

Somerset

6 miles southeast of Glastonbury

The main village street of Keinton Mandeville is composed of somewhat austere houses, but it is interesting as the birthplace of Sir Henry Irving, the Victorian actor-manager. His house, marked by a plaque, is one of a row facing the baker's shop. Irving, the son of a local tradesman, achieved fame at the age of 33 when he played in *The Bells* at London's Lyceum Theatre. He was the first actor to be knighted, and his ashes are in Westminster Abbey.

A few miles to the south is Lytes Cary, a medieval manor house typical of many others in the West Country: long ownership by one family, decline in the 18th and 19th centuries and resurrection in the 20th. It was the home for the Lyte family from the 13th–18th centuries; Henry Lyte was a pioneering botanist and translator of *Lyte's Herbal*.

KENNETT, EAST AND WEST

Wiltshire

6 miles west of Marlborough

A half-mile walk along a footpath from the A4 leads to the 4500-year-old West Kennett Long Barrow, the largest chambered tomb in England. The walk to the long barrow is a pleasant stroll which crosses the slow-moving River Kennet, passes through a kissing gate and climbs a gentle hill to a semicircular forecourt at the entrance to the tomb.

The entrance is startling. Massive standing stones guard the narrow passageway, but it is just possible to sidle past the largest and enter the chamber. Inside are five burial chambers, two on each side and one at the far end, where the remains of some 20 adults, one youth and at least a dozen children were found when the barrow was excavated in 1956. Because of its size – the barrow is 330 ft long, 80 ft wide and 10 ft high – it is thought that it served as a mausoleum for something like 1000 years.

On the return walk the view of the landscape is dominated by the great, green cone of Silbury Hill on the other side of the A4. It is the largest man-made prehistoric mound in Europe and stands 130 ft high and more than 200 yds around the base. Its flat top could comfortably accommodate the giant circle of Stonehenge, and its purpose may have been to serve as a plinth for a similar stone circle. Recent excavations have shown that it was built in four stages, between the period 2145 BC and 95 BC. But that is all that is known for certain, and Silbury Hill remains one of the great archaeological mysteries.

At the moment, visitors are not allowed on the hill, but there is a good viewing area.

The mystical stones of Avebury lie to the north, with the stone-lined West Kennett Avenue stretching southeast from them, and all around are the green hills and vales of Wiltshire. Overton Hill is the terminus of West Kennett Avenue, and it is marked by a large monument known as The Sanctuary. It dates from the very beginning of the Bronze Age. But it apparently had replaced a previous timber structure of Neolithic times, evidenced by six concentric circles of post-holes. An attempted reconstruction has shown that this was probably of more than one period.

After they had completed their examination of the site, the excavators erected concrete blocks in the former stone sockets and concrete pillars in the post-holes, so that the whole pattern of The Sanctuary is now visible for inspection.

For the visitor who wishes to appreciate more than the archaeological aspects of the Marlborough Downs, a 4 mile each-way stroll along one of the loveliest parts of The Ridgeway – in total, an 85 mile route through the North Wessex Downs and Chilterns – may be the answer. The walk starts at Overton Hill, and climbs steeply over downland, rising to 663 ft in the first half mile. Sarsen stones litter the fields and the humps of round barrows come into view like small islands – the lonely graves of Bronze Age people who lived here about 3000 years ago.

The path climbs steadily to Hackpen Hill, 892 ft at its highest point, and the view broadens to take in the sweep of rippling hills and downlands. Here and there, copses of beech break up the otherwise treeless contours. The trees were planted to make windbreaks in the 18th century and are now a natural part of the landscape. Along the route are a variety of wild flowers – yellow rock-rose, the common milkwort and the occasional, thrilling orchid.

There is another long barrow at East Kennett, about 2 miles southeast of Silbury, but this one has not been excavated. It lies in farmland, and its distinctive hump is crested with tall trees. It looks, and is, a lonely place, and whoever sleeps within it, sleeps undisturbed.

A 2 mile walk along The Ridgeway, south from East Kennett village, leads to the point where the Wansdyke rides high on the back of Pewsey Downs, before plunging into a valley where the ditch becomes lost in a tunnel of thickly woven trees in West Woods. The tangle of trees and undergrowth is almost impenetrable here, and there is an eerie silence save for the sighing of the wind in the tall trees. In places the dyke can be seen much as it was when it was built, a massive bank about 25 ft high with a deep ditch on the northern side. It is thought to date from the 5th century AD, and originally ran some 80 miles from the Bristol Channel to the Vale of Pewsey. No one knows who built it, though its function was clearly to keep out invaders from the north. Its name is thought to come from the Saxon – Woden's Dyke – since Woden was the god of tribal boundaries. It has also been suggested that it was the work of Ambrosius Aurelianus, the last of the Romano-British generals, to keep out invading Saxons who were hard on the heels of the departing Romans.

SILBURY HILL *Between East Kennett and Avebury stands a huge, flat-topped cone, whose purpose still puzzles archaeologists. It is the largest man-made mound in Europe.*

KEWSTOKE

Avon

2 miles northeast of Weston-super-Mare

The most exciting approach to Kewstoke is along the coastal toll-road north of the Knightstone Pavilion at Weston-super-Mare, which enters a steep wood overlooking the Severn Estuary. In 1852, in a recess in the church wall, a wooden cup was found, stained with human blood and said to have belonged to the martyred archbishop, Thomas Becket. The cup is now in the County Museum, Taunton.

A series of stone steps, known as the Monks Steps or the Path of St Kew, leads to a hilltop from which the Welsh hills are visible across Sand Bay.

KILMERSDON

Somerset

2 miles south of Radstock

Kilmersdon is an estate village, mostly owned by Lord Hylton of Ammerdown House, 1 mile to the east. It lies tucked neatly away in a combe, with a little brook forming the northern boundary, creating a delightful break with the world beyond.

There are a handful of new houses, but these are visible only from the surrounding hills. From road level, the village appears as a symphony of grey and green, the silvery stone of the buildings blending with the rich green of the meadows and, in spring, contrasting with the dandelions that bloom in profusion or the occasional yellow field of rape on the hills.

Its brightest gem is the Church of St Peter and St Paul. Even a casual glance shows that both money and care have been lavished on it over the centuries, and the 20th-century contribution is an unusual triangular lych gate designed by the architect Sir Edwin Lutyens (1869–1944). But happily the church has not been 'improved' out of recognition by its benefactors. The result is that it constitutes a practical guide to church architecture over the centuries, with work from almost every period – a Norman window, door and frieze; a 97 ft medieval tower with carved angels and fearsome beasts; a door with its date of 1766 studded in nails and a Pre-Raphaelite stained glass of 1878. The highlight is the 15th-century screen in front of the north chapel. Apart from the church, there is also a plain, handsome Nonconformist chapel, a quaint disused lock-up – a temporary jail for drunks and other minor miscreants – and an 18th-century inn, the Jolliffe Arms.

But it is the total ambience that stays in the mind. Climb the steep hill on the far side of the brook for a general view. From here, too, you can see the neighbouring farms linked by a barely visible network of lanes, as well as the bulk of Ammerdown House. Lutyens also designed the gardens at Ammerdown, which are periodically open to the public.

The house itself was built in 1788 to the design of the architect James Wyatt, and Thomas Samuel Jolliffe, MP, moved here in 1791. He is commemorated by a stone column, 150 ft high with a lantern at the top, across the valley. It was built by his family in the 1850s and to make trebly sure that the Jolliffe name is never forgotten, the inscription on the base is carved in three languages.

A short walk across open fields on a public footpath from Kilmersdon leads to Babington Wood. The wood, with a tributary of the Somer running through the centre of it, makes a pleasantly secluded retreat.

KILVE PILL

Somerset

3 miles northwest of Nether Stowey

At the northern end of the Quantocks the hills tumble down to Bridgwater Bay, and low cliffs shelter the creek called Kilve Pill. A lane from the village of Kilve near the Hood Arms leads down to the creek, following the course of a stream between breeze-rippled fields of tall grass and corn. The path opens out to a rocky beach below the blue-grey cliffs of shale and

limestone. Coiled fossils shaped like flat snails – called ammonites – are embedded in the rock-face, which was once quarried for building stone. Between 1924 and 1926 oil was also extracted from the blue-grey oil shales around the Pill. There is a path along the cliff top, but the edge is jagged and crumbling and care should be taken when walking here.

Early this century, the shore near Kilve was the frequent scene of 'glatting'. At the time of very low tides, the locals would go out with sticks and terriers to find and collect conger-eels hiding in the rock pools.

Smugglers used the creek in the 18th century, and hid their brandy kegs in the lime-kilns which can still be seen in fields along the shore. They also used the abandoned 14th-century manor house which stands close to the footpath and about 500 yds from the beach. The building was given in 1329 by Simon de Furneaux, and housed five priests who sang masses for his soul. Abandoned in the 15th century, parts of the house, including the Chapel, were used for storing farm implements. Now, its ivy-covered walls, built from the local limestone, are gaunt ruins as the result of a fire. It is said to have been caused by smugglers when they set light to their brandy kegs to thwart the Excise officers. A hollow in the field nearby is the site of the priory fishpond.

KING'S WOOD
Somerset
1 mile northwest of Axbridge

Below Shute Shelve Hill, and on the eastern side of Wavering Down, lies one of the unexpected pleasures of the Mendips. King's Wood, on a minor road west of the A38, stretches for about half a mile, and is a marvellous place to be at any time of the year – especially in autumn, when the dying leaves provide a spectacular canopy of colour.

Yet this has not always been a pleasant spot. In the 17th century, Shute Shelve was the site of a gibbet, and travellers on the old Bristol to Exeter road, which passes close to the wood, would have heard the clank of chains as the grisly remains of the unfortunate victims swung in the wind.

The soil in King's Wood is deeper than on the other side of Wavering Down, so a wide range of trees grows here: oaks, ashes, beeches, cherries, sycamores, maples, small-leaved limes and Scots pines.

This beautiful stretch of woodland also has many wild flowers, especially in early spring before the tree foliage blots out the sunlight. Then the wood is a riot of colour with bluebells, primroses, dog's mercury, wild arums and wood anemones growing in large numbers. The rarer herb paris also grows here, as do the hart's-tongue fern and common polypody.

A walk west of King's Wood, along the crest of a ridge, leads towards Wavering Down, Compton Hill and Crook Peak. The path follows a dry-stone wall which forms the boundary between Somerset and the comparatively new county of Avon. However, the line it follows is even older – it divides the parishes of Compton Bishop and Winscombe, and was defined in Saxon times as an important estate boundary.

There is a gentle approach to Crook Peak from the village of Compton Bishop, three-quarters of a mile southeast of the summit. Alternatively, there is a stiff climb up a bridleway from the minor road which skirts

the western flank of the hill. The limestone strata slopes gently south to the green Somerset plain, across which, 10 miles away, runs the low east-west ridge of the Polden Hills. On clear days, far away to the southwest, the purple-clad slope of Dunkery Hill on Exmoor can be seen.

The peak, which takes its name from the ancient British word *cruc*, meaning 'a pointed hilltop', is well named. It stands 628 ft above sea-level, its limestone head worn to a jagged edge by centuries of erosion by the elements. The limestone contains many marine fossils from the time when the area was covered by the sea.

On the southern slopes, where erosion of the rocks has produced a limestone-pavement effect, there are yellow rock-roses, wild thyme, quaking grass, tormentils and rare species, such as the spring cinquefoil, the delicate bee orchid, autumn lady's tresses, slender-leaved thistles, and white horehound. Badgers have their underground setts in cracks in the rocks. They appear at dusk to feed on worms, beetles, blackberries and other food found on the hill.

The open downland is a nesting place for stone-chats, skylarks and meadow pipits. Although they do not nest there, wheatears can sometimes be seen feeding. Butterflies, notably marbled whites, common blues and dark green fritillaries, are also plentiful.

KINGSTON
Dorset
4 miles southwest of Sturminster Newton

The tiny village of Kingston contains an 18th-century inn, The Scott Arms, which is said to be haunted. The ghost is that of an old woman who has been seen sitting with her back to the bar after closing time, drinking from a mug. During the summer of 1970, a couple staying at the inn claim that they saw her hazy figure standing at the foot of their bed. No one knows who the ghost is.

The Church of St James was built of local materials in 1880 by G. E. Street. It is one of his finest churches and shows French influence. The imposing central tower is a notable feature; the chancel is vaulted. The fittings are also Street's work and include some impressive ironwork.

KINGSWOOD
Avon
4 miles east of Bristol centre

A royal forest that covered the whole of south Gloucestershire gave Kingswood its name. Now only a protected stretch of the Avon Valley remains.

Three centuries of expanding industry have turned a once-tiny village into a spreading development of some 31,600 people on the edge of Bristol. It began with coal-mining in the 17th century, and for 200 years the pits were worked. But when they closed, the Kingswood cottagers, who had made hob-nailed boots for the miners, had to sell their boots elsewhere.

Kingswood was a stronghold of Nonconformism in the 17th and 18th centuries, and John Wesley was among the revivalists who preached from Hanham Mount. A symbolic beacon, 80 ft high, stands on the site and a classical Chapel stands in Blackhorse Road. The parish church is *c.* 1820.

L

LACOCK
Wiltshire
3 miles south of Chippenham

All the character and atmosphere of medieval England are packed into Lacock's streets. The village is entirely owned by the National Trust and is a happy jumble of styles – no building is later than the 18th century, and many date from two or three centuries earlier. It is popularly acclaimed as one of the most beautiful villages in England.

The buildings crowd together in cheerful disorder. Whitewashed half-timbered houses are wedged between greystone and red-brick cottages; steep-sided gables jut above moss-flecked, stone-tiled roofs; and upper storeys thrust boldly forward over the pavements. In High Street, Porch House has two gables and close-set uprights in its timber frame; the Red Lion Hotel dates from the 18th century and has a frontage of mellow brick. In East Street there is a 14th-century barn with curved timbers.

These are some of the gems of Lacock, but its two glories are St Cyriac's Church and Lacock Abbey. St Cyriac's is mainly 15th century, and has a lofty nave with a traceried window above the chancel arch. A fan-vaulted side chapel contains the intricately carved tomb and monument of Sir William Sharington, who died in 1553. Sir William acquired Lacock Abbey in 1540, when it was one of the last religious houses to be dissolved by Henry VIII. It had been founded as a nunnery in the 13th century by Ela, Countess of Salisbury, and when Sir William Sharington adapted it as his manor house he retained all the abbey's features – the sacristy, kitchen, cloisters and chapter house – and all are still there. He also built a curious octagonal tower overlooking the Avon.

It was from the battlements of the abbey, that Olive Sharington leaped in despair in 1574, denied marriage to John Talbot from Worcester by her father. She was saved by her billowing petticoats and her lover, who was nearly killed when she landed on him. But on his recovery the marriage took place, Olive's father observing that 'since she had made such leaps she should e'en marry him'. The house was altered in Gothic style in 1753.

Lacock Abbey passed to the Talbot family through marriage, and it remained with them until 1958. The house was actually ceded to the National Trust by the last descendent, Matilda Talbot, in 1944.

Visitors wandering among Lacock's ancient streets and buildings reach instinctively for their cameras at every turn, and it was at Lacock Abbey that William Henry Fox Talbot carried out his experiments in the 1830s, which later formed the basis for modern photography. His first recognisable photograph, showing a detail of the abbey and its oriel window, can be seen in the house. There is a museum containing some of Fox Talbot's work and equipment in a 16th-century barn at the gates of the abbey.

At the Lackham College of Agriculture is a museum of agricultural tools, farm machinery and granaries. The museum is normally open on selected open days.

LECHLADE
Gloucestershire
10 miles northeast of Swindon

Georgian houses line the streets of Lechlade, which takes its name from the River Leach. This flows into the Thames beside the Trout Inn just below St John's Bridge. Lechlade Bridge, known as Halfpenny Bridge, from the days when there was a halfpenny toll, is the highest navigable point on the Thames for cabin cruisers. Old wharves, now lined with pleasure-boats, once catered for barges carrying stone to London for St Paul's Cathedral in the 17th century.

LECKHAMPTON HILL
Gloucester
2½ miles south of Cheltenham

Part of Leckhampton Hill's dramatic quality lies in its bare, spectacular limestone cliff and the teetering rock column called the Devil's Chimney, said to arrive straight from Hell, which seems to hang in space over the Severn vale below. It was from the cliff quarries on this hill that the beautifully dressed stone for Regency Cheltenham was cut. The village of Leckhampton itself has a 14th-century church and manor house. The former has interesting brass monuments. A steep footpath climbs up from the B4070 at the northern foot of the hill and divides. The route to the west goes round the hill below the summit and provides the most impressive view of the Devil's Chimney set in the cliff below the summit from which there are views southwest to the Forest of Dean and west to the Black Mountains in Wales. On the summit, above the Devil's Chimney, is the grassy site of an Iron Age fortification, where coins have been found revealing later Roman and Saxon occupation.

A flat, metalled path leads east from the hilltop and, initially, takes a wide, meandering course over the plateau of Leckhampton Hill. It eventually turns southeast through cornfields to join a minor road leading west past a quarry on to the B4070. East of the quarry, a path leads north to join the footpath below the summit, and so provides a circular route round the hill. Leckhampton Hill is carpeted with wild flowers – the vivid pink buds and blue petals of Viper's bugloss can be found here, also blue tufted vetches, pink sainfoin, moon daisies, rock-roses and woody nightshade. Pink and white dog-roses abound, and in autumn the black sloe berries with their blue bloom appear on the blackthorn bushes.

Flocks of goldfinches and, in winter, long-tailed tits, visit Leckhampton Hill, scourged by cackling magpies. The common blue butterfly and the meadow brown are often seen, and the chalkhill blue can be found where there is horseshoe vetch. Yellow charlock and pink field bindweed grow in the cornfields.

Seven Springs, about 1½ miles southeast, burbles from the Cotswold Hills. It is the source of the Churn River, and is thought by many to be the true head of the Thames.

LIDDINGTON CASTLE

Wiltshire
4 miles southeast of Swindon

In the fading light of evening, the bold outlines of Liddington Castle are dramatic. The earthen ramparts jut out against the sky, and long shadows pick out the faint outlines of wide ditches curling round the southern side. This was an Iron Age hill-fort, a rough and hummocky expanse covering more than 7 acres and sprawling across the brow of a 910 ft high hill.

The path to the castle which takes off from The Ridgeway is lined with aromatic clusters of purple marjoram, and lesser bindweed twines its white and pink cups among the hedgerows. The banks of the castle are clad in lush green grass dotted with yellow carline thistle – a plant that can withstand the attention of grazing cows. A dip in the bank on its north-western side was probably an entrance to the fort, and the best views of the surrounding countryside are from the top of this bank.

Ignoring the grey swathe of the M4 motorway to the east – it is decently buried in a cutting to the north – the view takes in the western end of the Vale of White Horse and the Cotswold Hills rising mistily beyond the red-brick sprawl of Swindon.

LITTLECOTE HOUSE

Wiltshire
2½ miles northwest of Hungerford

Littlecote House, the gabled Tudor manor house of 1490–1520, became the home of Sir John Popham, later Lord Chief Justice, in 1589. In the Great Hall are the finger stocks he was said to have used to make sure prisoners stood still in the dock. Period furniture, tapestries, plasterwork and panelling enrich the house.

His grandson, Colonel Alexander Popham, was a supporter of Cromwell, and raised his own force, known as Littlecote Garrison. The helmets, cuirasses and buff buckskin jerkins they wore now hang in the Great Hall.

In the early 18th century, William George, steward of the Littlecote Estate, found in the manor house deer park the remains of a Roman villa, including a large mosaic floor. George died shortly afterwards and the site was lost. Archaeologists have been excavating the area since 1978.

LONG SUTTON

Somerset
17 miles northwest of Sherborne

Sleepy Long Sutton lies a quarter of a mile south of the Ilchester to Taunton road, and is typical of this low-lying part of Somerset. The cottages have walls built of local lias, a grey stone tinged with blue, and windows dressed in honey-coloured Ham stone. The heart of the village has everything you would expect to find in the depths of rural Somerset; a green, a church, a manor farm, a school, an inn – the Devonshire Arms – and a post office. The inn, facing the green, has more the appearance of a manor house than a country inn, even to the coat of arms of the Dukes of Devonshire above the porticoed entrance.

Like the rest of the village, the 15th-century Church of the Holy Trinity is built of lias stone with Ham stone dressings. Inside, it is a blaze of colour, for the 15th-century pulpit and rood screen have been gaily painted in red, green, gold and blue; not even the Jacobean font cover has escaped the restorer's brush. The nave is spanned by a magnificent timber roof supported by carved wooden angels carrying shields.

On the main road, north of the village, stands the Friends' Meeting House. It is dated 1717 – a time when the Quakers formed the strongest Nonconformist movement in Somerset. The immaculately scrubbed benches and panelled screen at the entrance create an atmosphere of order and peace. The Court House, which dates from the Tudor period or earlier but was altered in 1658, stands a few hundred yards to the west. It has mullioned windows, set at different levels, and a porch with a rounded arch.

LONGLEAT HOUSE

Wiltshire
4 miles west of Warminster

The wonderful mansion known as Longleat House is one of Britain's great Elizabethan stately homes, begun in 1568 for Sir John Thynne, an ancestor of the Marquess of Bath who owns it today. The house was designed by Robert Smythson, but building was not finished at Thynne's death in 1580. The lions roaming among visitors' cars in the park draw the weekend crowds; and the house itself – symmetrical except for its great hall at one side, with a flat roof with domed pavilions, and a large number of windows in its three-storey facade – has a rich collection of furniture, paintings and books. It also has a ghost, that of the Green Lady, Louisa Carteret, whose lover was killed in a duel by her husband, Thomas Thynne, the second Viscount Weymouth, and buried in the cellar. The mourning shade of Lady Louisa has been reported walking up and down the top-floor corridor. Early this century, a man's skeleton, wearing 18th-century clothes, was discovered under the stone flags of the cellar.

Near the park, which was landscaped by 'Capability' Brown, is Heaven's Gate, a half-mile walk through woodlands bright with azaleas and rhododendrons in June, to a superb viewpoint looking down on Longleat valley below.

In the village of Horningsham, 1 mile south, is a thatched Nonconformist chapel – one of the oldest in Britain – built in 1568 by the Scottish builders who worked on Longleat.

LUCCOMBE

Somerset
17 miles west of Watchet

A modest plaque on the north wall of Luccombe church commemorates a hero who might have stepped from the pages of a West Country romance – perhaps *Lorna Doone*, which brought fame to the combes and moorland a few miles beyond Porlock.

Henry Byam was born in the village rectory and succeeded his father as rector. He was chaplain to the exiled Charles, Prince of Wales, and he took up arms in the Civil War, with his five sons as captains. However, he was defeated and captured in 1643 by Robert Blake, Parliament's all-conquering general in the west. Byam escaped to rejoin the fighting again, but his wife and daughter were drowned fleeing across the Bristol Channel. After the Royalists' defeat, Byam shared the exile of Charles II, while his arch-enemy Blake went on to glory as Cromwell's 'General at Sea', defeating the large and hitherto all-powerful Dutch fleet three times between May 1652 and June the following year, although he had almost no previous naval experience.

Byam emerged from exile and returned to England when the king was restored three years after Blake's death in 1657. He lived out his days until 1669 as rector of Luccombe once more. Byam's Church of St Mary was old when he was the incumbent, dating from the 1200s and with a fine original carved roof. Let into the floor is a brass effigy of 1615, depicting in all his finery a local worthy, William Harrison. In the churchyard are the remains of a cross, which was damaged by the Roundheads.

The name Luccombe means either 'enclosed valley' or 'courting valley', or may derive from the name of a 13th-century landowner, John de Lucume. Accessible only along narrow lanes banked with hedges, the village is set in a deep hollow between the high moor and soft pastures on which cattle and sheep graze. Many of its cottages are thatched and painted cream and some have old bread ovens in their walls.

A stream rising on Dunkery Hill flows through the village, skirting the front doors of many of the cottages before disppearing under a low sandstone bridge. Its gentle burble is frequently the loudest noise in this peaceful scene.

LULWORTH, EAST AND WEST

Dorset
3 and 4 miles south of Wool

West Lulworth is a tourist spot of such renown that its real grandeur is best appreciated out of season. The village includes Lulworth Cove, where the chalk cliffs suddenly end and two arms of Portland and Purbeck stone almost encircle a lake-like body of water. A not-too-arduous climb and walk westwards leads to the sheltered Man o' War Bay and to a huge limestone arch called Durdle Door, which juts out to sea.

East Lulworth, 2½ miles east of West Lulworth, is an attractive village dominated by the estates of the Weld family. Their castle, set in 600 acres of rich woodland, was gutted by fire in 1929. The adjoining Rotunda, built in 1786, was the first Roman Catholic church built by royal permission after the Reformation; George III consented on condition that it did not look like a church.

The road eastwards to Steeple along the ridge of the Purbeck Hills gives superb views towards the coast across the beautiful Tyneham Valley. But this road is on Defence Ministry land, so watch for the notices indicating whether the area is open or closed.

LYDIARD TREGOZE

Wiltshire
3 miles south of Swindon

Lydiard Mansion, a Georgian house near Swindon owned by Thamesdown Borough Council, was once the home of the St John family. Of medieval origin, the smooth, pedimented facade was rebuilt in 1745 and in more recent years has been extensively restored. Its rococo ceilings are particularly beautiful and its elegant

LYDIARD TREGOZE *Rebuilt in 1745, the mansion gives an impression of austere classicism.*

Georgian furnishings and paintings are well presented.

The Church of St Mary, standing in the parkland of the mansion, has a richly coloured triptych in a cabinet, some fine 15th-century Flemish stained glass, a screen, the St John family pew, an early 17th-century pulpit and monuments to the St John family. One of the most brilliant of the monuments is a gilded life-size figure of Edward St John, who was killed fighting for the Royalists at the second Battle of Newbury in 1645, and another has panels painted with a genealogical tree.

LYME REGIS

Dorset
20 miles southwest of Yeovil

The medieval port of Lyme Regis became a resort in the 18th century. It earned its royal title when Edward I used its harbour – later sheltered by the massive breakwater known as the Cobb – during his wars against the French in the 13th century. The Duke of Monmouth landed here in 1685 to lead his ill-fated rebellion against James II. Smugglers used the town, until the fashion for sea-bathing restored it to respectability.

The resort was a favourite of the novelist Jane Austen, who set part of the action of *Persuasion* in Lyme Regis. There are fine views along the bay, dominated by Golden Cap, at 626 ft the highest cliff on England's south coast.

The Philpot Museum contains the fossilised remains of an ichthyosaurus, a 30 ft long aquatic reptile of 140 million years ago. It was found in the fossil-rich cliff bordering the town. St Michael's Church, built about 1500, contains a carved 17th-century pulpit and a chained Bible.

Charmouth, 2½ miles east, is a resort with Regency houses and an old inn, the Queen's Arms, where Catherine of Aragon, Henry VIII's wife, stayed in 1501.

LYME REGIS *The almost mystic quality of the 18th-century maritime town has been immortalised in John Fowles'* The French Lieutenant's Woman *(overleaf).*

MAIDEN CASTLE

Dorset

2 miles southwest of Dorchester

The Celtic tribe who gave their name to Dorset – the Durotriges – made Maiden Castle their hilltop capital. But the fort, whose mighty multiple ramparts wind sinuously around a saddle-backed hill, was many centuries in the making.

Hardly discernible now is the New Stone Age camp that crowned the eastern summit long before 2000 BC; but a crudely shaped chalk idol, dating from this period and possibly the image of a mother-goddess, was found on the hilltop and can now be seen in the County Museum in Dorchester. Largely lost, too, is the enormous New Stone Age long-barrow burial mound that ran one-third of a mile along the top.

The first Celtic inhabitants, who arrived about 300 BC, fortified their single rampart with timber. It enclosed about 16 acres, and within its protection they lived in timber huts, laid out in streets, and stored their corn and water in large circular pits. The enclosure was enlarged to its present size of 47 acres – making it a small town – after 250 BC.

Maiden Castle as it is today dates from later Celtic times, largely from the 1st century BC, and was a response to the threat of a new weapon, the slingshot, that could kill at 100 yds against the 30 yds of primitive arrows. Extra lines of ramparts were added – and were raised as high as possible. You can still walk round an inner rampart that rises 50 ft above its ditch.

But none of these fortifications offered adequate defence against the ballistae – or giant crossbows – of the Roman 2nd Legion, which attacked in AD 43. The Durotriges were routed and suffered heavy losses. By AD 70 the fort was deserted, and the survivors driven down into the new Roman town of Durnovaria. Around AD 380, the hilltop was reoccupied by the people who built the mysterious Romano-British temple whose foundations can be seen there today. Some 300 years later, about AD 635, a sacrificial victim with a hole cut in his skull was buried in the bank-barrow. By whom and for what reason is unknown.

Poundbury earthworks, northwest of Dorchester, date from the same period as Maiden Castle, but are much smaller, covering about 20 acres. The site is surrounded by a single, low rampart.

MALMESBURY

Wiltshire

15 miles west of Swindon

When Henry VIII abolished the monasteries in 1539, the handsome Benedictine abbey at Malmesbury was sold off for £1517 to a local wool merchant, William Stumpe. He used many of the old abbey buildings for cloth weaving, but two years later presented the abbey's nave to the town as a new parish church.

The Benedictine abbey had been founded in the 7th century by St Aldhelm, its first abbot, and what remains is impressive. The church's Norman porch is considered one of the finest in England and has a richly decorated arch illustrating various Biblical themes. There is also a 15th-century screen and a musician's gallery.

The church also contains a 15th-century monument to the first Saxon monarch to rule the whole of England, King Athelstan (AD 925–40), who is buried here. In a corner of the churchyard is the tower of the previous parish church, St Paul's, now used as the abbey belfry. St Paul's was already falling into ruin when Stumpe gave the town its new church.

Malmesbury stands between two branches of the River Avon, on the site of a fortified Saxon hilltop town. It claims to be the oldest borough in England – Alfred the Great granted it a charter in AD 880. About 60 years later King Athelstan gave some 500 acres of land to a number of townsmen who helped him defeat Norse invaders. This land, known as the King's Heath, is still owned by about 200 men living in Malmesbury who can trace their ancestry back to those who fought for Athelstan.

Water surrounds the base of the hill on which the town stands, and no fewer than six bridges lead to the steep slope of Market Square. At the centre is the elaborate late 15th-century Market Cross, which is not just a cross but an octagonal building. According to one chronicler, 'it is curiously voulted, for poore market folkes to stande dry when rayne cummith'. The fine vaulting remains and people still take shelter here. Grotesque gargoyles gape from the colonnaded corners of the old stone house. Nearby are Abbey House, built by William Stumpe on the site of the old abbot's house, and the arched Tolsey Gate, whose two flanking cells once served as the town prison.

Most of the older buildings are made of locally quarried stone. They include, at the bottom of the High Street, the mainly 17th-century St John's Almshouse, which has a late Norman arch. The Old Bell Hotel may have belonged to a Saxon castle, demolished in 1216, and incorporates what could be some walls of a 13th-century abbey guesthouse.

An 11th-century monk of Malmesbury, named Elmer, once tried to fly. He fastened home-made wings on his feet and hands; then he jumped off the abbey tower, frantically beating the air. It is said that he flew some 200 yds before crashing, breaking both legs and laming himself for life. Brother Elmer's epic flight of fancy has been commemorated in the abbey by a modern stained-glass window.

MARLBOROUGH

Wiltshire

10 miles south of Swindon

The town of Marlborough straddles the former stagecoach route from London to Bath, beside the River Kennet. It is the commercial centre of a large area of rural Wiltshire, and boasts shops of all kinds.

AVON MILL BRIDGE *Half a dozen bridges span the flowing River Avon, inviting travellers into Malmesbury.*

A VIEW OF TEN COUNTIES *The 1000 ft summit of May Hill is crowned by a spinney of pines.*

The broad High Street is lined on its north side with Georgian buildings with colonnades and tile-hung fronts. It has a reputation as having one of the widest main streets in the country. There is a Perpendicular church at both ends: St Mary's, from which a curfew bell is rung each evening – the tower still shows the scars of battle left after the Civil War, when the town fell to Royalists – and St Peter's, which has a Norman doorway. Behind, there are alleys with half-timbered cottages which escaped a fire in 1653.

Marlborough College, established in 1843, stands beside Castle Mound, where Stone Age and Roman remains have been found, and near Maerl's Barrow, which gives the town its name. An enclosed, arched bridge leads from the western end of the town to the public school.

On the downlands around Marlborough are many prehistoric remains, including the hill-fort of Barbury Castle, 4 miles northwest.

MARSHFIELD

Avon

6 miles north of Bath

A remarkable village shop existed in Marshfield until 1983. Bodman's Grocery and Drapery Store had been run by the same family since at least 1870, and the last Mr Bodman continued trading up to his death at the age of 90, having inherited the shop from his father.

In his last years, however, the place was more of a museum than a shop. The fixtures and fittings were unchanged from the early 1900s, and if Mr Bodman did not want to part with something in his stock that he had grown to like, he would simply refuse to sell it. So he preserved a little corner of old rural England.

On his death, villagers hoped that Bodman's might become an official museum, but market forces pre-vailed and antique dealers and curators moved in and the place was stripped. It stayed empty for a year and was sold to a local businessman who expressed the wish to retain 'the unique charm' of the shop.

The whole village is itself a remarkable survival. Its high street must be one of the longest in Britain, running for almost a mile, with the parish church at one end and the walled Crispe almshouses of 1619 – they are still in use – at the other.

Ranks of grey stone buildings, Georgian or Georgian-style, face each other across the street with scarcely a break along its length and without a hint of green. The effect could be claustrophobic, but it escapes this, probably because no two houses are exactly alike. They are large houses in the Cotswold manner, with door lintels and window frames seemingly designed to withstand a siege.

Two factors created Marshfield's prosperity: its position and its industry. The village lies along a ridge like a grey cap on the green head of the combe. Once there were 13 inns along its length, and even now three survive in a community of 1300 people.

Most of these hostelries were coaching inns – one survivor, the Catherine Wheel, is particularly stylish – for the village lay on the main Bristol to London road, a fact betokened by the precision of an 18th-century signpost which proclaims that it is '103 miles to London; 12 miles and one furlong to Bristol'.

Wool was the original creator of Marshfield's wealth and, later, malting the local grain for brewing. So skilled did the maltsters become that they were in demand for miles around – not simply because they knew their trade, but because they knew how to deal with excisemen. A house in the High Street has peepholes through which, it is said, the excisemen could be observed as they snooped around.

Although the main part of the village is a conservation area, a large new development is tucked away behind the imposing Church of St Mary, which has two choir chapels and a spectacular tower with a pierced open parapet.

The name Marshfield seems odd for a place perched

on high ground, but 'marsh' is derived from march, or border. Until 1974 the borders of Wiltshire, Somerset and Gloucestershire met nearby.

MAY HILL
Gloucester
3 miles south of Newent

The breezy summit of May Hill is a perfect spot for short but rewarding walks. For miles around, the topknot of dark trees on its broad dome is an easily spotted landmark. Tracks crisscross the hill, mounting gradually up the springy turf between the bright splashes of gorse and the bracken fronds towards the crowning cluster of tall pines. The trees were planted to commemorate Queen Victoria's Golden Jubilee in 1887. In 1977, and again in 1980, there were further plantings to commemorate the Silver Jubilee of HM The Queen, and the 80th birthday of HM The Queen Mother.

The hilltop, at almost 1000 ft, is a superb viewpoint offering glimpses into ten counties on the best days. Green waves of wooded hills roll westwards to merge with the mountains of Wales. To the east, the long line of the Cotswolds rises suddenly from the broad Vale of Gloucester, where the Severn meanders seaward through a fertile landscape of farms and villages. The Forest of Dean lies to the southwest, but what catches the eye most is a huge loop of water where the Severn curls, and at low tide the silvery sheen of silt.

Newent Woods cover the northeast side of the hill. They are sunny with drifts of daffodils in spring and then sweet with perfume from the thick carpet of bluebells in early summer. By ancient custom, rival parties of young folk from Newent village used to walk up through the woods to the top of the hill on May Day and there do battle, summer's supporters against winter's. Summer's friends were always victorious in the fight, and would triumphantly carry fresh summer greenery back to the village.

MEARE
Somerset
4 miles northwest of Glastonbury

The site of one of the lake villages built in the swamps during the Iron Age, the villagers' homes at Meare probably had timber foundations, daub and wattle walls and thatched roofs; and each building was supported by a central pole. Finds are in the County Museum at Taunton and the Tribunal at Glastonbury. In the Middle Ages the Abbots of Glastonbury owned Meare, and the manor house was their summer retreat. It dates from the 14th century, as does the curious stone Fish House, used by local fishermen to salt and store fish for the summer palace of the Abbots of Glastonbury.

MELBURY OSMOND
Dorset
5 miles south of Yeovil

Thatched, stone cottages line the slope which leads down to Melbury Osmond's water-splash, a shallow, paved ford with a footbridge across it. The name Melbury is derived from the Old English word for 'multi-coloured hill'. The title is fully justified in the spring, summer and autumn – when the leaves on the enveloping wooded hills display their greenery, or turn to bronze and gold.

At the highest point in the village is the yew-surrounded Church of St Osmond, with the 17th-century former rectory nearby. The nave, rebuilt in 1745, has a fine circular, stained-glass window – but little survives of its original furniture, except two coffin stools. The wall of the chancel bears a stone carving of a weird-looking animal believed to be a representation of Abraham's ram caught in the thicket.

Melbury Osmond is approached along a winding, sunken lane, its banks draped with hart's tongue fern and – in spring and summer – spangled with flowers.

Nearby Melbury Bubb, about 3 miles to the southeast, has the Church of St Mary, rebuilt in 15th-century style but with an original tower. It has a curious font depicting upside-down wrestling animals.

MELCOMBE BINGHAM
Dorset
10 miles west of Blandford Forum

Gateposts, crowned by heraldic eagles, announce the entrance to the manor house called Bingham's Melcombe and the footpath to the Church of St Andrew. Walking towards the manor house and its church is like stepping into a 19th-century romance. Indeed, the author Thomas Hardy immortalised several of the names associated with Bingham's Melcombe in his novel *Tess of the D'Urbervilles*.

One of the Bingham family married Lucy Turberville – from the family whose name Hardy altered to D'Urberville. Another Bingham, who was the rector of St Andrew's Church, appeared in the novel as Parson Tringham.

Straight ahead from the gateway stands the 14th-century gatehouse, with the church to one side. At the bottom of the churchyard Mash Water, a small stream also known as Devil's Brook, meanders slowly through woodland gardens beneath the grassy slopes of Combe Hill.

The Bingham family lived at Bingham's Melcombe for more than 600 years, until 1895. The present Purbeck and Ham stone house, breathing an air of well-preserved prosperity, dates mostly from the Tudor period, but parts were refurbished in about 1720. It is not open to the public but, from the path to the church, visitors can glimpse the terraced garden which rises behind it and which has one of the finest yew hedges in England. It was planted in the reign of Elizabeth I, and is more than 20 ft high and 20 ft wide. There is also a well-preserved Tudor bowling green. The ghostly Turberville coach is said to drive through the garden on Midsummer night.

The 14th-century Church of St Andrew houses many memorials to the Bingham family – one of them to Thomas Bingham, 'deare childe', who died aged seven months in 1711. A touching plaque dedicated by his mother expresses the wish that his dust might never be disturbed.

The village of Melcombe Bingham itself lies 1 mile to the northwest and can be reached by road or by public footpath. It is a happy gathering of Dorset roadside cottages – some of them thatched – which straggle along to join up with the hamlets of Higher and Lower Ansty.

MELKSHAM

Wiltshire
6 miles south of Chippenham

An industrial town, Melksham lies on the banks of the Avon. Only a few woods survive of forests which were once a favourite hunting ground of the Plantagenet kings. By the 17th century, Melksham was one of the great weaving towns of Wiltshire, and good 17th- and 18th-century houses in Canon Square recall this period of prosperity. In 1815 the discovery of a chalybeate spring fired enthusiasm to turn Melksham into a spa; the original Pump Room survives, much altered, on the Devizes Road. But the scheme was destined to fail.

Three miles west of Melksham is the village of Great Chalfield, whose moated, late Gothic manor house has Tudor overtones. The house is approached through an arched gateway, and its oriel windows reflect the sunlight on to the courtyard's polished yellow-grey stones. The great hall and screen remain as Thomas Tropenell built them in 1480. The house is owned by the National Trust.

MELLS

Somerset
3 miles west of Frome

The road into Mells winds past steep green banks and crumbling garden walls, radiant with flowers in the spring. It is a village of grey and yellow stone cottages, some thatched, set among greens and trees and forming an appealing group with the 15th-century church, Elizabethan manor and the 15th-century Talbot Inn. It retains a particular appeal because it is a workaday place, not a formal exhibit.

A short cul-de-sac leading to St Andrew's Church is lined with cottages whose front doors open on to the road. The churchyard has two old yew trees, and among the graves is that of the Catholic theologian Monsignor Ronald Knox, known for his translation of the Bible completed in 1955. He died at Mells in 1957.

The church has a 104 ft high tower, added in the 16th century, a nave with lovely crested screens, and a chapel built by the Horner family who have lived at the manor since the 16th century. The centre of the chapel is dominated by an equestrian statue by Sir Alfred Munnings, in memory of Edward Horner who fell at Cambrai in 1917.

John Horner is said to be the 'Jack Horner' of the nursery rhyme. In the 16th century, when Henry VIII was dissolving the monasteries, the Abbot of Glastonbury is supposed to have sent the king the deeds of Mells Manor – a gabled and mullioned-windowed Tudor house – hidden in a pie, hoping that the gift would save Glastonbury Abbey from destruction. But the gift-bearer, Jack Horner, removed the deeds – 'the plum' – and kept them for himself. No firm evidence has been found to support this story, and the rhyme did not appear until 1725. The house was extensively restored in 1900, but retains its Elizabethan style of gabled roofs and mullioned windows.

There are four prehistoric camps near Mells. The nearest is Wadbury Camp, bounded by Mells stream and by ditches and stone walls. The others are Tedbury Camp, whose earth rampart is still as much as 15 ft high in places; Newbury Camp and Kingsdown Camp, part Roman, part Iron Age.

MERE

Wiltshire
7 miles northwest of Shaftesbury

Mere has two old coaching inns. The Old Ship has an interesting 18th-century sign associated with the badge of John Mere, a merchant adventurer who in the 14th century founded a chantry in the church for the singing of masses, and so gave the village its name. The Talbot is now modernised, but the old inn acted as a refuge for a disguised Charles II after the Battle of Worcester.

The pinnacled Church of St Michael has a rich and beautiful decorated interior and a Perpendicular tower. The octagonal font, fine rood and chapel screens are of the same period. There are brasses of 1398 and 1426 and medieval stained glass. Just outside is a Tudor chantry where the Dorset poet William Barnes had his own school. On the downland slopes outside the town are ridges which may have been Roman vineyards.

MIDSOMER NORTON

Avon
9 miles southwest of Bath

The small town of Midsomer Norton derives its name, not from River Somer, which flows through the town, but from Midsummer Day, the date of the festival of the church's patron saint, St John the Baptist. In the church is a statue of Charles II, who is said to have hidden in nearby Welton Manor during the Civil War.

MILBORNE PORT

Somerset
3 miles northeast of Sherborne

Once noted for the number of its mills, the small village of Milborne Port was a port, or borough, returning two members to Parliament. The remains of a medieval cross stand in the centre of the village. The old guildhall, near the market hall, incorporates a Norman doorway, and the church is partly Saxon and early Norman.

At the east end of the village, on the Salisbury road, stands a Queen Anne mansion, Ven, formerly the seat of the Medlicott family. On the lane to Milborne Wick traces of a prehistoric camp can be seen.

About 3 or 4 miles south, across the border into Dorset, lies Purse Caundle Manor, a charming 15th-century manor house with 16th-century additions. Of the five medieval rooms, the finest are the Great Hall with its minstrel gallery and Tudor fireplace, and the Solar or Great Chamber, which has a beautiful wagon roof. Several audible phantoms have been reported, among them the sound of chanted plainsong.

MILTON ABBAS

Dorset
6 miles southwest of Blandford Forum

In the 1770s, Joseph Damer, Earl of Dorchester, had the medieval Benedictine abbey, from which the village takes its name, rebuilt into a magnificent new house. Proud of his house, he was displeased that its view of the wooded countryside was interrupted by

MILTON ABBEY *The Benedictine abbey church dates from the 14th and 15th centuries; the 18th-century house is now a school.*

the market town of Milton Abbas. He was so annoyed by this 'oversight' that he decided to have the town – which stood on his property – demolished. In the face of fierce local opposition, he razed the 'eyesore' of homes and commercial buildings. About 1 mile away, in a wooded valley, he erected a large 'model' village. And on part of the site of the old town he built an ornamental lake to enhance the beauty of the surroundings. Such drastic measures to improve the landscape were not uncommon in the 18th century, but Horace Walpole's opinion of Lord Milton, 'the most arrogant and proud of men', is no surprise. Today, Milton Abbas is much as Lord Dorchester created it towards the end of the 18th century, and his house is now a public school, Milton Abbey, set in a landscape of romantic solitude created by 'Capability' Brown.

Most of the thatched, cob cottages are washed in white or pale yellow. They are equally spaced and lie back from the road behind large unfenced front gardens, which together give the effect of a village green. The houses have flower borders in front, and long strips of kitchen garden behind. The rear gardens reach a steep escarpment which is crowned with trees. The main street cuts through the green, and in the centre of the village stand some 17th-century brick-and-flint almshouses, which Lord Dorchester had moved from their original site. At the lower end of the main street, in the old brewery buildings, is a museum devoted mainly to farming.

Opposite the almshouses is the 18th-century Church of St James. It was designed in late-Georgian Gothic style to fit in with the appearance of the new village.

The abbey church was built on the site of land given by Henry VIII to the lawyer who arranged his divorce from Catherine of Aragon. It was restored in the 19th century by Sir Gilbert Scott, architect of London's Albert Memorial. The choir, railing and transepts only remain; the nave has disappeared. Three-hundred yards to the east, a long flight of grass steps leads up to St Catherine's Chapel, dating from Norman times. A museum of brewing and agriculture is now housed in what was once the village's own brewery.

MINEHEAD
Somerset
Resort on Bristol Channel

Every May Day Eve a colourful hobby horse dances down to Minehead quay, accompanied by accordion and drum. For the next three days, it prances its way around the district accompanied by the music. The horse consists of a 9 ft long frame covered with painted canvas and ribbons; its antics are controlled by a dancer concealed inside. It is probably the survival of an ancient spring fertility rite, though local legend gives it a different origin, ascribing it to an old ruse used to frighten away Viking pirates.

Minehead has safe beaches, a large sea-water pool and attractive parks. Quay Town huddles by a 17th-century harbour.

MONKTON COMBE
Avon
2 miles southeast of Bath

A hamlet of ancient stone cottages in a deep wooded combe beside a small river, Monkton Combe was formerly a manor of the Priors of Bath. It is overlooked from the north by Combe Down, which commands splendid views of Bath and surrounding hills. There is an 18th-century stone lock-up in the village and one of John Rennie's fine aqueducts, built in the classical style in 1804. It carries the Kennet and Avon Canal over the Avon in a single arch.

Half a mile southeast is Midford Castle, beautifully set in wooded grounds. It was built c. 1775 to an unusual design – the shape of a clover-leaf – said to commemorate a gambling triumph of its owner, Henry Roebuck; his success was based on a lucky ace of clubs.

MONTACUTE
Somerset
4 miles west of Yeovil

A magnificent Elizabethan mansion, an ancient church, the remains of a medieval priory and narrow streets lined with buildings of golden Ham Hill stone, combine with more than 1000 years of history to make Montacute a village of exceptional interest. Its roots go back to a 7th-century settlement; 200 years later it was known as Bishopston – now the name of the street that runs north from the church.

Immediately after the Battle of Hastings, Count Robert de Mortain, half-brother of the Conqueror, built Montacute Castle on top of 60 ft St Michael's Hill, which dominates the village to the west. The name Montacute derives from the Latin *mons acutus*, meaning 'steep hill'. No trace of the castle remains, and the wooded slopes are now crowned by a folly tower built in 1760.

The stronghold was later given to a newly founded Cluniac priory, and many of the castle's stones seem to have been used when the priory was built. The priory's battlemented gatehouse survives, with adjoining buildings, and now forms part of Abbey Farm. Though not open to visitors, the gatehouse can be seen from the churchyard. The monks kept Montacute for more than 400 years, until Henry VIII closed it down and sold it in 1539.

Much of St Catherine's Church, standing where Middle Street turns north to become Bishopston, is 15th century, but the chancel arch and several other features date from the end of the 13th century. Inside are monuments to the Phelips family, who had links with the village from the mid-1400s.

The beautiful Montacute House was built for Sir Edward Phelips by William Arnold, a Somerset mason whose other notable works include Wadham College, Oxford. Sir Edward (who had inherited the former priory estates from his father in 1588) was a successful lawyer, and built the house between about 1590 and 1601, when he became an MP. By 1604 he was Speaker of the House of Commons, and made the opening speech for the prosecution in the trial of Guy Fawkes in 1606. The house, like most of the village, is built of Ham Hill stone and is one of the finest Elizabethan mansions in Britain, with an immense gallery 189 ft long running the whole length of the second floor. It contains a valuable collection of furniture and china, portraits, tapestries, plasterwork and panelling.

MONTACUTE *The great mansion was begun about 1590, though its Tudor west front, cannibalised from another house, is about 50 years older.*

The grounds present a fine aspect of deep yew hedges and golden stone terraces. Some of the Atlantic cedars are 50 ft high. When the Phelips' fortunes fluctuated, many of the family treasures were sold off. After being leased several times, the house was bought by a Mr Cook and presented to the National Trust in 1931. The most famous tenant was Lord Curzon, Viceroy of India and later Foreign Secretary, who lived there from 1915 to 1925. His bath, in a mock Jacobean cupboard in the corner of his dressing room, survives.

The village itself is most attractive. Many of the buildings in Bishopston have stood since the 17th century, with stone-mullioned windows and mellow red-tiled roofs that contrast with that of Montacute's only thatched building, Monk's House (formerly The Gables), built in the 15th century. The Borough is a spacious square, the heart of the village, where the 18th-century Phelips Arms and the Old Bakery still stand. Nearby are the wisteria-clad Montacute Cottage and The Chantry, adjoining buildings from the 16th century. The Chantry belongs to the National Trust, having once been a school and later the post office.

Many of the South Street Cottages were weavers' homes when the glove trade flourished in the 18th century. The Baptist chapel in South Street, which dates from 1880, is one of the few recent buildings in the heart of the village. In Townsend is the one-time Baptist manse, a 16th-century building that later became the Shoemakers' Arms and is now a private house.

MUCHELNEY
Somerset
1 mile south of Langport

The Benedictine abbey of Muchelney was possibly founded in the 8th century and housed about 20 monks. The ruins include the refectory, common room and kitchen. It lies outside the village of Muchelney on a minor road off the Bridgwater road.

In the village itself is the Priest's House, one of very few pre-Reformation priests' houses to survive in England. The internal arrangement is identical to that of much more substantial houses of the 14th and 15th centuries, with a hall that once was open to the thatched roof.

NAUNTON

Gloucestershire
5 miles west of Stow-on-the-Wold

The north Cotswold Hills are almost bare of trees along the tops, but miles of dry-stone walls follow their contours, giving some shelter to the wheat crops that in summer shimmer like a yellow eiderdown from one horizon to the other. The Stow to Cheltenham road runs along the top of a high ridge, and Naunton looks like a child's model village in the dip below. The little Church of St Andrew stands at the west end, and stone cottages are threaded like beads along the fine string of the River Windrush.

Local lore tells mischievously that Satan and his devils founded Naunton when they flew over the Cotswold Hills and let fall an imp. Unable to fly because of a broken wing, the imp built himself a cottage from local stone.

A more likely story, based on archaeological finds, is that Naunton's sheltered and well-watered site was first settled in Neolithic times. The Saxons called the place *Niwetone* – New Town – and a relic of their settlement is a small Saxon cross, carved in stone and set into a wall below the tower in St Andrew's. Do not miss the pulpit of about 1400, carved in stone with patterns of Gothic arches and tracery.

The little green outside the church is shaded by huge beech trees growing from the gardens of two large houses. The infant Windrush, clear, gravel-bedded, and fast-flowing, is channelled under a bridge and then between stone walls before emerging to run through little paddocks, dotted with cowslips in spring, where ponies, cows and sheep graze.

A footpath, starting almost opposite the Black Horse Inn, follows the river as it weaves through the village, past several cottage gardens and orchards. Many of the stone cottages are hung with roses, wisteria and pears trained to grow against their walls.

One of the oldest of the buildings is the square and gabled dovecote which stands beside the river. It was probably built in the 15th century and can accommodate up to 2000 doves.

Naunton's long main street often echoes to the clatter of horses' hooves, for no fewer than three packs of foxhounds hunt in the area. The Cotswold Farm Park, 2 miles north at Temple Guiting, contains a unique collection of rare breeds of domestic animals that include some sheep called Cotswold Lions.

NETHER STOWEY

Somerset
10 miles west of Bridgwater

Bypassed in 1969 by a new main road, the village of Nether Stowey has returned to its former calm. For two years – 1796 to 1798 – Coleridge lived here with his wife and baby son in a cottage now owned by the National Trust; the poems he wrote in it include 'The Ancient Mariner' and 'Kubla Khan'.

Adjoining the local church is Stowey Court, a manor house dating in part from the 15th century, with a fine 18th-century gazebo (garden house). A stream flows down beside the road from the circular mound of a ruined castle, and the houses stand behind little bridges over the stream.

Dodington Manor House, 2 miles to the northwest, is partly medieval. Above the village is Dowsborough hill-fort, an oval high-banked prehistoric earthwork.

The winding way between Nether Stowey and Crowcombe constitutes a magnificent scenic drive, with plenty of stopping places of interest along the route. It is called the Old Coach Road, and is sign-posted south about 1 mile west of Nether Stowey on the A39. Thick woods crowd in on the right-hand side of the road for about half a mile, where a sharp right turn takes the road up past Five Lords Combe. From this corner, a path leads across a field to a small quarry – a place with the sinister-sounding name of Walford's Gibbet. On a clear day, there are fine views across the Bristol Channel to Wales.

The Old Coach Road continues past Five Lords Combe on the left – a splendid Quantocks woodland of mixed oak and beech. At the top of the combe the road turns sharp left to run across open moorland. At this turn, on the right-hand side, a path leads up through the woods to the hill called Dowsborough. Some local people call it Danesborough, though the fort on top is Iron Age and has no connection with Scandinavian invaders.

The oval, 7 acre fort occupies the higher end of the narrow ridge. Its defensive banks and ditch follow the natural contours of the land. The ditch is now full of scrub oak and the ramparts are crowned with heather. Like all Iron Age sites, little is known about the people who lived here some 2000 years ago. This air of mystery adds to the character of Dowsborough, with its superb views across the Bristol Channel.

From below Dowsborough, the road continues to a junction at which stands a signpost with the name Dead Woman's Ditch. However, there is nothing morbid about this place; many pleasant walks lead off in all directions into the hills and combes round about, and there is adequate roadside parking.

About 1 mile beyond the road junction is Crowcombe Park Gate, which lies at the top of the combe above Crowcombe village. From this point, there are superb views of Fire Beacon hill, half a mile to the south, and Wills Neck – the highest point in the Quantocks – 2 miles to the southeast. The drive down the combe to the village is beautiful, with wooded banks on either side which are bright with bluebells in late spring and clothed in ferns and wild flowers in summer.

Walford's Gibbet today is a pleasant spot on a hillside, but its name recalls a tragedy of 200 years ago. John Walford was a well-liked local charcoal-burner whose true love was Ann Rice, but he married half-witted Jane who visited him in the woods, and whose two children he fathered.

One night in 1789 as the couple were going from their cottage above Bincombe to buy cider at the Castle of Comfort Inn, they quarrelled. He struck and killed her with a fence stake, then, panic-stricken, left her body in a ditch. He was arrested, tried and found guilty. On his way to be hanged, Walford was allowed to make a final farewell to Ann. As was the custom, his body was gibbeted at the scene of the crime.

NEWENT
Gloucester
8 miles northwest of Gloucester

Wild daffodils grow thickly around the old market town of Newent in spring; they have even colonised the central strip of the Ross Spur motorway. Near the town is a falconry centre where this ancient hunting art has been revived. The birds can be seen being handled, in ground training and at work in the sky.

The 16th-century timber-framed market hall is well preserved and there are several 18th-century houses and a medieval spired church. The lead was removed from the church roof by the Royalists in 1644 during the Civil War, to make bullets to repel Roundhead attacks, and after a heavy fall of snow in 1674 the roof collapsed, destroying the nave. It was rebuilt after Charles II made a grant of 60 tons of wood from the Forest of Dean.

Taynton House, 3 miles south, has three interesting barns, one of which dates from 1695, and Upleadon, southwest about 2 miles from Newent, has a Norman church – St Mary the Virgin – with a timber-framed 16th-century tower. It is particularly notable for a tombstone in its churchyard to James Broadstock, a local blacksmith who died in 1768. His stone proclaims:

> My sledge and hammer He's reclined
> My bellows too has lost its wind
> My fire extinct, my forge decayed
> And in the dust my vice is laid
> My coal is burnt, my fire's gone
> My nails are drove, my work is done.

NORTHLEACH *Medieval aspects of the village are cherished.*

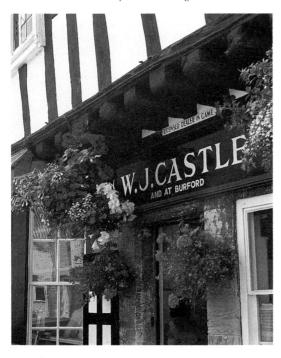

NEWLAND
Gloucestershire
4 miles southeast of Monmouth

The spacious Church of All Saints in Newland, Forest of Dean, has aisles almost as wide as the nave, giving it the local name of the Cathedral of the Forest. It was built mainly during the 13th and 14th centuries, but has later additions and was restored in the 19th century.

It contains a strange and unique brass showing a helmet with a miner as a crest. He carries a pick, and has a candle in his mouth. Sir John Greyndour, Sheriff of Gloucester, went to France with Henry V in the early 15th century. There, with a company of Forest of Dean miners, he helped to capture Harfleur, and became its governor. He was granted the miner's crest by the king to commemorate the exploit.

The church also has a monument, with a recumbent effigy of a bowman, dating probably from the early 17th century.

NORTHLEACH
Gloucestershire
10 miles northeast of Cirencester

Sheep grazing in the churchyard and sheep depicted on memorial brasses inside the church tell the story of Northleach – a wool centre of the Cotswold uplands which, in medieval times, was as important as Cirencester. As in so many other Cotswold villages and towns, its church is a memorial to the days when the wealthy wool merchants lavished their riches on a place in which they could give thanks for their good fortune, and go to their final rest in suitably splendid surroundings.

The Church of St Peter and St Paul was largely rebuilt in the 15th century, in the delicate Perpendicular style of the period that gloried in pinnacled buttresses, tall windows and lofty towers. At Northleach the tower rises 100 ft above a two-storey south porch with a vaulted ceiling which is claimed to be the loveliest in England.

The clerestory over the chancel arch was built by John Fortey in the 15th century; his is one of many brasses inside the church. The memorial of Thomas Bushe, who died in 1526, includes the arms of Calais in France, a reminder that this was the port to which the fleeces were sent. The stone pulpit is Perpendicular, the font is carved with faces.

Northleach's wood industry declined after the Abbey of Gloucester, which held the manorial rights, was dissolved in the mid-16th century. However, its market, established by the abbey in 1200, went on and the place became a miniature market town with its own annually elected bailiff and constables. For a few years in the mid-18th century the coaching trade brought renewed prosperity.

The High Street is lined with many houses whose fine fronts in pale gold Cotswold stone were added at several dates from the mid-1500s onwards. The Wheatsheaf Hotel is a particularly attractive example.

At the crossroads, where the Foss Way crosses the old Oxford to Gloucester road, stands the grim facade of a House of Correction built in the 1780s. Such establishments were used as an alternative to prison or transportation, and minor offenders were sent there in the pious hope that a short dose of hard labour would make them see the error of their ways. For the 37 inmates the 'short, sharp shock' consisted of various tasks which, in the 1820s, included working on a treadmill. Each prisoner had a ground-floor day cell and first-floor night cell. He was also allowed to wash. Men did not have such rights in the formal prisons of that time.

The building now houses a fascinating Museum of Rural Life, though it includes one cell block preserved in its original condition. Also on display are farm implements, a superb collection of carts and a steam tractor, and a range of domestic items.

North of the crossroads some 5 or 6 miles is Notgrove, where a Neolithic transeptal-chambered long barrow is located. It has two chambers on either side of the gallery and a fifth at the inner end. The gallery leads in from a forecourt. Beyond these chambers, excavation revealed a further circular chamber, now concealed, which is an unusual feature in barrows of this type.

NORTON ST PHILIP
Somerset
5 miles north of Frome

Nine men of Norton St Philip were bound to stakes and burned alive after the Battle of Sedgemoor ended the Monmouth Rebellion in 1685. So says Geoffrey Coombs, the village contractor and undertaker, in whose family memories of the horror remain quite fresh. Geoffrey's ancestor Thomas Coombs was one of the men burned; and three other families in the village are descendants of three more. Eight of the men had languished almost 12 months in a dungeon before a judge – possibly the notorious Judge Jeffreys himself – arrived to exact terrible retribution from the pro-Monmouth villagers. Their gaol is now the Dungeon Bar of Norton's superb half-timbered George Inn, which has stood at the village crossroads for more than 500 years and is reckoned to be one of the oldest inns in Britain. The ninth man was an innocent bystander who held open the gate of the George when the men were led out and was bundled away with the others to be burned in an orchard just east of the village on the Trowbridge road, says Mr Coombs.

There is no official record of these burnings, though mention has been made of 'hangings' in Norton. But Mr Coombs has examined the parish records and found that the church paid 12 shillings for 100 bundles of faggots for 'ye execution'. Other sources attribute the buying of faggots to the provision of fuel for boiling oil and tar, used to tar the prisoners as a milder retribution than execution.

It is all fairly recent history for the Coombs family, which has lived in the village since records began in 1220. At home Geoffrey has a cannonball, picked up by one of his ancestors after a skirmish when Monmouth rebels barricaded the roads into Norton against the soldiers of James II. It has been used as a doorstop by the family ever since.

On show in the George is a section of oak beam replaced during renovations, in which is embedded a lead musket ball. It could be the assassin's bullet which local history says missed the Duke of Monmouth – illegitimate son of Charles II and pretender to the throne – when he stayed at the George on the night of June 26, 1685, just 10 days before Sedgemoor. Or it could have been fired during that skirmish nearby,

when fierce fighting took place in Chevers Lane – still called 'Bloody Lane' by villagers. An earlier visitor to the George was Samuel Pepys, who dined there with his wife while on his way to Bath in June 1668.

The pub, with its mullioned and bow windows, and its small courtyard and timbered balcony at the back, has hardly changed since Elizabeth I reigned. Cloth merchants met there in those days, when the village was a centre for the wool trade, had town status and was said to have 'the most noted cloth fair in the west'. Daniel Defoe called it Phillips' Norton in his list of Somerset's principal clothing towns.

The village is 1 mile west of the Bath to Warminster road, about halfway between the two towns. Its houses are grouped closely together in the friendly medieval manner. From about 1230 until the Dissolution of the Monasteries by Henry VIII it belonged to the great Carthusian priory of Hinton Charterhouse, $1\frac{1}{2}$ miles north. The George, in its original simple stone form, may have served as a guest house for the monks: the upper part is believed to have been added as a wool store and extra accommodation.

The Church of St Philip was originally 13th century, but the present building was donated by a wealthy local merchant, Jeffrey Flower. He apparently took a hand in the design, and his fertile imagination produced a tower like no other in England, with oddly arched windows and elaborate niches. He died in 1644. Pepys admired the bells and called them 'mighty tuneable'. Treasures inside include magnificent wrought-iron gates to the chancel and handsome screens of carved oak. St Philip's is said also to contain the grave of Siamese-twin sisters, the Fair Maids of Foscot. Pepys describes their tombstone, which he saw in 1668, as being carved with the figures of girls, who had 'two bodies upward and one stomach'. They were born in Foxcote, a hamlet $3\frac{1}{2}$ miles to the west. The carved faces from the tombstone are set into the wall inside the tower.

NUNNEY
Somerset
3 miles southwest of Frome

A wooded fold among the valleys which ripple down from the eastern flank of the Mendip Hills is the picturesque setting for Nunney. It is a fairy-tale setting, with greystone, red-tiled houses grouped around a ruined medieval castle. A 10 ft deep moat and a stream surround the castle, forming an island which is maintained as a bird sanctuary.

The castle is reached by a footbridge. Owned by English Heritage, it is open to the public. It was built in the 14th century by Sir John de la Mare, and is said to have been modelled on the Bastille in France. All four sturdy towers are almost intact externally. During the Civil War the castle was a Royalist stronghold, but eventually fell to Cromwell's artillery.

One of the 30 lb iron cannonballs that demolished the castle walls is in All Saints Church, a 13th-century building greatly restored in 1874. In the south corner of the church there is a room containing a model of the castle as it appeared when built in the 1370s. The family tombs of the de la Mares are also in the church.

The early-18th-century Manor Farm near the castle is built of the same grey stone, as are the cottages bordering the stream. Some of the cottages bear dates from the 1600s and 1700s.

OARE

Somerset

6 miles east of Lynton

It was in the little Church of St Mary, at Oare, that Carver Doone shot Lorna in R. D. Blackmore's famous novel *Lorna Doone*. Indeed, few people would have heard of Oare had Blackmore not bestowed immortality upon it. The village lies deep in an Exmoor valley less than 2 miles from the sea, yet bears little relation to the coast which can be reached only by winding lanes. The scenery in this remote corner of Exmoor is superb. Oare Water tumbles riotously through the narrow valley, a green ribbon amid towering round-shouldered hills that in autumn are carpeted with glowing heather.

Those wishing to envisage the dramatic scene when Lorna was shot at her wedding should remember that the church, though small, was even smaller in the 17th century, the period in which the novel is set. No more than a dozen people could have got inside, and Carver would have been only a yard or two from the bride when he shot her at the altar. The west tower was rebuilt and the chancel enlarged in the mid-19th century, and the box pews put in a little earlier. Doone country and the Badgworthy Water – where the novel's hero, John Ridd, stumbled into his adventures – lie approximately 2 miles to the southwest. There was a John Ridd serving as churchwarden at Oare as recently as 1925.

Stoke Pero and Culbone are equally remote hamlets, respectively 5 miles southeast and 2½ miles east of Oare. The Church of St Beuno at Culbone is England's smallest parish church still in regular use – it is 35 ft long and 13 ft wide. It was once at the heart of a community of charcoal burners. It dates from the 12th century, but on the north side is a two-light Saxon window cut from a single slab of sandstone.

ODSTOCK

Wiltshire

3 miles south of Salisbury

In the southeast corner of Odstock's churchyard is the grave of a legendary local figure, Joshua Scamp, a gipsy who was wrongfully hanged for horse-stealing in 1801. Scamp became a martyr among his people, and each year they assembled around his grave on the anniversary of his death, after first drinking lengthily to his memory in the nearby Yew Tree Inn.

One year, the rector and his churchwardens decided to stop the riotous celebrations by locking the church door and uprooting a briar rose which the gipsies had planted by Scamp's grave. The thwarted gipsies put a curse on anyone who should in future lock the church door and, after sudden death befell two who defied the curse, the rector threw the church

key into the River Ebble, where it is said still to lie.

Another briar rose has been planted by Scamp's grave, marked by a headstone now splitting with age, and the Yew Tree Inn still flourishes in this tiny village of stone and flint cottages. St Mary's Church – largely rebuilt in the 1870s in flint and stone – sits alone at one end of the village street. At the other end of the village is the parsonage, a 17th-century house that was once an inn where Oliver Cromwell is said to have stayed.

OKEFORD FITZPAINE

Dorset

7 miles northwest of Blandford Forum

Locals persist in telling the story of how an orphan was adopted by the nearby village of Child Okeford. Shilling Okeford, now the village of Shillingstone, is said to have contributed a shilling towards the child's upkeep while Okeford Fitzpaine gave five pence. Though this is a charming explanation for the names of the three villages, 'Fitzpaine' is not, in fact, a corruption of 'five pence': the village owes its name to the Fitzpaine family, who were lords of the manor in the 14th century.

Parts of the Church of St Andrew, including the west window, date from this period, although most of the church was rebuilt in 1866, using fragments from the older church. Inside, there is a fine 15th-century stone pulpit and an east window dedicated to the memory of George Rivers Hunter, rector of the parish for 52 years from 1820 to 1872.

The church clambers up a mound overlooking the 18th-century rectory and a jumble of thatched village

OLD SARUM Earthworks and cathedral foundations are all that remain of a once great Roman and Norman centre.

roofs. Behind immaculately tended borders stand cottages built of a whole range of different materials. One cottage in particular, St Lo House, is composed of distinct sections: a flint wall, then a stone section with mullioned windows and, finally, a section of timber-framed red brick. The different types of construction and the uneven lie of the land on which the village is built lend Okeford Fitzpaine a charmingly individual character. Even the telephone box is painted green to blend in with its surroundings.

The heart of the village is called The Cross: and here, next to the school, a tiny and venerable fire engine is preserved in a purpose-built shelter. Dated 1895, it belonged to the Okeford Fitzpaine Parish Council and was operated by the see-saw action of shafts on either side driving a pump.

Okeford Hill towers behind the village. It is linked by a ridge to Bulbarrow Hill, at 901 ft the second highest hill in Dorset. From here it is possible, on a clear day, to see the Needles, off the Isle of Wight.

OLD SARUM
Wiltshire
2 miles north of Salisbury

The forerunner of modern Salisbury and site of the original Roman fortress of Sorviodunum. Old Sarum is deserted today. But there is still a strong atmosphere of its vanished glory. The huge circular mound of multiple earthworks, covering 56 acres, was probably first used as an Iron Age camp. The Saxons called the stronghold Searobyrg, meaning 'dry town'; in the Domesday Book, Salisbury is recorded as 'Sarisberie'.

Norman invaders quickly realised the camp's strength, and the inner earthworks are of Norman origin. A small town grew up and the first cathedral was completed by Bishop Osmund, a nephew of William the Conqueror. It was taken down when the See was moved to Salisbury, but the lines of the cathedral's foundations are still visible on the turf.

Old Sarum was one of the so-called 'rotten boroughs' abolished by the Reform Act of 1832, in which only ten voters returned two MPs: one was the constituency's most famous representative, William Pitt the Elder, the 18th-century Prime Minister, whose membership is commemorated by a plaque on the site, erected in 1931.

OZLEWORTH
Gloucestershire
2 miles east of Wotton-under-Edge

The small village of Ozleworth has the Church of St Nicholas, whose main feature is the hexagonal Norman tower, which is thought to have Saxon origins. There is a pretty south door ornamented with carved foliage. Restoration was carried out in the 19th century. Newark Park is 16th century, altered by James Wyatt *c.* 1790.

A few miles to the northeast is Lasborough Park or Manor, a Cotswold stone house, built in 1609, with a garden noted for its herbaceous borders and shrubs. It can be seen by appointment.

Meandering lanes wind northwards from Ozleworth to footpaths that circle over lonely turf, west through Newark Park and Tor Hill, and back south through Wortley to the Alderley, Hillesley and Lower Kilcottall enchanted valleys. Finally, the route emerges through Midger Wood Nature Reserve (managed by the Gloucestershire Trust for Nature Conservation) and up on to the suddenly 20th-century A46 – relieved only by the abrupt sight of Nan Tow's Tump, one of the largest and most mysterious Bronze Age round barrows in the Cotswolds. About 9 ft high and some 100 ft in diameter, crowned with trees, the barrow is believed to contain the skeleton of Nan Tow – a local witch who was buried upright.

OZLEWORTH BOTTOM *The smallest of hamlets nestles in a green valley near the Avon border* (overleaf).

P

PAINSWICK
Gloucestershire
16 miles northwest of Cirencester

Painswick churchyard is a mass of yew trees in all imaginable shapes and forms. Of the 100 or more trees, some have grown together to form multiple arches; others are trained as hedges, skilfully clipped to give square sides. Many are freestanding, some of them proud under bouffant hairstyles sweeping the ground; others are standard trees, clipped to form neat cones above wide trunks. Several have been there since 1714. Yews in pairs straddle one path through the churchyard and meet overhead – looking almost like married couples tripping hand in hand from the altar.

As if the yews were not enough, the magnificent stone tombs in St Mary's churchyard confirm that here is no ordinary village. This assembly of mainly 18th-century table and pedestal tombs is unique in Britain; and complemented by the dark foliage of the yews they make the churchyard resemble a sculpture garden.

Brass plates on the sides of some are elegantly engraved with the names of their occupants – the Lovedays, the Packers, the Pooles – families of rich merchants and clothiers.

Painswick's heyday was between the 14th and 18th centuries, when the village – a town at that time – grew rich from the wool trade and was a centre of cloth making. The wealthy built magnificent houses in creamy-white stone quarried from Painswick Hill, a mile to the north. Several of the more interesting houses are in Bisley Street.

The elegant 18th-century front of Byfield House masks an earlier building of Tudor origin. Humbler cottages – but still built of the same creamy stone – line Vicarage Street. The street slopes downwards giving views of the Cotswold Hills, where a few sheep graze in hedged fields generously wooded with beech and oak. In medieval times these hills were unfenced, and Painswick merchants could gaze contentedly out at great flocks roaming them under the watchful eyes of their shepherds.

However, the atmosphere was not always one of peace and plenty, judging by the stocks of St Mary's Street which are shaped like a pair of spectacles. The stocks were put here in the mid-19th century 'for the punishment of those who carry on carousels to the annoyance of neighbours'.

The church manages to hold its own within the incomparable frame of its churchyard. The 15th-century tower, housing a famous peal of 12 bells, was topped in 1632 by a spire which reaches to 172 ft. Annually, on the first Sunday after September 18, a 'clipping' ceremony takes place, when the children of the village hold hands to encircle the church and dance around it, singing hymns. Afterwards the children, who are garlanded with flowers, each receive a traditional Painswick bun and a silver coin. The ceremony had nothing to do with shearing sheep – it was once an ale-swilling dance!

Half a mile outside the village, on the Gloucester Road, stands the handsome Palladian mansion, Painswick House. It has a good collection of furniture and some fine Chinese wallpaper. The house is open throughout August.

The hamlet of Paradise, just north of Painswick, was named by Charles I. While Charles was bombarding Gloucester he stayed there and described it as the most delightful spot he had ever seen. The local inn, inevitably called the Adam and Eve, was at that time called The Plough.

PEN HILL
Somerset
3 miles northeast of Wells

A walk of about 3 miles, from Pen Hill to Rookham, follows the southwestern face of a ridge above the Somerset Plain. Following the bridleway from the parking area near the transmitter crowning the hill, the view takes in Queen's Sedge Moor and Glastonbury Tor, the steep hill crowned by the 15th-century tower of St Michael, looming above the town. Beyond are the Blackdown Hills and the Quantocks. On a clear day, Dartmoor can also be seen, its outline rising darkly on the horizon. Immediately beneath the hill lies the ancient city of Wells, crowned by the delicate square towers of the cathedral and St Cuthbert's Church.

On Pen Hill, the Old Red Sandstone has broken through the limestone layer covering the Mendip plateau, resulting in a landscape that is pastoral and well wooded. Ash trees and oaks mingle among the stately stands of conifers, and pheasants scuttle in and out of the woods which line the bridle-path.

PEWSEY
Wiltshire
6 miles south of Marlborough

William Cobbett, in his *Rural Rides* published in 1830, was attracted to the Vale of Pewsey's 'villages, hamlets, large farms, towers, steeples, fields, meadows, orchards and very fine timber trees scattered over the valley'. Little has changed since Cobbett's day in the green valley of which Pewsey is the centre. Pewsey has a mixture of Wiltshire thatched cottages and Georgian houses, and at the crossroads a statue of King Alfred looks across the River Avon. Attractive villages surround the town, and prehistoric barrows line the high southern escarpment of the Marlborough Downs to the north.

The vale itself runs between Devizes and the hills just north of Pewsey. On its northern edge, a ridge of hills lies like a ribbon of fresh green paint, the treeless slopes softly rounded as they sweep down to the valley floor where hamlets and farms are shielded from the north winds by this 900 ft high arm of the Marlborough Downs.

From the road along the north side of the valley there are distant views of Bishop's Cannings Down,

ST MARY'S CHURCHYARD *The long-dead of Painswick slumber beneath sculptured yews and carved table-top tombs.*

then Easton and Horton downs. But at Allington they begin to loom larger – Clifford's Hill, Tan Hill and Milk Hill have their lower slopes close to the road, and footpaths to their summits.

At Alton Barnes crossroads the northbound road climbs almost to the summit of Walker's Hill. A path from the roadside provides a stiffish but short climb to a long barrow called Adam's Grave, from which there are fine views across the valley and along the Downs. On the slopes of Milk Hill there is, inevitably, the figure of a white horse, carved in 1812. Northwards the view takes in Silbury Hill.

Just below the brow of Walker's Hill, on the northern side, a footpath from the road leads to a New Stone Age camp on Knap Hill and to the steep slopes of Golden Ball and Draycot hills.

PILTON
Somerset
21 miles north of Sherborne

Although almost 20 miles inland, Pilton – or Pooltown as it was called in Saxon times – was once a harbour on the edge of a low-lying tidal lake which stretched to the sea. Legend claims that Joseph of Arimathea, who came from the Holy Land in the 1st century to convert the British to Christianity, landed here and built a small mud-and-wattle church on the banks of the Whitelake, which courses through the village.

The present Church of St John the Baptist, said to stand on the site of Joseph's church, dates from the 12th century. Its churchyard clambers up the steep dip in which the village is set – a haphazard assortment of greystone cottages on either side of the

stream. The Whitelake gurgles alongside cottage gardens, passes under a stone bridge and then opens out under the shade of chestnut trees in the meadows of the Manor House grounds.

Silhouetted against the sky on the other side of the hollow stand the gaunt remains of a medieval tithe barn which once belonged to the Abbey of Glastonbury. Although its thatched roof was destroyed by lightning and fire in the early 1960s, the stonework is in good repair. Its gables still carry the carved emblems of the four Evangelists – the God-man for St Matthew, the lion of Judah for St Mark, the sacrificial ox for St Luke and the eagle for St John. The barn lies on private property but may be visited by written application to Mr Peters, of Cumhill Farm.

From the barn, there are fine views of the village and the surrounding countryside – west towards the tower which caps Glastonbury Tor, 6 miles away, and north back over the village and its pinnacled, turreted church. The Norman south door to the church was taken down in the 19th century and the present replica later installed. The bottom stage of the tower was built in 1196 and the top part was added in 1490. But the church's greatest treasure is the 15th-century timbered, tie-beamed roof, which is bathed in light by the clerestory windows. Carved wooden angels with wings outspread hover at the centre of each beam, which is itself supported by angels carved in stone.

Beneath the church stands the Manor House – in a curious and capricious blend of styles. The front is Georgian with a Venetian window, castellations and corner pinnacles; while Gothic windows on the south side overlook the stream. The manor has a vineyard, planted in 1966 and 1968, producing three white wines which have achieved international recognition. In a good year such as 1976, with its long, hot summer, 17,000 bottles are produced. Villagers help to harvest the grapes in late autumn, and the vineyard is open to the public occasionally.

POOLE

Dorset
4 miles west of Bournemouth

The heart of Poole is a 15 acre area beside the harbour crammed with buildings of historic interest. There are 80 houses, a church, six pubs, the old Guildhall, the Custom House, 30 shops, and other buildings, all maintained or restored to harmonise with one another. This part of town has a miraculously untouched 18th-century atmosphere about it.

Fine parks, a magnificent harbour, gently sloping sandy beaches and the unspoilt scenery of the countryside add to the charm of Poole.

The town developed as a port in the 13th century, on one of the largest shallow-water anchorages in Britain, and the largest natural harbour in the world, measuring about 95 miles around. It became a base for pirates, then fishermen, and in the 18th and 19th centuries for timber trading with Newfoundland. It is still used commercially – by coasters – but is primarily a centre for leisure craft of all types. The town itself has grown from its early origins in the wool and luxury goods trade into a busy commercial and industrial centre as well as a resort.

On the quayside the Town Cellars, a group of 15th-century warehouses, contain a maritime museum. The nearby lifeboat museum has models, paintings, documents and other relics illustrating 150 years of the Royal National Lifeboat Institution. The Poole Pottery on the quayside is open to the public.

The 18th-century Guildhall and medieval Scaplen's Court both serve as museums of local history. The Guildhall houses ceramics of the 18th century, glassware and collections of local interest; Scaplen's Court, in addition to the latter, also includes items relating to archaeology and industrial archaeology, arms and armour. Of particular interest is the unique 33 ft long dug-out canoe built by Iron Age fishermen. It was discovered in the mud of Poole Harbour in 1964.

In the middle of the harbour lies Brownsea Island, which is owned by the National Trust. In 1907 it became the birthplace of the Boy Scout movement when Lord Baden-Powell held a camp there for about 20 boys. The island, which is covered by heath and woodland, has a nature reserve.

PORLOCK

Somerset
5 miles west of Minehead

A series of hairpin bends and a 1-in-4 gradient make Porlock Hill a spectacular road down into Porlock village. Small, whitewashed houses with tall chimneys crowd in on the narrow, twisting main street, their gardens glowing with fuchsias, roses and creepers. Perhaps even more attractive are neighbouring West Porlock and Porlock Weir, 1 mile and 1½ miles down the road leading westwards out of the village. Both hamlets lie under the shoulder of a huge wooded hill which skirts the coast for several miles.

Porlock merits an unhurried visit, being surrounded by romantic countryside and other more remote hamlets, with many pathways to delight the explorer on foot. One fascinating walk is along a path going west from Porlock Weir. The path leads for some 2 miles along a ledge, through dense woods at the edge of the sea, to the 35 ft long church at Culbone – claimed to be the smallest medieval church in England – which has stood since Norman times. Porlock's own parish church of St Dubricius dates mainly from the 13th century, although it does have a fragment of a Saxon cross fixed to the west wall of the nave. In the 14th-century arcade is the alabaster effigy of a knight who fought alongside Henry V in France in 1417 – John Harington. He lies beside his wife on a superb table tomb, his hands clasped in prayer over his badge, and his head supported by angels.

At the east of the village is the 15th-century Doverhay Court, now a museum and information centre. A mile along a minor road to the northeast is Bossington, another attractive village of thatched cottages.

PORTISHEAD

Avon
8 miles west of Bristol

The small resort and port of Portishead is sited on the Severn Estuary, on a wooded hillside near the mouth of the Avon. The old village, of which several houses survive, grew up around the church and the manor house, The Court. The high tides which sweep up the Severn Estuary, particularly at the Spring Equinox, are a spectacularly dramatic feature of the coast upstream from Portishead.

PORTLAND

Dorset
4 miles south of Weymouth

Thomas Hardy called Portland's narrow, rugged peninsula 'the Gibraltar of Wessex'. All the level surfaces of the 2 mile wide and 4 mile long mass of almost treeless rock are scarred with quarries; the light-brown, rough-textured Portland stone has been enhancing important buildings ever since Sir Christopher Wren used it to build St Paul's Cathedral. Today most of the quarries are abandoned, their ledges softened with turf and wild flowers.

Because of Portland's vulnerable position, two castles were built to fortify it. The earliest, the Bow and Arrow – or Rufus – Castle built by the Normans above Church Ope Cove, is now in ruins, but Portland Castle, built in 1520 by Henry VIII, has been well preserved and still stands on the northern shore. The castle was manned again in the 16th century, at the time of the Spanish Armada. It was occupied by Royalist forces during the Civil War and fell to Parliamentary troops in 1646. The design is based on a segment of a circle, with inner and outer fortifications and a moat. The officers of the garrison had their living quarters in the tower and wings. The men lived in barracks in the courtyard, which was originally roofed.

Modern Portland is a major naval base, using a massive harbour and breakwater which were completed in 1872 after taking 23 years to build. From Church Ope Cove, there are some fine cliff walks with impressive views; Portland's highest point (496 ft) gives good views westwards along the Chesil Beach and eastwards to the Purbeck Hills. One of the old twin lighthouses on Portland Bill, built in 1869, is now used as a bird-watching station; the other is a private residence. The present fine lighthouse, erected in 1906, is typical of the period. There is good bathing for careful swimmers from Church Ope Cove.

POWERSTOCK

Dorset
4 miles northeast of Bridport

Flights of terraces make up the village of Powerstock, with the almost square, greystone Church of St Mary standing on the topmost layer. Around the church, at different levels, are stone cottages and large houses – some of them with thatched roofs. Glebe House, a few hundred yards to the north of the church, has the ruins of a 17th-century tithe barn in its grounds.

Powerstock is overshadowed by the 827 ft high Eggardon Hill, with its remains of a complex Iron Age fort. It has three banks with intermediate ditches. The visible hollows in the 20 acre central area are grain storage pits.

On another hilltop to the southeast of the village is the earthwork of Powerstock Castle. The castle was built in Norman times and was later converted into a hunting lodge for King John, who hunted in Powerstock Forest.

St Mary's is a Norman structure which was largely rebuilt in the 1850s. The impressive 12th-century chancel arch with four rows of ornament remains, and it has a row of gargoyles – probably Norman – while on the inside of the south porch are some fine 15th-century carvings of figures in relief, including a Virgin and Child, and a king with a staff and book. Just outside the door are the remains of a 13th-century dole table, from which loaves of bread were given to the poor.

PRIDDY

Somerset
4 miles northwest of Wells

A stack of disused hurdles on the green in the centre of the village of Priddy high in the hills preserves the villagers' rights to have their 600-year-old annual summer fair. But the most impressive sight near Priddy is 1 mile to the north, the Priddy Circles, a Bronze Age complex of four circles, each of which is about 200 yds across. They are set in a straight line about 1 mile long, the circle at the north end being divided from the next by a gap wider than the average. These monuments, like Stonehenge, have ditches on the outside rather than the more usual interior ones.

Half a mile to the south, a gentle path over the B3135 leads to Ashen Hill, a Bronze Age barrow cemetery. Like many prehistoric sites, it is an austere setting. The scattered community of Priddy is situated high up on the limestone plateau, about 800 ft above sea-level, and is exposed to the cruel ravages of the winter winds. Centuries of trampling by human and animal feet – to say nothing of the work of rabbits – has reduced the barrows to a fraction of their original size. But they and their prehistoric neighbours a short distance south on North Hill, Priddy Nine Barrows, form a landmark which can be recognised for many miles around. In the 19th century some of the Priddy Nine Barrows – there are only seven, in fact – were excavated. They were found to contain burned bones and, in one case, beads similar to those found in Egyptian tombs.

Stands of beeches and firs dot the hillside, adding colour and variety to the landscape. There is plenty of wildlife, including badgers in the neighbouring Mendip woods, but they are seen only at dusk.

PUDDLETOWN

Dorset
5 miles northeast of Dorchester

The charmingly named Puddletown lies on the River Piddle – or Trent – and has a pleasant 15th-century church, St Mary's. It has a good interior, and the panelled nave roof is 15th century. The gallery, box-pews and canopied pulpit are of the 17th century. In the south chapel are many monuments and brasses of the 15th and 16th centuries and in the west window is stained glass by Sir Ninian Comper.

Three miles east, on Affpuddle Heath, a tall tree grows from the 50 ft depths of a smooth-sided crater measuring 150 yds across, known as Cull-peppers Dish. The tree and crater resemble a huge mortar and pestle, and may have been named after the 17th-century herbalist Nicholas Culpeper. The crater is a swallow-hole – one of 200 or so on the heath – a subsidence caused by underground streams eroding chalk.

In the northern part of heath, the many little bridges and decaying sluice gates tell of the once-intricate system of water-meadows around the River Piddle. The controlled flooding of these meadows in spring resulted in early grazing for stock, because the incoming water, warmer than the soil, advanced grass growth.

To the south, tracks lead down from the heath through Forestry Commission conifers and past Rimsmoor Pond to the bridle-path to Clouds Hill. Here the National Trust maintains the cottage that was the home of Lawrence of Arabia from 1923. He bought it while, as Private Shaw of the Royal Tank Corps, he was stationed at nearby Bovington Camp. Later he transferred to the RAF, and on his discharge in 1935 returned to live at Clouds Hill until his death a few months later at Moreton, 2 miles northeast. He is buried in the small, cheerful church at Moreton, which has chancel windows which were engraved by Laurence Whistler in 1958.

PURTON

Wiltshire
5 miles northwest of Swindon

The Church of St Mary is unique among English churches in that it has both a central tower with spire and a western tower with pinnacles. Tradition explains that this is because the two sisters who had the church built could not agree on its design, so they struck this peculiar compromise. But in this case tradition is mistaken; the spire was built about 1325 and the western tower 150 years later. Inside many details indicate the Norman origins of the building, which was altered during the 14th–15th centuries. There are mural paintings, including a 17th-century Death of the Virgin and fragments of medieval glass.

Halfway between Purton and Purton Stoke is a bend in the road called Watkins' Corner. Allegedly, it is haunted by the ghost of a man called Watkins, who was hanged there for a murder to which his father later confessed. As he swung from the gallows, a fearful storm blew up, which so frightened the hangman's horse that it bolted and threw him, breaking the hangman's neck.

POOLE *A view from the other side of the bay, over a windswept golf course, towards the harbour* (overleaf).

QUANTOCK FOREST
Somerset
Between West Bagborough and Nether Stowey

Though large areas of Quantock Forest are now conifer plantations belonging to the Forestry Commission, it dates back to Saxon times and was a royal hunting ground. Ash trees formed much of the old forest – the nearby village of Aisholt takes its name from them – and there are parts of the forest where they still grow, along with oaks, beeches and cedars.

A forest walk of about 5 miles starts from Triscombe Stone, the highest point at 1047 ft above sea-level. The lowest point on the walk is at Pepper Hill Farm, some 600 ft below. Although the route takes in some beautiful broad-leaved woodland in the parkland round Pepper Hill Farm, much of it is through conifers, which are not to everyone's taste. There is no denying, however, the magnificence of stately Douglas fir, Sitka spruce, Japanese larch and Scots pine – especially on a warm, summer's day when sunlight shafts through the trees and the scent of pine is heavy on the air.

There is another walk through Quantock Forest, starting at Seven Wells, where streams threading their way off the heights attract herons, dippers, kingfishers and wagtails. At Adscombe Farm, on the fringe of the forest, are the remains of a chapel built in the 10th century by the monks of Athelney Abbey.

OLD GROVE *Beech and ash form the most ancient part of Quantock Forest, today joined by fir and pine.*

QUANTOXHEAD, EAST AND WEST
Somerset
3 miles east of Watchet

A partly Jacobean manor resembling a medieval castle stands on a hillside overlooking the grassy coastal plain around East Quantoxhead at the northern end of the Quantock Hills. Court House, just behind the church and built of local stone, is the home of the Luttrells of Dunster Castle, a family which has links with the village going back more than 700 years. No part of the parish has ever been sold since it was granted by William the Conqueror to Ralph Paganel – a direct ancestor of the Luttrells.

The village is reached by way of a winding high-banked lane leading north off the Minehead to Bridgwater road past squat, deeply thatched cottages. In the very centre is a duck-pond, raised slightly above road level and brimming with clear water.

A footpath from the car park leads to the Church of St Mary, some 13th-century features of which were retained when it was largely rebuilt in the 15th century. The porch has a 'coffin squint', an aperture through which the waiting priest could watch out for the approach of a funeral party. There is some fine medieval panelling inside, with carved bench-ends and several memorials to bygone Luttrells, one of whom was rector here for 71 years. More picturesque cottages and a footpath from the pond lead across a field to the rocky shore half a mile away.

West Quantoxhead, 1½ miles to the southwest, has some handsome houses and an imposing mansion, St Audries – now a girls' school – built in the Tudor style in the 19th century, at the same time as the pinkish-buff stone Church of St Etheldreda – also called St Audrey – which has an elegant tapering spirelet.

The pocket-sized patch of Forestry Commission woodland known as Staple Plantation is at the foot of Beacon Hill, about ¼ mile west of West Quantoxhead. Barely half a mile square, it lies in an easily accessible

EAST QUANTOXHEAD *Old farm buildings and spring blossom lighten the view south towards the Quantock Hills.*

corner of the Quantocks on their northwestern fringe, where the ancient Devonian sandstone rocks give way to the lush farmland of West Somerset. From the car park at Staple Plain, above West Quantoxhead, a pathway drops down between silent conifers, with westward views over the Brendon Hills, and Exmoor's lofty Dunkery Hill, a purple mound in the distance.

Staple Plantation is at its best in autumn, when the beech and sweet chestnut turn to copper and gold against the never-changing green of the conifers. Beyond the woodland, Weacombe Combe runs east to Bicknoller Post, its flanks of bracken providing perfect camouflage for red deer which occasionally venture from the heights to raid the orchards and gardens in the hamlet of Weacombe. The hamlet lies at the bottom of the path from Staple Plain, at the southwest end of the plantation.

RAMSBURY
Wiltshire
6 miles east of Marlborough

Ramsbury is a picturesque village on a wide stretch of the River Kennet. The river flows through the park of Ramsbury Manor, built in 1680 by John Webb, the son-in-law of Inigo Jones. It was in this house that Cromwell laid his plans for the subjugation of Ireland. The town has many Jacobean and Georgian buildings, an impressive parish church with Anglo-Saxon foundations, and a charming pub, The Bell.

RINGSTEAD BAY
Dorset
5 miles east of Weymouth

The massive chalk headland of White Nothe, called Nose locally, protects Ringstead Bay to the east. On the southwest side, the formidable stone rampart of the Isle of Portland shelters both Ringstead and Weymouth bays.

The deserted medieval village of Ringstead lies about 1 mile east of Osmington Mills, where John Constable painted his picture of Weymouth Bay. The village is now no more than a collection of grassy mounds and the ruined fragment of a church. Why it was deserted local records do not say.

The villagers may have succumbed to the Black Death. A more likely story is that they were the victims of French raiders in 1420, during the Hundred Years' War.

A coastal path climbs eastwards about 2 miles to White Nothe, across sloping downland overlooking a long sweep of pebbled beach, sheltered in places by ledges of rock running into the sea. Even the tumbled layers of the Burning Cliff in no way disrupt the bay's idyllic and tranquil atmosphere. The Burning Cliff is so called because the dark, sulphurous oil-shale – or Kimmeridge coal – of which it is composed, ignited spontaneously in 1826 and smouldered for four years.

After a series of wooded gullies, the final climb up White Nothe is very steep, but for those who make it there are superb views.

ROUNDWAY HILL
Wiltshire
1 mile northeast of Devizes

A beechwood crowns Roundway Hill, its majestic trees standing sentinel-like over verdant downland. Clover springs from the long grass, and there are wild flowers such as blue speedwell and yellow goat's beard. Here, the walker can relax beneath the trees or take in the views of the Marlborough Downs to the northeast, where they sweep down to the River Kennet and extend beyond to the Vale of Pewsey.

Roundway was the scene of a Civil War battle on July 13, 1643 when Prince Maurice, brother of Prince Rupert, led a Royalist force to victory against the Roundheads. The battlefield, on Roundway Down, is out of sight from the top of the hill, tucked away in the fold of the Downs about 1 mile north of the car park at the foot of Roundway Hill. Legend tells that, on the anniversary of the battle, the dead cry out from the nearby ditch where they were buried.

THE OSMINGTON HORSE *A carving of George III on horseback charges across the chalk hill near Osmington Mills.*

S

ST ALDHELM'S HEAD
Dorset
5 miles southwest of Swanage

The grey wall of rock that sweeps westwards from Swanage reaches its climax at St Aldhelm's Head, a towering 350 ft cliff thrusting boldly out into the Channel. A few yards back from the cliff-edge a small Norman chapel dedicated to the evangelist St Aldhelm (c. 640–709), a Saxon Bishop of Sherborne, stands solitary on the windswept grassy plateau, heavily buttressed against the gales. Where a stone cross now stands on its roof, there was originally a fire basket whose bright glow warned sailors of the tide-race off the headland.

Westwards from the cliff the rock collapses in spectacular disarray, and strangely fretted towers and pinnacles rise from the green undercliff, wreathed in wild flowers. The Dorset Coast Path follows near the cliff-edge to Emmetts Hill overlooking Chapman's Pool, a quiet cove in a deep cleft bordered on the west by Houns-tout Cliff.

ST BRIAVELS
Gloucestershire
5 miles west of Lydney

A castle that never saw a battle dominates St Briavels, standing high on a spectacular bluff above the Wye Valley. The castle dates from the 13th century, and during the reign of King John was used as a hunting lodge. The keep fell down in the 18th century, but the twin-towered gatehouse survives and provides one of the best-sited and most interesting Youth Hostels in Europe. There are wonderful views across the Forest of Dean and marvellous walks.

The Church of St Mary is Norman and later, and outside the church the St Briavels Bread and Cheese ceremony is held every Whit Sunday. After Evensong, a local forester stands on a wall and throws pieces of bread and cheese to the churchgoers below. The custom is said to be 700 years old, and the villagers who catch the food retain the right to collect wood and graze animals in nearby Hudnalls Wood.

A well-preserved 7 mile stretch of Offa's Dyke runs near St Briavels. It was built by Offa, King of Mercia, together with a ditch and earth rampart, in the 8th century, to define and defend the boundary between his territory and Wales. It runs for nearly 170 miles from the River Severn to the Dee, with some gaps where there was originally thick forest.

SALISBURY
Wiltshire
21 miles northwest of Southampton

Long before the Romans came to Britain an Iron Age camp stood on a hill a few miles south of Stonehenge. The Romans strengthened it and called the place Serviodunum. Then the Normans built a castle and a cathedral on the site and called it Sarum. Bishop Herbert Poore found that Sarum was not big enough to accommodate the authority of both church and castle, and decided to build a new cathedral to the south. The bishop died before he could carry out his plan, but his brother Richard, who succeeded him, began to build the new cathedral in 1220. Around it grew a community which was called New Sarum and is known today as Salisbury.

Bishop Richard Poore completed the cathedral in the remarkably short time of 38 years and, as a result, it is built largely in a single style, unlike many other medieval English cathedrals. The tower and spire, a combined height of 404 ft, the tallest in England, were added in 1334. Its central piers stand on foundations only about 6 ft down in swampy ground.

The west front, is the most lavishly decorated. It has row upon row of statues in niches. The present statues are Victorian replacements of the originals.

Inside, graceful columns of Purbeck stone line the high-vaulted nave and the many windows add to the airy, yet dignified, interior. The nave is rich in monuments, tombs and effigies. The oldest tomb is that of William Longespée, Earl of Salisbury, who was buried in the cathedral in 1226. He was a witness at the sealing of Magna Carta by King John, his half-brother, in 1215, and the copy he brought back to Salisbury is on display in the Charter House. It is one of only four surviving originals of the document.

The miniature fan-vaulted north aisle of the nave has a clock dating from 1386 and claimed to be the oldest working clock in the world. It has no dial, and chimes the hours.

Beneath the spire is a brass plate, set into the floor and engraved 'AD 1737 the centre of the tower'. It marks the result of a check made 50 years after Sir Christopher Wren had discovered that the spire was leaning $29\frac{1}{2}$ in. off centre. Wren's solution was to straighten it with iron tie-rods. When these were replaced in 1951 it was found that the spire had moved no further.

The chapter house, which is octagonal and has a graceful central column, is decorated around its walls with 60 scenes from the Old Testament involving about 200 carved figures – splendid examples of the medieval stonecutters' art.

The cathedral was built before the town, and so Church authorities had to build houses for the clergy. These were contained within a walled square – the largest and finest cathedral close in Britain. It is entered through medieval gateways, and many of the buildings inside, such as the Bishop's Palace and the Deanery, are also medieval.

Some private residences in the close date from later periods. Mompesson House was built in the early 18th century for Thomas Mompesson, a rich Wiltshire merchant. Malmesbury House, built in 1327, was given a new interior and facade between 1640 and 1749. Both houses are open to the public and have rooms furnished and decorated in 18th-century style. An elegant stand of almshouses, Matron's College, were built by Bishop Seth Ward in the 17th century.

South of the cathedral stands the Bishop's Palace, built in the 13th century. The view of the cathedral from the palace gardens was portrayed by John Constable in a famous painting now in the Victoria and Albert Museum. The palace was considered sufficiently isolated by Charles II to use for his court during the Great Plague of 1665. Today it is used by boys of the cathedral choir school.

Outside the walls of the close the city streets were laid out in a grid pattern. In most of them can be seen timbered houses and inns, overhanging gables and bow-windowed shops. Among the outstanding black-and-white half-timbered buildings are the 15th-century House of John A'Port in Queen Street, the 16th-century Joiners' Hall in St Ann Street, a 15th-century inn, the Haunch of Venison, and a 14th-century inn, the Rose and Crown.

Salisbury has a large market square and a modern shopping precinct, the Old George Mall, which blends unobtrusively with the older buildings around it. The hexagonally buttressed Poultry Cross is a 15th-century reminder of Salisbury's once large poultry market.

The city's churches are almost as old as the cathedral. St Thomas's dates from 1238 and, with its tower and cap spire, is far enough away from the cathedral not to be dominated by it. St Martin's chancel dates from 1230.

The Salisbury and South Wilts Museum, in King's House, The Close, exhibits many finds from Stonehenge, together with pottery from Old Sarum and the surrounding district, a Roman mosaic pavement, and a collection of English pottery, china and glass.

Salisbury is an important market town and a good touring centre, from which peaceful riverside drives radiate in every direction. The splendid Avon, which rises near Devizes, becomes navigable at Salisbury, after three other rivers have joined it. One mile below Salisbury in the Avon water-meadows, is Britford, a village with splendid views of the spire of Salisbury Cathedral. It has charming old houses, including the 18th-century Bridge Farm and The Moat, a partly-Georgian, partly-Gothic Revival house.

Longford Castle is another mile further south, and is largely 16th century, built to a triangular pattern. It has a notable collection of paintings.

East of the city the River Bourne winds through wooded downs and picturesque villages named after the river. To the west lie the valleys of the Wylye and the Nadder, separated by the wooded heights of Grovely Wood and the Great Ridge, along which can be traced the route of a Roman road plunging westwards towards Bath, the Roman city of Aquae Sulis.

The Wylye Valley delighted Izaak Walton, 17th-century author of *The Compleat Angler*, and the light reflected from its placid water-meadows inspired many of Constable's paintings. The Nadder Valley is fringed by the parklands of old country mansions, and along both valleys are many unspoilt little hamlets and prosperous farmlands, where well-fed cattle graze.

SALT WAY AND SALTER'S HILL

Gloucestershire
2¼ miles east of Andoversford

The most walkable section of the Salt Way begins just north of the A436, about 2½ miles east of Andoversford. It leads north for 7 miles and ends just beyond Hailes Abbey, north of Winchcombe.

Salt was an essential meat preservative in medieval times, when people had to slaughter their cattle, sheep and pigs in the autumn because there was not enough feed for the animals during winter. Salt became an important commodity and, for centuries, packhorses loaded with it travelled to towns throughout England from coastal saltpans and inland mines such as those at Droitwich in the old county of Worcestershire. One of the 'salt ways' runs across a high ridge of the Cotswolds on what was probably a prehistoric path. Remote, windy and sunny, the airy narrow road that skirts the vale of Sudeley to the west and the gentle Windrush valley to the east is still called the Salt Way. Salter's Hill lies 2 miles east of Winchcombe on the northern section of the Way.

On the west slope of the ridge above the vale of Sudeley there is a planted woodland of conifers. Along the path through the wood the grassy banks are vivid with rock-roses and bright blue tufted vetch. The path starts on the wet side of the Salt Way 3 miles north of the A436. From it, swallows can be seen swooping and diving in the immensity of air over Winchcombe, the valley of the River Isbourne, wooded Sudeley Castle and the blue reaches of Cleeve Common far beyond.

At its northern end, the Salt Way is a footpath and leads to Salter's Hill. Beyond the hill the path dips down to Salter's Lane and into a precipitous valley with patterns of fruit blossom covering the orchards on the facing hill in spring. From the path there is a rare view of the ruins of Hailes Abbey, owned by the National Trust and built in the 13th century for the white-robed Cistercian monks.

SANDFORD ORCAS

Dorset
3 miles north of Sherborne

At the top of a winding lane up a combe north from Sherborne is a striking view towards the Somerset plain. If you then go down the steep hill on the other side, you come suddenly on the beginning of the straggling village of Sandford Orcas which follows a stream down the valley. This contains a number of cottages and houses built of golden Ham Hill stone, some with stone mullioned windows and leaded lights.

Near a road junction at the lower end of the village several streams converge to flow eventually into the River Parrett.

On a rise beyond the centre of Sandford Orcas, the church and Manor House form a fine pair of early-Tudor buildings. The Church of St Nicholas has a Norman font and a 15th-century tower, and its small chapel contains a number of monuments. Among them is one dated 1607 to William Knoyle, whose family once owned the village.

The small, 16th-century Manor House is complete with arched gatehouse, stable court and walled garden. It was formerly the home of Edward Knoyle, who inherited Sandford in the early 1530s. There may well have been an earlier 11th-century manor house on the same site – the property of the Orcas family – who, in the 12th century, gave the village the second half of its name. The house contains period panels, furniture, woodwork, china, glass and rugs.

A few miles to the southwest is Trent, whose Church of St Andrew is of 13th-century origin. Additions include the 14th-century south tower and spire, and a fine Perpendicular rood screen, still with its vaults. There are several monuments and 16th- and 17th-century stained glass. The pulpit is probably Dutch c. 1600, and the pews and decorative bench-ends are said to have been saved by the canny villagers from destruction by the Puritans. Lord Fisher, the 99th Archbishop of Canterbury, who died in 1972, is buried in the churchyard.

SAVERNAKE FOREST
Wiltshire
½ mile southeast of Marlborough

In the Middle Ages, Savernake was a wilderness of bracken and heathland that had been a royal hunting ground from before the Norman Conquest. In 1540 it was acquired by the Protector, the Duke of Somerset. At one time Jane Seymour's father was its hereditary warden. It still remained hunting land with small coppices providing shelter for the deer and their 'vert', or winter feed. The 2000 acres are now leased to the Forestry Commission by the Marquess of Ailesbury, and is the only English forest that does not belong to the Crown.

Timber was always a byproduct but there was no systematic replanting. By 1675, the trees were so decayed that a navy surveyor found only three or four fit for use. A few of these ancient trees survive – the big-bellied oak on the A346 Salisbury road is the easiest to see.

Today's forest of stately beeches and oaks was the inspiration of the 18th-century landscape gardener 'Capability' Brown; he devised a 4 mile long Grand Avenue that ran arrow-straight through the forest, and about halfway along its length he created a 'circus' from which radiated eight walks.

Brown's Grand Avenue may have been as formal as a processional way 200 years ago, but time has given it an air of informality. The road is narrow, and although the great beeches climb like columns in a cathedral nave, they have been joined by new trees that crowd the road edge and arch in leafy tunnels. Occasionally the grandeur returns, especially at the circus where tall pines intermingle with the beeches and the young intruders are held at bay. Once again the cathedral-like atmosphere prevails, with the sun filtering through windows mullioned by slender branches. The Avenue begins at Forest Hill on the A4, and runs northwest to southeast.

Informality can be found, too, in many other walks and drives in the forest, especially in the Postern Hill Walk just off the A346 at the western end of the forest. Here the venerable beeches give way to a trim, 30-year-old plantation of oaks, young beeches and rowan trees. Bluebells carpet the woods in early summer, when chiffchaffs, willow warblers and whitethroats arrive. Another drive – Long Harry – has trees 90 ft tall, where rooks and jackdaws add their raucous calls to the fluting notes of blackbirds and thrushes.

Primroses, wood anemones and wood sorrel flourish in the woods in spring, and rosebay willowherb and wood sage dapple the glades in warmer weather. Pale bird's-nest orchids grow in the deep shade beneath the beeches.

You may catch a glimpse of a fallow deer, with fan-shaped antlers and spotted summer coat, as it slips silently into a thicket. And a fluster of brightly coloured feathers across a forest path marks the scurrying retreat of a pheasant.

SEDGEMOOR
Somerset
Near Bridgwater, between Polden Hills and the River Parrett

Sedgemoor is a low-lying, marshy region stretching from the Mendips to Taunton and Ilminster. It is intersected by numerous dykes or 'rhines', cut for drainage purposes, and its willows are used for the local industry of basket-making.

North of the village of Westonzoyland is the site of the Battle of Sedgemoor which ended the Duke of Monmouth's rebellion against James II in 1685. This fierce and bloody hand-to-hand struggle was the last major battle to be fought on English soil.

SELWORTHY
Somerset
3 miles west of Minehead

Thatched cottages are grouped around a pasture at Selworthy, reached by a lane where oak, ash and holly branches intermingle overhead.

The village is sheltered from the fierce sea winds by 1013 ft Selworthy Beacon, rising above it to the north. To the south, across a green valley, lies Exmoor and its highest peak, 1705 ft Dunkery Beacon – the best view of which can be seen from the steps of the largely 14th-century Church of All Saints. The church is perfectly proportioned, rich in stone carving and tracery, and has three magnificent wagon roofs, all lavishly decorated. There is a 14th-century tithe barn in the grounds of the former rectory.

Selworthy parish incorporates a number of outlying hamlets. Within easy walking distance are Lynch, 1¼ miles to the northwest, and Bossington, half a mile further on. Lynch has a 16th-century chapel of ease, built for the convenience of worshippers living some distance from their parish church, and at Bossington a stream gurgles into the sea over a pebble beach. Allerford, half a mile southeast of Lynch, has a two-arched packhorse bridge. At Tivington, under a wooded hill 1½ miles southeast of Selworthy, there is another, and lovely, chapel of ease. Dating from the 14th century, and thatched, it has a cottage attached at one end. All these hamlets have thatched cottages with cob walls of clay and straw mixture washed in pastel shades.

SHAFTESBURY
Dorset
20 miles west of Salisbury

Standing more than 700 ft high on a ridge of green sandstone, Shaftesbury is the only hilltop town in Dorset. Its summit can be reached by way of Gold Hill – steep, curved and cobbled – with old stone cottages on one side, a buttressed, medieval wall on the other, and breathtaking views of the surrounding country-side and the Blackmoor Vale. It figures under its old name, 'Shaston', in the novels of Thomas Hardy.

Perched at the peak is St Peter's Church, dating partly from the 14th century with later additions. It has

DORSET'S ONLY HILL TOWN *The green, grey and white houses of Shaftesbury climb up a 700 ft hill* (overleaf).

fine 18th-century panelling and a 17th-century iron poor box. The church is also used for music recitals and concerts.

The Town Hall, next to it in the High Street, was built in the 1820s in semi-Tudor style. A small passageway leads from the High Street to Park Walk, which contains the ruins of a Benedictine abbey for nuns founded in about AD 888 by Alfred the Great. The king's daughter, Aethelgifa, was the first abbess, and she is thought to have presided over about 100 nuns.

The assassinated Anglo-Saxon boy king, Edward the Martyr (about AD 963–78), was buried in the abbey and thousands of pilgrims visited his tomb which they believed had miraculous healing powers. After the abbey's dissolution in the late 1530s, Edward's relics were thought to be lost. But in the 1930s the ruins were excavated, and a lead box was found containing the bones of a teenage boy. These were assumed to be those of Edward, and there is a small shrine to commemorate him on the site.

There is also the oft-reported ghost of a monk, who is thought to know the secret resting place of the abbey's fabled treasure, buried on the orders of the abbess just before the Dissolution in 1539. He has been seen walking round the abbey before vanishing through a wall. Since his body is invisible from the knees downwards, it is thought the old ground level was lower than at present.

The Abbey Ruins Museum contains carved stones and tiles from the excavated abbey, while the Local History Museum commemorates Shaftesbury's button industry, and contains a manual fire engine dating from 1744, complete with leather hose and buckets.

Below the abbey ruins is the parish of St James. It is named after St James's Church, built in the late 1860s at a cost of £3350. Close by is St James Street, with its terraces of stone cottages. It opens into St Andrew's Pump Yard, where an ancient pump stands.

As well as elegant town houses, Shaftesbury has its share of pretty thatched cottages – many of which are on Gold Hill, and in Bell Street, Angel Lane and St James Street. The Westminster Memorial Hospital, between Abbey Walk and Magdalene Lane, was built in the 1870s in memory of a local landowner, Richard, 2nd Marquis of Westminster.

Shaftesbury also has two unique historical attractions: the Byzant and the elaborately carved Chevy Chase sideboard. The Byzant, a curious ornamental relic, was carried by the townsfolk when they paid an annual courtesy visit downhill to the lord of the manor of neighbouring Gillingham; Shaftesbury's water came from springs at Enmore Green which fell within the borough of Gillingham. The Byzant was decked with ribbons, feathers and up to £200 worth of jewellery. The ceremony ceased in 1830 and the Byzant can now be seen in the museum. The Chevy Chase sideboard, housed in the Grosvenor Hotel, celebrates the Battle of Chevy Chase, which took place near Otterburn, Northumberland, in 1388.

SHEPTON MALLET

Somerset
18 miles south of Bristol

The first part of the name Shepton Mallet is derived from the Old English *scaep tun*, a sheep enclosure. 'Mallet' preserves the family name of the post-Conquest owners of the manor.

SHEPTON MALLET *The Old Market Cross, c. 1500, stands outside the 15th-century Shambles or Meat Market.*

In the Middle Ages, Shepton Mallet was famed for its woollen cloth and stockings. Now the town is best known for cider, cheese, gloves and shoes, and as the home of the Bath and West Agricultural Show, held each June.

The Church of St Peter and St Paul has a 16th-century carved barrel ceiling, and a stone pulpit from the same period. The market cross dominates the market place, where the remains of the medieval Shambles – a rare wooden shed which acted as a meat market – can be seen. Several 17th- and 18th-century houses survive in the maze of little lanes that descend the hill to the northwest of the market place.

The walls of one of the caves in the hills north of Shepton Mallet are said to bear the marks of a terrible visitation by the Devil. A long time ago, a poor woman named Nancy Camel lived in the cave. Seeing her poverty, the Devil offered Nancy riches and a life of ease in exchange for her soul. She yielded to temptation, and though she continued to live in her cave, she never worked again and never appeared to lack for anything.

She grew old, and at last the time came for her to fulfil her part of the bargain. One stormy night, Satan brought a great horse and cart to carry her to Hell. People nearby heard piercing shrieks, the crack of a whip and the creaking of wheels, and next morning Nancy had vanished. The cavern walls were stamped with the impression of a horse's hooves and the tracks of cartwheels, which are still faintly visible to this day.

SHERBORNE

Dorset
6 miles east of Yeovil

The Elizabethan courtier, writer and explorer Sir Walter Raleigh had close associations with Sherborne's two castles – the old and the new. The Old Castle, set on a rocky knoll to the east of the town, was leased to Raleigh by Elizabeth I in 1592, and seven years later she gave him the freehold. At first Raleigh tried to convert the 12th-century fortress into a suitable home, but he found it impractical for his needs and decided to build himself a new castle instead.

He chose a site some 400 yds south of his original residence, and put up the present Sherborne Castle where an earlier Tudor hunting lodge once stood. The new building, dating from 1594, had four elaborate storeys, with tall chimneys and mullioned windows. One day, while sitting in the castle grounds quietly smoking his pipe, Sir Walter is said to have had a bucket of ale poured over him by an over-zealous servant. The man thought that his master – who a few years previously had popularised the smoking of tobacco from Virginia – was on fire.

Raleigh's castle looked like something out of a fairy tale, and later additions made it look even more romantic. In 1625 its owner, Sir John Digby, 1st Earl of Bristol, added four wings and four turrets. This gave the castle an 'H' shape – said to be in honour of Prince Henry, James I's gifted eldest son, who died in 1612. Then in the 18th century the celebrated gardener 'Capability' Brown laid out 200 acres of wooded grounds, flooding Sir Walter's formal gardens to make a serpentine lake between the two castles. The Old Castle was destroyed by Parliamentary troops in the Civil War, but its ruins are still here. Sherborne Castle is open on some days during the summer.

Sherborne lies amid green countryside on the north bank of the River Yeo. The town dates from the 8th century, and is a gracious blend of mainly Georgian, Regency and Victorian buildings. The town abounds in old inns too, and since the mid-16th century, when Sherborne public school was refounded in part of the abbey buildings, the town has been noted for its fine schools. There are ten of them in all, including Lord Digby's School for Girls, which occupies a handsome Georgian house in Newland.

The town's main shopping area is Cheap Street, at the bottom of which is The Conduit, used by the Benedictine monks as a wash-house and moved to its present site after the Dissolution in 1539. From there Church Lane leads past the abbey to the Almshouse of St John the Baptist and St John the Evangelist. Henry VI granted the Bishop of Salisbury a royal licence to build the almshouse in the mid-15th century, and the bishop appointed a 'Perpetual Priest' to pray for the souls of its inmates – 12 poor men and four poor women. The almshouse contains a fine triptych – either German or Flemish – its lovely colour due to the use of tempera. The chaplain is now the vicar of Sherborne Abbey, whose choir and nave have superb fan-vaulted ceilings – the choir's fan vault is · the earliest in England.

The abbey contains all the 35 available colours (flags) of the Dorsetshire Regiment (now the Devonshire and Dorset Regiment). It also has the world's heaviest ring of eight bells – a total weight of nearly 8 tons. The tenor bell is thought to have been given to the abbey by Cardinal Wolsey in 1514.

At the bottom of the town, near the railway station, are Pageant Gardens. These were laid out with the profits of the Sherborne Pageant of 1905. This grand affair, master-minded by Louis Napoleon Parker, dramatist, composer and master at Sherborne School, had an immense cast of 900 and was the mother of all modern pageants. In the 1960s Sherborne was the setting of the film musical *Goodbye Mr Chips*. Sherborne also appears in the novels of Thomas Hardy (1840–1928) as Sherton Abbas.

SHERBORNE

Gloucestershire
5½ miles west of Burford

In early summer there seem to be bees everywhere in Sherborne, buzzing around the colourful cottage gardens and visiting the dazzling yellow fields of rape that chequer the broad Cotswold Hills around the village. There are hives in gardens, and Sherborne honey is often available at one or two cottage doors.

The village sits comfortably beside its stream, the Sherborne Brook, and little terraces of two or three stone cottages are strung out, with plenty of space between them, for almost a mile along the valley. They have stone-slate roofs, stone-mullioned windows and stone hoods above the doors; and they stand back behind generous front gardens crossed by stone paths and framed by stone walls. The gardens are a delight. In season they are filled with neat rows of cabbages, beans and onions intermingled with garden flowers to make a riot of contrasting texture and colour.

At first sight there seems nothing special about the small cottage numbered 88 at the crossroads to the east of the village. But look again. The stone archway around the door, decorated with zigzag patterns, came from a Norman church that once stood in the village. The wisteria-hung post office is worth another look – in the publess village, it is licensed to sell not only stamps but 'Beer, Stout and Cider, to be consumed off the premises'.

Midway along the main street is a group of grander buildings around Sherborne House. The monks of Winchcombe Abbey built a small chapel on this site in AD 811. Later a separate monastery was established. In 1552 the site was bought by Thomas Dutton, who had a mansion built on it. The Dutton family became noted for their lavish hospitality in Elizabethan times. On one occasion Elizabeth I was entertained here and the household accounts show that the cost of 'Makynge Readye' for her visit was £5.18s. (£5.90), a princely sum then – equivalent to more than £885 now.

John Dutton, 2nd Lord Sherborne, commissioned the architect Lewis Wyatt to rebuild the house in 1830. Wyatt retained the style of the earlier stone facade with classical columns separating the tall, mullioned windows. In recent years the house has been a school and a meditation centre. Now it has been divided into flats and is not open to the public.

The Church of St Mary Magdalene, attached to Sherborne House, can be visited by taking the road that passes to the right of the stable blocks. The church houses a remarkable collection of monuments of the Dutton family. A macabre effigy of John Dutton, who died in 1656, is shown wrapped in his shroud, but standing upright. An inscription announces that he was 'one who was master of a large fortune and owner of a mind aequall to it.'

The sculptor Rysbrack's marble carving of Sir John Dutton, dated 1749, shows him leaning nonchalantly on an urn, wearing a Roman toga and sandals. There must have been some red faces when this memorial was unveiled, for the name of Sir John's grandfather, a Mr Barwick, was wrongly inscribed: the word 'John' is scored out, and 'Peter' carved above it.

Although Sherborne House is now in private hands, the village, surrounding park and agricultural land are owned by the National Trust.

THE SLAUGHTERS
Gloucestershire
10 miles west of Chipping Norton

Beautiful villages of great character and charm are plentiful in the Cotswolds, but few can equal the mellow, picture-postcard attractions of Lower and Upper Slaughter. A mile apart, with the River Eye running through them, the 'twins' are memorable clusters of rich, honey-coloured stone buildings which blend perfectly into the rolling landscape of the Gloucestershire countryside.

Many of the buildings date from the 16th and 17th centuries. Lower Slaughter has several relatively new houses, some of which have windows with stone mullions and small, rectangular panes edged with lead. No houses have been built in Upper Slaughter since 1904, although some cottages in Baghot's Square, by the churchyard, were remodelled by Sir Edwin Lutyens in 1906.

Lower Slaughter's tree-shaded main street runs beside the river. The southern side is notable for Manor Farm, with its creeper-clad walls and mossy roof. The farm, enlarged in 1688, stands almost opposite what is now the Manor Hotel. Originally known as the Manor House, it was built in the mid-17th century for Sir Richard Whitmore, Sheriff of Gloucestershire and MP for Bridgnorth. Its 16th-century dovecote is one of the largest in Gloucestershire.

Members of the Whitmore family, including several distinguished soldiers, are commemorated by brass tablets in St Mary's Church. It was rebuilt by Charles Shapland Whitmore in 1866–7, but stands on medieval foundations.

From the church, a short and enchanting riverside walk leads to The Square, where picturesque cottages bunch round an old water trough whose spout is shaped like a lion's head. Flanked by cottages on one side and low, stone footbridges on the other, the path continues to the early 19th-century corn-mill – which worked into the 1960s and retains its water-wheel. It now incorporates the village shop, bakery and post office, and has practically the only brickwork to be seen in Lower Slaughter.

Mill Cottage, Malthouse Cottage, Ivy Cottage and their neighbours make Malthouse Lane a stroller's delight as it doubles back to The Square. As the administrative centre of a 'hundred' – an ancient form of local government – Lower Slaughter was the seat of a court which sat every three weeks from the Middle Ages until the 17th century. The village prison was in use until 1630, a century after the local scaffold had claimed its last victim. It is commemorated by Gallow's Piece, a field southwest of the village.

Some of Lower Slaughter's most attractive buildings line the river's southern bank. Dene House, its ground-floor windows peeping out from 'frames' of trimmed

box, stands next to the trim Victorian school which is now a private house. Their near-neighbour, Washbourne's Place, takes its name from a 15th-century owner and overlooks the main bridge.

Upper Slaughter stands on a gentle, grassy hill above Slaughter Brook and was once dominated by a Norman castle. The remains of a motte and bailey have survived behind the early-18th-century Home Farm, and stand in the centre of the village. Pottery from the 11th to 13th centuries has been found on the castle mound.

SOMERTON
Somerset
4 miles northwest of Ilchester

Somerton, once Somerset's county town, is attractively situated near the River Cary; the buildings round the market place constitute one of the most appealing townscapes in Somerset.

The church and some 16th-century houses on the north side of the market place face the 18th-century former town hall and two medieval inns, one of which preserves part of a gallery. The octagonal market cross was rebuilt in 1673. West of the market place are the Hext Almshouses, built in 1626.

STANTON
Gloucestershire
3 miles southwest of Broadway

The villages of Stanton and Stanway, tucked under the western escarpment of the Cotswolds, are perhaps at their loveliest in the evening light. A short, easy stroll out from Stanway's avenue of oak trees – called The Liberty and a favourite haunt of nuthatches and owls – leads to a footpath to Stanton, one of the most perfect Cotswold villages. The path heads north across open fields at the foot of the steep escarpment. The walk from Stanway passes a fine Tudor country house, with a Jacobean gateway, and a medieval tithe barn.

Stanton itself, which is not on the road to anywhere, is a meandering, many-gabled street of Elizabethan and 17th-century cottages with a wayside cross and Gothic manor house. The long main street climbs the gentle Cotswold foothills to end at the Mount Inn. On either side of the street the houses are of golden stone with steeply pitched gables, and were built around 1600. Yet their appearance today is much as it was when they were built, thanks to the efforts of the architect Sir Philip Stott who owned the estate from 1906 to 1937.

Sir Philip's former home, Stanton Court, is a fine Jacobean house with beautiful grounds. The gardens are sometimes open to the public on Sundays during the summer. The original manor house, Warren Farm House, is partly 16th century. Also of medieval origin is the village cross, another fine example of Stott's restoration work.

Furnishings by the architect Sir Ninian Comper can be seen in St Michael's and All Angels Church. His rood screen of 1923, organ loft of 1918 and a number of windows blend well with the church's Norman architecture. The east window, destroyed by prisoners shut in the church during the Civil War, was also restored by Comper. Some medieval pews survive – grooves in their ends are said to have been made by the leashes of dogs brought inside by shepherds.

A footpath and bridleway climb steeply out of Stanton up to Shenberrow Hill and its airy, ramparted Iron Age fort standing in the lee of the lofty ash trees on the ridge above. The path crosses farmland as it climbs, following the contours of the curving hill, and views drop away behind to Bredon, Dumbleton Hill and the Malverns, golden in the evening sun. Sheep graze on the hill, and kestrels can sometimes be seen hovering. On the descent from the fort, pink and white dog-roses can be found in bloom in summer, and primroses in spring.

The circuit uphill and down round the fort is not clearly marked and it is easy to stray from the path here, but the descent from the fort is well trodden and the path emerges at the eastern end of the village.

A couple of miles to the southeast lies the village of Snowshill, with its 16th- and 17th-century manor house. It contains a collection of clocks, musical instruments, armour, scientific instruments, toys and dolls, bicycles, spinning wheels and fire-fighting equipment – over 15,000 items in all. Owned by the National Trust, it is open to the public April to October.

STANTON DREW One of three stone circles, known as 'The Devil's Wedding', lies in verdant pastureland.

STANTON DREW
Avon
7½ miles south of Bristol

The three circles at Stanton Drew date from the early Bronze Age (c. 2000–1600 BC). The central and largest has 27 of its original stones and is about 360 ft across. Southwest of it is a circle of 12 stones, and north lies a circle of eight stones. The central and northern circles each have an avenue which joins to lead to the river. Nearby, behind the Druids Arms Inn, is a 'cove', a three-sided enclosure similar to one at Avebury, Wiltshire. Its precise significance is not known.

Local legend claims that the monuments represent a wedding party who were turned to stone for continuing their revelry into Sunday morning, hence the local epithet, 'The Devil's Wedding'.

STEEPLE ASHTON
Wiltshire
4½ miles south of Melksham

The impressive west tower of the mainly 15th-century Church of St Mary the Virgin at Steeple Ashton was crowned by a 93 ft spire until 1670, when lightning struck it. Stone lierne vaults (vaults with short ribs

connecting the main ribs) roof the north and south aisles – a rare feature in a parish church. The chancel was rebuilt in 1853. There is a partly panelled roof to the nave, and some medieval stained-glass fragments.

The vicar's library, in a room above the south porch, includes a 15th-century Latin Book of Hours, an illustrated book of prayers for fixed times of the day.

STEEPLE LANGFORD
Wiltshire
5 miles northwest of Wilton

A village in the Wylye Valley with thatched brick cottages contrasting with the even older traditional chequered-flint houses. The Norman church contains a Purbeck marble Norman font and a 'squint' aperture in the wall, and nearby there are several interesting houses of the 16th and 17th centuries.

From the church there is an attractive short walk southwest across innumerable streams to join a minor road leading into Hanging Langford, a hamlet which seems to hang on to the lower ledges of the hills bordering Grovely Wood.

STINSFORD
Dorset
1 mile east of Dorchester

Stinsford is set in the wooded valley of the River Frome, which is a favourite place for trout-fishers. The main house in the village is the red-brick and gabled Stinsford House, a few yards from the 13th-century Church of St Michael.

In 1972 the remains of a great man of letters, C. Day-Lewis, the Poet Laureate, were buried in the churchyard, close to the resting-place of Thomas Hardy's heart. Stinsford is known to be the 'Mellstock' of Hardy's poems and novels – including *Under the Greenwood Tree*. His home was in Higher Bockhampton, to the northeast of Stinsford. At Stinsford Cross, on the south side of the A35, is what is thought to be a Roman milestone.

STOGURSEY
Somerset
7 miles northwest of Bridgwater

Formerly called Stoke Courcy, Stogursey was the *stoc* (estate) of William de Courci, a Norman knight. The only surviving part of the Benedictine priory that once stood here is the church, now the parish church of St Andrew, which contains some fine Norman work, including a font. There are also 16th-century bench-ends and several monuments, including one from the 14th century to William Verney, who holds his heart between his hands.

Near the village stand the remains of a castle, whose destruction probably began during the Wars of the Roses.

Just outside the village is Wick Barrow, a Bronze Age burial mound which has long had associations with the pixies. A ploughman working near the mound, who repaired a tiny peel – a type of flat wooden shovel used in bread baking – after hearing a tiny voice bewailing its breakage there, was rewarded by a beautiful cake hot from the pixies' oven.

STOKE ABBOTT
Dorset
13 miles east of Axminster

Ravine-like lanes, guarded by silvery-barked beech trees and fringed by hedgerows aglow in early summer with ragged robin and bluebells, lead the traveller to Stoke Abbott, lying in a fold of the Dorset hills.

In the middle of the village is the New Inn, whose sign depicts monks tending cows and reads: 'The former name of this village was Abbot Stock and is said to relate to the dairy farm of the manor of the abbots which no longer exists.' Dairy farming is still the major occupation. There is hardly a building in the place that is not a delight, from the cottages with absurd little thatched hats over their doors to the big stone farmhouses festooned with lilac and wisteria in summer. The village street curves serenely up a hillside. About halfway up the street, at the bottom of Norway Lane, is an oak, still fairly slim by local standards, yet it was planted to commemorate the beginning of Edward VII's reign in 1901. Beside it, a pair of springs gush forth, one into an ancient trough and the other from the mouth of a stone lion. A notice warns that the water is unfit for drinking.

About the crest of the hill there is a handsome group of 17th and 18th-century farms, the Old Rectory and the Village Hall, formerly the village school. Between them, well-trodden by cattle, a lane runs to a farmyard and to the Church of St Mary in its steep churchyard. Here brown and white sheep graze among the tombstones, several of which bear gaily painted carvings of weeping willows.

Many of the graves are sheltered by the branches of a yew of immense girth, dignity and age. In fact, it is probably a near-contemporary of the church, and that was remodelled in the 13th century. Inside is a beautifully carved Norman font and a memorial tablet in the porch to William Crowe, rector and poet, who died in 1829.

Crowe was a delightful old gentleman who liked to climb nearby Lewesdon Hill – one of a great ring of hills. Another, Waddon Hill, still bears the marks of a fort built about AD 43, nearly a century after the Roman invasion. Resting on Lewesdon Hill's high, wooded summit, Crowe 'garnered worthy thoughts, the fruit of frequent musings', according to his monument. One May morning, he composed a blank-verse poem upon its slopes. He found that:

> 'Above the noise and stir of yonder fields
> Uplifted on this height I feel the mind
> Expand itself in wider liberty ...'

One can readily understand why so many liked him.

The good parson was also Public Orator of Oxford University, and had to go there regularly. But, having little of this world's goods, he used to walk the distance of over 100 miles, carrying his clothes over his arm and composing Latin speeches as he went.

STOKE SUB HAMDON
Somerset
5 miles west of Yeovil

Meadowland divides Stoke Sub Hamdon into two parts – West Stoke, where most of the people live, and East Stoke, where the Church of St Mary stands. To the south is Ham Hill, sometimes called Hamdon Hill, now a country park. It is covered by a network of earthen ramparts, ridges and terraces created largely by a succession of peoples who fortified it in prehistoric times. But part of its outline is a legacy of centuries of quarrying for its honey-coloured stone.

The stone houses in the village, even the smaller cottages, have mullioned windows and well-proportioned gables and date back to the 17th century. On a road leading north from West Stoke stands The Priory, a complex of buildings begun in the 14th century to house priests from a long-vanished chantry. The Priory is now preserved by the National Trust.

The church itself has a Norman chancel and chancel arch, with a 15th-century nave with panelled timber roof, carved bench-ends of the same period, and an iron-framed hourglass by the Jacobean pulpit. Traces of 15th-century mural paintings, representing four angels, remain on the upper walls of the nave, and in the massive transept walls are squints – holes cut to allow a view of the altar.

STONEHENGE

Wiltshire
2 miles west of Amesbury

Viewed from the main road, the world-famous Bronze Age site of Stonehenge appears minute against the vastness of Salisbury Plain. But once the visitor has walked, by a tunnel under the road, towards the first circular ditch, the whole perspective changes and human figures look like pygmies beneath the standing stones, the largest of which is 21 ft high.

The outer ditch is the oldest part of Stonehenge, probably constructed before 2150 BC. About 475 years later, a double circle was erected of 80 bluestones brought more than 200 miles from the Prescelly Hills in southwest Wales. It is believed they were floated on rafts across the Bristol Channel, then dragged over tracks of logs to Salisbury Plain. In 1650 BC the bluestones were taken down and two rings of sarsen stones (from 'Saracen', or 'foreign', though brought this time from no further away than the Marlborough Downs) were erected in the formation that survives today: an outer ring of standing stones, 14 ft high, with lintels across the top of them, and an inner horseshoe of five pairs of uprights with lintels. The great sarsens were probably sawed with wooden levers, rollers and thong ropes, and the lintels raised on a timber platform that was gradually heightened. Mortise-and-tenon joints cut into the stone ensured that the lintels were firmly joined to the uprights.

Later still, some of the bluestones were set up again in a line between the two rings of sarsens and in an inner horseshoe. The largest bluestone – the so-called Altar Stone – was set at the very centre, where it still lies. From the Altar Stone the eye is drawn towards the Heelstone, 256 ft away; it is over the peak of this stone that the sun rises on June 21, the longest day of the year, and this has led many experts to believe that the site had a religious purpose in connection with sun-worship. Most of the missing stones disappeared from the Middle Ages onwards, as farmers and others used the site as a quarry.

Stonehenge, completed c. 1250 BC, is the finest Bronze Age sanctuary in Europe and retains a powerful atmosphere of mystery and awe. This sense is heightened when the sun casts the shadows of the huge upright stones towards holes near the outer ditch.

STOURTON

Wiltshire
3 miles northwest of Mere

Unfenced lawns in front of neat stone houses border the road at Stourton, an estate village laid out in a deep, wooded valley leading down to a lake. Cars are normally left in a large car park on the plateau above the valley, the walk down through the trees being only a few hundred yards. Though always lovely, Stourton is especially so in the early spring when the daffodils are in bloom, and a few weeks later when the rhododendrons and azaleas glow with colour.

The great house of Stourhead was completed in 1724. It was built in Palladian style by Colen Campbell for a banker, Henry Hoare. The library and picture gallery were added a few years after, and about 20 years later, Henry Hoare's son laid out pleasure gardens, lakes and temples in one of the finest landscape designs in the 18th century.

In 1946 the owners of the house, the Hoare family, presented it to the National Trust. The house has an outstanding collection of works of art and furniture by Chippendale the Younger, carved woodwork by Grinling Gibbons, paintings by Angelica Kauffman, and sculpture by Michael Rysbrack. The shores of the lake are edged with magnificent rhododendrons, beeches and tulip trees.

There is a good $1\frac{1}{2}$ mile walk along footpaths from the 14th-century High Cross, which was brought from Bristol in 1765, down to the lake and across the bridge, then through the Grotto and past the Pantheon and up to the woodland-sheltered stone rotunda of the Temple of the Sun. The best views of the area are from the 790 ft Kingsettle Hill, with its triangular 160 ft tower built by the Hoares in 1772 to commemorate King Alfred's victory over the Danes in AD 879.

STOW-ON-THE-WOLD

Gloucestershire
9 miles west of Chipping Norton

Stow is set on a round hill some 750 ft above sea level. From here the ancient wool town looks southwest to the Cotswolds. Apart from the Roman Foss Way, four other roads meet at Stow – which has been an important junction since pre-Roman times.

The town is built mainly of Cotswold stone, and its buildings are grouped around a series of spaces – which give Stow a gracious sense of openness and comfort. In old English, the town's name means 'the meeting-place on the hill', and from 1107 to the turn of the present century a Thursday market attracted farmers and traders, as well as travellers.

Daniel Defoe (1660–1731), author of *Robinson Crusoe*, once attended one of the twice yearly Sheep Fairs in the late 17th century, and recorded that more than 20,000 sheep were sold. The Sheep Fairs later became Horse Fairs, and were held annually until 1985 when they moved to nearby Andoversford.

The Square has a medieval cross, and a carved headstone added in 1878. The carving on the cross's north face shows Robert de Jumièges, Abbot of Evesham, receiving the town's charter from William Rufus in the late 11th century.

The town stocks once stood near the cross, but were moved a short distance away to the Green in the 1870s when the civic centre, St Edward's Hall, was

being built. The Gothic-style hall has a figure of St Edward the Confessor in a niche above the main door. The hall cost just over £4000 to build – and the money came from unclaimed deposits in a local savings bank.

The nearby Talbot was built before 1714 and acted for a time as the Corn Exchange. The brass box on the front of the hotel was where farmers used to leave packets of grain to be tested for quality. On the left of the hotel is one of the narrow alleys known locally as 'tures'. Several tures lead into The Square – on market days sheep were brought through them in single file so that they could be counted.

Two of Stow's main thoroughfares – Sheep Street and Shepherds Way – are reminders of the days when sheep were the town's main livelihood. Branching off Sheep Street is Church Street, on the bend of which is the Masonic Hall, built of rubble masonry in 1594 to house St Edward's Grammar School. The school had been founded in 1475 and stayed here until 1848.

Behind it stands the parish church of St Edward – this could be the St Edward who, according to local legend, lived a hermit's life on the hill, long before the town existed. The church was built by Normans and was added to in the following centuries, giving its interior a variety of architectural styles. In the churchyard the graves of three wool merchants are topped with wool bales carved in stone.

A walk through the churchyard and back into The Square leads to Stow's most unusual building – known as the Crooked House, dating from about 1450 and now an antiques shop. Because of subsidence, the upper part of the house leans steeply to one side as though about to collapse of old age.

STRATTON-ON-THE-FOSSE
Somerset
4 miles southwest of Radstock

The village of Stratton is noted for its nearby Roman Catholic abbey and school, Downside. A Benedictine community of English Catholics founded at Douai in 1607 moved to Shropshire during the French Revolutionary Wars in 1795 and finally settled at Downside in 1814. The present abbey, dating from 1872 and the early part of this century, is chiefly the work of Thomas Garner and Sir Giles Gilbert Scott, architect of Liverpool's Anglican Cathedral.

STREET
Somerset
2 miles southwest of Glastonbury

In the early 19th century James Clark hit upon the idea of lining slippers with sheepskin. His brainwave transformed Street into a busy town, and the shoe firm he founded now employs about one-third of Street's population.

A museum housed in Clark Brothers' shoe factory traces the history of shoe-making since the firm was founded in the 1830s. On display are materials, tools, benches, machines and photographs. One section illustrates footwear of the past, back to Roman times.

There are good walks over the hills, with fine views

ROMANCING THE STONES *Stonehenge, one of England's most popular sites, has an air of Druidic mystery.*

across the moors to the Mendip and Quantock Hills and to the Bristol Channel. The view is outstanding from Ivythorn Hill, a 90 acre wooded estate owned by the National Trust, 3 miles south of Street. Southeast of the town, on Windmill Hill, stands a tall monument to Admiral Lord Hood (1724–1816), who distinguished himself in naval actions against the French.

STROUD
Gloucestershire
8 miles south of Gloucester

The narrow old streets of Stroud climb steep hillsides on a site where five Cotswold valleys meet. Clothmills, powered by fast-flowing streams, were operating in the area in the early 16th century, and by the 1820s there were more than 150 of them. Stroud-water scarlet, a cloth used for military uniforms, was renowned throughout the world. Today, only six mills remain, but these produce fine-quality cloth.

An interesting architectural feature are the Subscription Rooms, built in the early 19th century, incorporating the George Room Art Gallery. The rooms have a *porte-cochère* with Tuscan columns and a balustraded balcony above.

Above the town is Minchinhampton Common, a 600-acre National Trust property giving fine views over the Golden Valley.

Woodchester Roman Villa is about 2 miles south, and is one of the largest archaeological sites of this type in Britain. It covers 26 acres and was excavated in 1796. It is generally covered with earth for preservation, but is occasionally opened. About 4 miles beyond is Nailsworth, where lived W. H. Davies (1871–1940), the 'supertramp' poet.

Four miles southwest of Stroud is Nympsfield Long Barrow, in which between 20 and 30 people were buried between 3000 and 2000 BC. Funeral fire rituals were probably held in the chamber forecourt.

An area of high, open grassland and mixed woodland owned by the National Trust lies just northwest of Stroud and contains the much-loved local Haresfield Beacon with the finest of all viewpoints on the southwestern edge of the Cotswold escarpment. Gloucester lies below with its limestone outlier of Robins Wood Hill; the Severn is a wide swathe of often muddy silver to the southwest, and beyond the Forest of Dean are the blue, distant peaks of the Welsh mountains.

Haresfield Beacon is a natural promontory fortification, 700 ft high, and lies secluded above swathes of dark woodland that clothe the slopes on either side of it. Many people have used this perfect military site to their advantage, including the Romans who had a large camp here after the Iron Age settlement. In the last century some 3000 Roman coins were unearthed on Haresfield Beacon.

The beacon lies on the Cotswold Way, and the National Trust has waymarked the footpaths from the spot. In one direction, the Way leads northeast for three-quarters of a mile to Cromwell's Siege Stone. It is dated 1643 and commemorates the successful defence of Gloucester against Charles I and the Royalists. About 1 mile further on is an unusual hexagonal-shaped farmhouse.

In the other direction, the Cotswold Way follows the deeply indented ridge southwards, past a topograph (direction finder) overlooking the Severn valley, and then into beautiful Standish Wood.

In summer, local people fly kites and model aeroplanes from the beacon's steep rim, but despite the distant murmur of the M5 motorway far below in the Severn vale the National Trust's 348 acres allow plenty of room for space, peace and solitude. Kestrels hover, treecreepers, nuthatches and woodpeckers frequent the woods, there are primroses and bluebells in spring and dog-roses everywhere in summer.

STUDLAND HEATH

Dorset
3 miles north of Swanage

The ancient wilderness of Studland Heath, glowing with gorse and heather, is about 1 mile north of the village of Studland. It butts up against the sparkling creeks and inlets of Poole's vast, landlocked harbour, and the 1570 acres of the heath are under the protection of the Nature Conservancy. There are two nature trails starting from the Knoll car park. One leads over beach and sand-dunes, the other through woodland and swamp.

The sand-dunes trail first follows the superb crescent of Studland's beach, well sheltered and with wide white sands, one of the finest bathing beaches in Britain. Shells to be found along the waterline include Pandora shells, about $1\frac{1}{2}$ in long and with a mother-of-pearl sheen; they are found only here, at Weymouth and in the Channel Islands. From the beach the trail turns inland over three lines of dunes which grow greener the further they are from the sea. These sand-dunes demonstrate how the peninsula has been built up over 250 years from a small spit of land – the wind sweeping sand inshore and plants gradually colonising and anchoring the newly created dunes. Marram grass helps to hold the sand firm. Tree lupins favour sandy soil, while the Scots pine grow in damp hollows.

The most seaward dune is known as the Zero Ridge. The centre one is called the First Ridge, because it was the nearest dune to the sea when the area was surveyed in the 1930s. The third, innermost, ridge dates from the 18th century. From Shell Bay, at the north end of Studland, the car ferry crosses to Sandbanks, near Poole. At the southern end, a footpath over Ballard Down leads to Swanage.

The woodland trail passes close to the south end of Studland's Little Sea, a mile-long freshwater lake edged with sallow, reedmace, yellow flag and bog bean. Until 350 years ago it was a coastal bay, but developing sand-dunes have now completely cut it off from the sea, and drainage from inland streams has gradually replaced the salt water.

A wooden hide, reached along a short path from the ferry road, overlooks the lake, where in winter thousands of wildfowl, such as wigeon, pochard, goldeneye and shoveler, may be seen. Summer visitors include sedge and reed warblers, which can be heard singing in the reed beds. Britain's three lizard and three snake species are all found on the reserve.

STURMINSTER NEWTON

Dorset
8 miles northwest of Blandford Forum

Sturminster Newton is the market centre for the Stour farmlands. A graceful six-arched 15th-century bridge over the river carries the dire warning of 'Transportation for life' for those who damage it. The 17th-century town mill is still working, churning its waters into white-flecked foam. The wooden-porticoed Mill House on the road to Blandford Forum faces a thatched house of character. A little further on is Newton House; its Georgian facade, with a curious medallion frieze over the front door, hides its much greater age.

William Barnes, Dorset's 19th-century poet who wrote 'Linden Lea' and is noted for his use of the pure dialect of his county, was born at nearby Pentridge Farm. Thomas Hardy wrote *The Return of the Native* in a greystone mansion, Riverside, on the outskirts of the town. Sturminster Newton is made colourful by many bow-windowed buildings of brick, stone and cob. There are also good thatched, timber-traced houses leading up to the pretty market square where, on Monday mornings, crowds of farmers overflow into the station yard and surrounding streets. The thatched White Hart Inn is 18th century, and the Perpendicular church has been enriched by modern artists.

Nearby, about 3 miles to the north, is Marnhull, whose Church of St Gregory is of a fine cruciform with a west tower. Originally constructed in the 12th century, it was refashioned in the 14th and enlarged in the 19th. The bowl of the font is made from the old village preaching cross.

SUDELEY CASTLE

Gloucestershire
8 miles northeast of Cheltenham

Catherine Parr, the sixth queen of Henry VIII, is buried at Sudeley Castle; in 1547, after Henry's death, she married her former lover, Lord Seymour of Sudeley, but died here in childbirth the following year. The castle was a headquarters of Charles I during the Civil War and was besieged in 1643 and again in 1644. The ruined banqueting hall dates from c. 1450; the chapel of the same date contains the tomb of Catherine Parr. The castle houses much fine furniture, tapestries, needlework and china: the pictures include works by Constable, Rubens, Turner and Van Dyck. Double yew hedges, 15 ft high, are a feature of the garden.

One and a half miles to the northwest is Winchcombe, whose Church of St Peter has grotesque carved heads beneath the battlements. It was built during the 15th century, when Winchcombe grew prosperous from the wool trade. Some of the embroideries on the 14th-century altarcloth are said to have been done by Catherine of Aragon, while she was staying at Sudeley Castle.

SWANAGE

Dorset
9 miles southeast of Wareham

Stonework and street furnishings brought from London in the 19th century are an intriguing feature of Swanage, on the Isle of Purbeck. The town, once a Saxon port, is referred to in the Domesday Book as 'Swanic'; and a granite column on the front commemorates King Alfred's naval victory in AD 887 over the Danish fleet in the sweeping bay now lined by a safe, sandy beach. The facade of the Town Hall came from the Mercers' Hall, Cheapside, designed by a student of Sir Christopher Wren in 1670; and the clock-tower near the pier was originally erected at the end of London Bridge in honour of the Duke of Wellington.

One mile south are the dramatic grey cliffs of Portland stone that rise from the waves at Durlston Head. And in the park above the cliffs is a man-made rock formation – known as the Durlston or Great Globe – which is a chart of the world cut from 40 tons of Portland stone and surrounded by stone slabs carved with cosmic information and quotations from the poets. It was carved in the 1880s by George Burt, a local quarryman who made his fortune supplying paving stones for Victorian London.

The Dorset County Council's Country Park here has a 'stone trail', a nature trail and geological models that tell the story of the local rocks. A path leads down through holm oaks and tamarisk to a cliff-edge sea-bird sanctuary, and then strides on towards the Anvil Point Lighthouse, descending into the gully where the Tilly Whim Caves emerge. Rock falls have forced the closure of these old quarry workings, but the great wall of Portland stone, divided into gargantuan blocks by natural joints, remains awe-inspiring.

There are other impressive quarry caves at Winspit, 4 miles to the west. This is an idyllic spot on a sunny day, with its great stone stacks and the sea dancing over the ledges from which generations of quarrymen winched their stone into the barges waiting below. It can be reached along a 1¼ mile track from the village of Worth Matravers.

THE SWELLS
Gloucestershire
1½ miles west of Stow-on-the-Wold

An elegant bridge, an old mill still with its wheel, and an attractive millpond make a charming introduction to Upper Swell, which has even more of interest to offer in the shape of its manor house and tiny church at the centre of the village.

The manor house dates from the 17th century and has a fine Jacobean, two-storey porch with columns, mullioned windows and a roof of Cotswold stone. Only a few feet away stands St Mary's Church, mostly Norman, with its original plan of chancel, nave and porch, and crowned with a bellcote. The River Dikler flows behind church and house, reappearing at the millpond, where swans, coots and ducks gather.

Another mill is the Donnington Brewery, 1½ miles north of Upper Swell, which has been a brewery since 1827 and was a flour mill and a cloth mill for 150 years before that. Its brew can be sampled at the Golden Ball in Lower Swell, a village larger than its neighbour and also boasting a hotel, the Old Farmhouse. In the early 19th century, Lower Swell might have become a 'spa', had not the local chalybeate (iron) spring lost its strength. Dating from the time are Spa Cottages, a group of three houses with a carved facade, standing on the east side of the Dikler and, like all the houses in Lower Swell, built of Cotswold stone.

The road climbing to Upper Swell leaves the village by the Church of St Mary the Virgin, a Norman building extended northwards in the Victorian period. Between the two villages there is a view, restricted in summer, across the valley to Abbotswood, a grand house of 1902 by the architect Sir Edwin Lutyens. He also designed the gardens, known for their exceptionally magnificent flower displays and shrubs, open to the public several days each year.

SWINDON
Wiltshire
70 miles west of London

The initials GWR, standing for Great Western Railway, stamped themselves indelibly on the town's history from the middle of the last century, turning Swindon from an agricultural settlement into an industrial centre and goods terminus.

In 1835 it became a station on the GWR London to Bristol line, and a few years later was chosen as the site of a locomotive works. When other lines were built, Swindon became a major junction and eventually the largest town in Wiltshire. In the hey-day of steam, the locomotive works were among the largest in the world, covering 320 acres and employing 12,000 workers. These had their own specially designed village, maintained today by the council because of its historical interest.

The Great Western Railway Museum, housed in a former Wesleyan chapel, which used to be a railway rooming house, displays famous locomotives, signalling equipment and other railway relics, and has a room devoted to the 19th-century engineer Isambard Kingdom Brunel, who established the GWR.

The town art gallery contains paintings by Graham Sutherland, Ben Nicholson and other modern artists, including one by L. S. Lowry.

SYDLING ST NICHOLAS
Dorset
7 miles northwest of Dorchester

Every road to the valley of the Sydling Water is lovely, but perhaps the finest way is over the hills from Piddletrenthide and Cerne Abbas, catching a glimpse of the Cerne Giant on the way. The valley is a green bowl carved out of the soaring, furze-patched Dorset hills. Long before the Romans came, and for several centuries after their departure, the steep slopes above the Sydling were dotted with farmsteads. But now all that remains of them are marks and lines that show and fade with the seasons, visited only by cattle and sheep.

Sydling St Nicholas, at the valley's heart, is of a respectable age even by Wessex standards. Probably it evolved as ploughs became strong enough to cope with the heavier valley soils, and there it has remained.

The principal building material is yellow stone, either by itself, or divided by double courses of split flint which is sometimes encased in frames of pink brick. Most of the cottages are capped by wheat reed thatch, a delightful material that lies close and sleek like an animal's fur, pale gold when newly put on and darkening to caramel as it weathers. In the High Street is the smithy, dated 1800, which has been run by the same family for three generations.

At the top end of the village is a neat, white swing-gate that looks as though it might lead into someone's garden, but is in fact the entrance to the churchyard. The Church of St Nicholas has yellow stone walls, topped by gargoyles to carry the rainwater off the roof. One of these had a minor role in the film version of Thomas Hardy's *Far from the Madding Crowd*, in

SWANAGE *White ducks waddle alongside the town pond, bright against grey, locally quarried stone (overleaf).*

which it was seen gushing water on to the grave of
Fanny Robin. The village also appears as 'Sidlinch' in
Hardy's story *The Grave by the Handpost*.

The interior of the church, much of which dates
from 1430, was considerably damaged during the
Cromwellian period, so that only fragments of its once
glorious stained glass still remain. However, not even
an Ironside trooper could make much impression on
the massive 12th-century font, which may well be
carved from a Roman capital. More surprisingly, the
chalice, the 400-year-old 'Sydling Cup', has also survived. There are a number of charming 18th- and
19th-century monuments to the Smith family, lords of
the manor for many years.

Over the wall from the churchyard there is an
enchanting glimpse of the gardens of Sydling Court,
with ancient, moulded yew hedges running up the

*SYDLING WATER The little river runs through the valley and
alongside the stone cottages of Sydling St Nicholas.*

hillside and tall trees full of cawing rooks. The Court
passed into the possession of Winchester College at
the Reformation. Among its many tenants since then
were the Elizabethan soldier-poet Sir Philip Sidney and
his mother-in-law, Lady Walsingham. She was the
second wife of Queen Elizabeth's Principal Secretary,
Sir Francis Walsingham, the founder of her Secret
Service.

Near the entrance of the lane leading to the church
is the stump of the old market cross, and behind it are
the handsome mullioned windows of the mainly Tudor
vicarage. The yews in the garden are thought to be
nearly 1000 years old.

T

TAUNTON
Somerset
43 miles southwest of Bristol

History has left its mark on Taunton, county town of Somerset, in its· many fine buildings and pleasant streets, though it is a history that was often bloody and cruel. It was the scene of bitter struggles during the Civil War of 1642–9, and in 1685 Judge Jeffreys held a 'Bloody Assize' in the castle when 508 supporters of the Duke of Monmouth's rebellion were tried and many were condemned to death. Others were deported to the West Indies.

The Norman castle retains part of its keep, which has walls 13 ft thick. The great hall where Judge Jeffreys presided is 120 ft long. The castle now houses the Somerset County Museum.

The gabled and half-timbered Tudor House in Fore Street bears the date 1578. It was the home of Sir William Portman, who took the Duke of Monmouth to London for his trial after the rebellion. Judge Jeffreys may have been entertained there while he presided at the 'Bloody Assize'.

The Church of St Mary Magdalene was built in the 15th century; the tower was considered unsafe in 1862 and was dismantled and rebuilt to the original design. The 163 ft high tower of red Quantock sandstone faces Hammet Street, a completely Georgian thoroughfare with white-porticoed houses. The tower of St James's Church, though smaller than its neighbour, is similar in style. The former Octagon Chapel in Middle Street was opened by Wesley in 1776, and a well-preserved medieval lepers' hospital is marooned amid the traffic in Hamilton Road.

Georgian architecture abounds in the High Street, blending with the 16th-century Municipal Buildings in nearby Corporation Street, which were originally a grammar school. At one end of the High Street is Vivary Park, entered by a gateway that is a riot of Victorian decorative ironwork.

Taunton takes its name from the River Tone, which flows through the centre of the town. The surrounding Blackdown, Quantock and Brendon Hills shelter the town and the rich Vale of Taunton Deane.

The warm climate and fertile soil of the vale are responsible for Taunton's best-known product – cider. The Taunton Cider Company's headquarters is just outside the town at Norton Fitzwarren. At Bradford-on-Tone, about 3 miles southwest of Taunton on the A38, is Sheppy's Farm, where cider-making by traditional methods can be seen each autumn and the farm museum is regularly open.

TEFFONT MAGNA AND EVIAS
Wiltshire
10 miles west of Salisbury

There are two Teffonts – Teffont Magna and Teffont Evias, so named after Ewyas in Herefordshire whose barons once owned the manor house. The two lie close together in the lovely Nadder Valley, and a tumbling stream – the Teff – gushes from the ground just north of Teffont Magna and flows through both villages. The name Teffont comes from the Anglo-Saxon words *teo*, boundary and *funta*, stream.

Teffont Magna is a charming village with thatched cottages clustering round the medieval Church of St Edward, where the 13th-century bell is kept on the windowsill. The stream is crossed by numerous miniature stone bridges. Fitz House, a gabled building of the 17th century, was once the collecting house for locally grown wool and its fine barn still stands.

Teffont Evias is one of the most delightful villages in the valley. Most of its cottages are approached by little bridges over the stream. Others are more imposing; cream-coloured Chilmark stone· has been used imaginatively to build a series of mansions within spacious, stone-walled grounds. A fine example is the beautifully proportioned Howards House which is now a private hotel. The nearby Chilmark quarry, now disused, provided stone for Salisbury Cathedral and for many of the old buildings in the Teffont neighbourhood.

Towards the end of the village the woods close in, almost overshadowing the early 19th-century parish church of St Michael and All Angels with its graceful and richly ornamented spire, 125 ft high. The adjoining turreted manor is a most imposing early 17th-century building with 19th-century additions, now converted into flats, which has its own private chapel in the church. Church and manor house together make a striking picture. A huge box hedge overhanging the stream marks the garden boundary.

TELLISFORD
Somerset
5 miles north of Frome

The village of Tellisford has strong connections with the Somerset wool industry. From the 14th to the 19th centuries, the River Frome provided power, first for fulling mills where cloth was pounded under hammers, and later also for spinning mills.

Wool and cloth were carried between farmers, weavers, mills and traders by trains of pack animals – horses or mules. The old cobbled pathway from the eastern end of Tellisford down to the river and across the narrow bridge was a packhorse route.

TEMPLECOMBE
Somerset
4 miles south of Wincanton

The village of Templecombe takes its name from the Knights Templar, who held the manor in 1185. Scanty remains of their preceptory (the name given to an estate of the Templars) are preserved in Manor Farm; the large fireplace in the kitchen is the most interesting survival. The church contains some narrow upright seats which have been called 'the most uncomfortable in Christendom'.

TETBURY

Gloucestershire

5 miles northwest of Malmesbury

An Elizabethan market town with fine old buildings, Tetbury is famous for its 17th-century town hall built on three rows of pillars, and for the Chipping Steps (Chipping is an Old English word meaning 'market') which lead to the old market.

At Beverstone, 2 miles west, are a fine Norman church and the ruins of Beverstone Castle where King Harold stayed in 1051, and which was held by the Berkeleys at the time when it was successfully besieged by King Stephen in 1145.

TEWKESBURY

Gloucestershire

9 miles northwest of Cheltenham

A tragic young Prince of Wales and a royal duke who may have helped to murder him lie entombed amid the splendours of Tewkesbury Abbey – possibly the finest parish church in England. Some historians believe that the 17-year-old Prince Edward died during the Battle of Tewkesbury in 1471. Others think he was captured, taken to the Cross House, at the corner of

TETBURY The 17th-century Market House, where wool was once weighed and sold, stands at a crossroads.

Tolsey Lane, and stabbed to death. The duke who was alleged to have been one of his attackers was George, Duke of Clarence – himself supposedly murdered six years later when he so spectacularly drowned in a butt of malmsey wine.

The main battle was fought in a field now called Bloody Meadow, off Lincoln Green Lane in the south of the town. Here most of the Lancastrians were massacred, but some fled to the nearby abbey – where they were butchered in the aisles by the Yorkists, despite the pleas of the abbot.

The Abbey Church of St Mary the Virgin was founded by a Norman lord, Robert FitzHamon, at the beginning of the 12th century. Stone from the Cotswolds was used, and the abbey's massive tower is 132 ft high and 46 ft square, the biggest Norman tower still in existence. The arch on the West Front rises 65 ft, the largest of its kind in Britain. The superb high altar, a 13 ft 6 in long slab of Purbeck marble consecrated in 1239, is one of the longest and oldest in the country. In the nave a decorated, vaulted ceiling is supported by 14 Norman pillars, and opposite the choir stands the Milton organ, one of the oldest still in use in Britain. Its pipework dates from 1610. But the abbey's greatest glories are the seven 14th-century stained-glass windows in the choir.

By the West Front stands Abbey House, the former lodging of the abbot. It is probaby late 15th century, but was restored in the late 18th century and returned to the abbey in 1883. It is now the vicarage. Beyond Abbey House is the 16th-century Gate House, restored in 1849.

The townsfolk were so proud of the abbey that in 1540 they bought it from Henry VIII for £453. This saved it from destruction at the Dissolution. Since then it has been sympathetically restored, and the medieval glass painstakingly cleaned.

Tewkesbury lies where the Severn and Avon rivers meet in the valley between the Malvern and Cotswold Hills. Parts of the bridge which crossed the Avon in the 13th century are incorporated in the present King John's Bridge. The town has numerous black-and-white timbered houses with leaded-light windows and overhanging eaves, balustrades and gables.

Tewkesbury's three main streets – High Street, Church Street and Barton Street – form a 'Y'. They are surrounded by a maze of small courts and narrow alleyways containing tiny, medieval cottages. Many of the inns and houses look much as they did at the time of the battle, and the conflict between the Yorkists and the Lancastrians is commemorated in The Ancient Grudge Hotel in the High Street. The building dates from shortly after the Prince Edward's death. Farther along the High Street is the House of Nodding Gables, once a depot and ticket office for stage coaches. A break in the supports has made one of its

THE ABBEY CHURCH OF ST MARY THE VIRGIN *Tewkesbury's parish church is as long as a cathedral. Begun in the early 12th century, its striking central tower dates from 1150.*

gables lean crookedly sideways, as if nodding off to sleep. The 16th-century Tudor House, now a hotel, has a priest's (hiding) hole in the chimney of what is now a coffee room.

In Church Street, the carefully restored Abbey Cottages originally consisted of 23 shops, built about 1450. During the day the shops were open to the street, and at night their counters were raised to act as shutters. One, the Little Museum, is furnished to show how the original occupants lived. Another is the John Moore Museum. Its timbered galleries display farm tools, old domestic utensils and other countryside mementoes. The museum is named after the local author and broadcaster John Moore (1907–67), whose many books include the autobiographical *Portrait of Elmbury*, a lightly disguised Tewkesbury.

The town's literary associations go back to Charles Dickens (1812–70) who set part of his *Pickwick Papers* (published from 1836 to 1837) in the 16th- and 18th-century Royal Hop Pole Hotel. Here Mr Pickwick and his friends did themselves well on bottled ale, Madeira and five bottles of port. Another literary connection is with the Victorian writer Mrs Craik (1826–87), who visited Tewkesbury several times. Her novel *John Halifax, Gentleman*, published in 1857, was woven around the town and its people.

TIDENHAM CHASE
Gloucestershire
4 miles northwest of Chepstow

Sprawling along the top of the eastern bank of the Wye are the former hunting grounds of the lords of Chepstow, Tidenham Chase. Well over 1000 acres of land were their exclusive preserve for hunting deer over the stretches of open land and through the thickets where birch, larch and yew are mixed now. The limestone table that supports the Chase thrusts through in places, giving pale grey vantage points for looking over the landscape. But these are eclipsed by three breathtaking viewpoints reached from the road that runs through the Chase from Chepstow.

Wintour's Leap towers 200 ft above the Wye, a massive grey crag over water that sweeps sharply round in a hairpin bend after encircling the Lancaut peninsula. The backwash as the water rounds the hairpin has worn away the tongue of land and made a pronounced hook at its tip. The leap is named after Sir John Wintour (or Winter), a Civil War hero who is said to have galloped his horse over the edge and swum across the river to escape from the Roundheads.

At the northern end of Ban-y-gor Rocks, three-quarters of a mile further up the road, is a double view – down the almost vertical wall of rock to the Wye, and in the other direction over the sloping fields to the Severn's broad estuary with the Vale of Berkeley and the Cotswolds beyond.

Offa's Dyke Path turns west from the road after a further half a mile and follows the original Offa's Dyke. Striding along above the steep, wooded slope you can admire the line chosen for the 8th-century boundary between Mercia and Wales. The view of the river, and of the Welsh borders beyond it, is superb. The Devil's Pulpit is 2 miles along the path. Below this natural rock platform and across the river lies a low green meadow bearing the elegant, soaring, grey ruins of Tintern Abbey. According to legend, the Devil used to visit the platform to shout insults at the Cistercian Monks.

TINTINHULL

Somerset
4 miles northwest of Yeovil

Tintinhull is a pretty old-world village, where the stocks may still be seen. Tintinhull House is a small and beautiful house built of Ham Hill stone in a delightful formal garden. It was built *c*. 1700, but a century later was given a new west front. The fine formal gardens, next to the village church, have been laid out and developed since 1900 and are now owned, together with the house, by the National Trust.

The Church of St Margaret of Antioch has old scratch dials on the outside walls which were used to indicate the time of mass. Inside there are pews with servants' seats attached to the bench-ends.

TISBURY

Wiltshire
10 miles west of Wilton

Tisbury village follows the line of a steep slope beside the Nadder. Its 200 ft long thatched tithe barn is one of the largest in England, and the Church of St John the Baptist, which dates mainly from the 13th century, has a fine panelled and carved roof. Its central tower had a spire until the latter collapsed in 1762. Inside, the font cover, pulpit and pews are 17th century; the communion rail is made from parts of a rood screen.

TOLLARD ROYAL

Wiltshire
8 miles southeast of Shaftesbury

The village of Tollard Royal tumbles down the side of a valley in the heart of Cranborne Chase, an undulating tract of chalk downland lying between Salisbury, Wimborne Minster, Blandford and Shaftesbury. Tangled copses and a belt of woodland running through the landscape are all that remain of the great primeval forest which once covered the area.

The oldest part, with hunting rights dating back to Saxon times, is the Inner Chase – 10 miles by 3 miles, to the northwest of the A354, centred around the hamlet of Tollard Royal.

Win Green Hill, 4 miles northwest of Tollard Royal, at 910 ft the highest point in Wiltshire, is now owned by the National Trust. Its summit is a perfect place from which to survey the wide sweep of the Chase.

Deer-poaching is as old as the Chase itself. For centuries the Chase was a battleground between an army of keepers and local farmers and poachers. Murderous affrays became so commonplace that keepers and some poachers, 18th-century 'bloods', even wore protective clothing – straw-lined, beehive helmets and padded jackets. But the sporting ardour of the 'bloods' cooled after 1736 when the penalty for a second poaching conviction was transportation.

Hunting rights ended in 1828, and much of the ancient forest – described by Thomas Hardy as the oldest wood in England – was eventually cut down. One of the loveliest parts that still remains is Chase Wood, which can be reached by road (to New Town) or track across Handley Common.

The Chase was a forest often hunted by King John, who had a small estate at Tollard – and so the village came to be called Tollard Royal. His name is commemorated in the village inn, King John's Hotel, and in King John's House which dates from the 13th century. The house was once the king's hunting lodge, and owes its present superb condition to General Pitt-Rivers, who owned it in the late 19th century. It is a tall, straggling but elegant part stone and part timber-framed building, standing in well-kept gardens behind the low green wall of an immaculately clipped box hedge. There is still a member of the Pitt-Rivers family

ST PETER AD VINCULA *The church at Tollard Royal is one of only three in England dedicated to the apostle in captivity.*

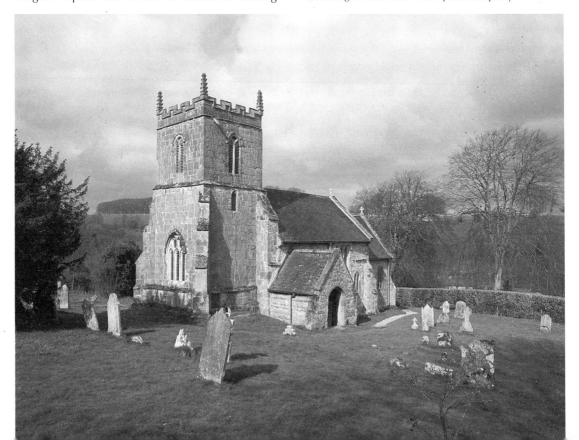

living in the house. General Pitt-Rivers, sometimes called the 'father of English archaeology', inherited the surrounding Rushmore Estate in 1880, and devoted the last 20 years of his life to excavating its many Bronze Age earthworks, with great enthusiasm.

The general also laid out the park on the Wiltshire border called Larmer Tree Gardens – the Larmer Tree being the spot where King John and his huntsmen used to gather. The original tree was probably a wych elm, but there remains only the stump, from which an oak tree now grows.

A lane leads up from the village to the Church of St Peter ad Vincula·('in chains') – one of only three such dedications in England, one of the others being the chapel at the Tower of London. The village church dates from the late 13th century and houses the tomb of General Pitt-Rivers.

The general's finds were exhibited in a museum in the village of Farnham, 3 miles southeast, until the 1960s when the museum was closed and the exhibits dispersed. Most went to Oxford, but in the South Wiltshire Museum in Salisbury there is a Pitt-Rivers Gallery with some scale models and finds from Cranborne Chase. The days when Farnham's Pitt-Rivers Museum was one of the most important in the country are commemorated by the local inn, the Museum Hotel, and by the museum building, which was originally a school for gipsy children and is now a private house. Outside the hotel stands the village stocks where miscreants were punished.

The whitewashed and thatched cottages of Farnham are in neat rows, their backs to the north winds and their lattice windows glinting as they reflect the late morning sunlight.

An ancient cedar dominates the churchyard of St Laurence's Church, which has a 12th-century nave and 15th-century tower. Flint and green sandstone have been used to give the tower an attractive chequerboard appearance.

TOLPUDDLE

Dorset

7 miles east of Dorchester

Wooden staves now prop up the old sycamore tree under which the six farmworkers known as the Tolpuddle Martyrs are said to have held some of their protest meetings in 1833–4. The tree stands on a steeply sloping triangle of grass not far from the centre of the village. The trade union martyrs were led by two brothers, George and James Loveless, and they were protesting against a reduction in their wages of 7 shillings a week to a starvation level of 6 shillings. They formed their own lodge of the Friendly Society of Agricultural Labourers to resist this third wage reduction in four years. For this, they were brought before a hostile judge and jury in Dorchester, in March 1834. They were found guilty of swearing unlawful oaths, and were sentenced to seven years' transportation to Australia. A public outcry later resulted in a pardon.

Memorials to the martyrs are found among the cob-walled cottages, 17th-century Manor House, and modern bungalows and houses which comprise the present-day village. Thomas Standfield's cottage, where the oaths were taken, still stands in the main street. Some of the martyrs were Wesleyan Methodists and, although the Methodist chapel has been rebuilt since their day, it contains a document of 1829–30 which mentions the Loveless brothers as local preachers.

In 1934 the Trades Union Congress built a small museum and six cottages, which were named after the Loveless brothers and their four comrades.

The stone-and-flint Church of St John the Evangelist stands nearby. It dates in part from the 13th century, and was much rebuilt in 1855. It contains a headstone to the martyrs by the 1930s sculptor and engraver Eric Gill. James Hammett, the only one of the martyrs to return from Australia and spend the rest of his life in Tolpuddle, is buried in the churchyard.

THE TOLPUDDLE MARTYRS *The town's famous sons, founders of the earliest trade unions, are commemorated by a local pub sign.*

TROWBRIDGE

Wiltshire

8 miles southeast of Bath

The administrative county town of Wiltshire has been a centre of the weaving trade since the 14th century, and by 1830 there were 19 mills in the town. One mill still makes the West of England broadcloth that is used for fine quality suits.

Trowbridge is a good base from which to tour the Wiltshire Downs and the Cotswolds. There are fine 18th-century stone houses, built by prosperous merchants, in Fore and Roundstone streets and in The Parade. Cottages of the less wealthy weavers can be seen in Yerbury Street.

The interior of the Church of St James was restored in the 19th century, but follows the style of the lavishly decorated church endowed by a wealthy cloth-maker in 1483. The spire dates from an earlier church built in the 14th century. A former rector, George Crabbe (1754–1832), who wrote the poem on which Benjamin Britten's opera *Peter Grimes* is based, is buried in the chancel. His memorial shows a deathbed scene.

The Town Hall has on its front wall a plaque commemorating Sir Isaac Pitman (1813–97), inventor of the shorthand system which bears his name. He was born in a house in Nash Yard, now demolished.

U

ULEY BURY FORT

Gloucestershire
2 miles east of Dursley

Beechwoods flank the hills around the village of Uley, built by cloth merchants in the 18th century. Above it looms a massive Iron Age hill-fort enclosing 32 acres of the lofty heights. Only the banked ditches of the outer rim are clear to walkers, the plateau top being used for arable crops. But the views from the summit are immense and give a sense of just how awesome this great fortress must have been when first constructed. Those masons and labourers must have themselves looked out at the dark curve of Stinchcombe Hill to the west and the lowland beside the Severn estuary. The spirit of these ancient Britons lingers on among the ramparts; on a day when the rain marches over that lowland the fort seems to come strangely alive.

Recent excavations have produced evidence of a wealthy population in the 1st century BC, including jewellery of bronze, glass and shale, iron currency bars and gold coins of the Dobunni – the tribe within whose territory the fort is situated.

About 1 mile north of the fort is Hetty Pegler's Tump, a Neolithic long barrow almost as fine as Belas Knap near Cheltenham. The barrow is 120 ft long and 22 ft wide, and its walls and ceiling are made of large stone slabs filled in with areas of drystone work. To enter the barrow the key must be obtained from Crawley Hill Farm, half a mile south on the B4066. Torches are needed to illuminate the burial chambers while crouching inside. Each of the four chambers is reached by a short passage. Some 38 skeletons were discovered in them in the last century. The barrow was named after the wife of a local landowner, but no one knows why; only that there was a Hester Pegler who lived locally in the 17th century.

HETTY PEGLER'S TUMP *The Neolithic long barrow, one of Britain's finest, lies about 1 mile outside Uley on the edge of the Cotswold escarpment.*

WAREHAM

Dorset
6 miles west of Poole

The early Britons settled on the site where the town of Wareham now stands. So did the Romans, but it was the Saxons who developed the town and named it Wareham (town by the weir). Wareham was the centre of conflict between the Saxons and the invading Danes, who sailed into Poole Harbour and up the River Frome.

During the Civil War the town changed hands constantly between Roundheads and Royalists, and suffered heavily as a result. Then, in 1762, fire destroyed many buildings. Wareham's architecture, therefore, is mostly Georgian, but some older relics remain. The Georgian planners also designed a spacious wide, main street.

The town walls were originally ancient British earthworks, later reinforced by the Romans. The section known as Bloody Bank was the scene of executions by the order of Judge Jeffreys after the Monmouth Rebellion in 1685.

The 8th-century St Martin's Church contains a fine effigy of Lawrence of Arabia in Arab dress, with his head supported by a camel. Lawrence lived in Clouds Hill cottage, 7 miles northwest of Wareham. The sculpture is the work of Eric Kennington, and was completed in 1939. A small but interesting museum has numerous Lawrence relics. St Mary's Church, overlooking the quay, contains the stone coffin of Edward the Martyr (d. 978) and a unique six-sided lead font. The church gives good views of the Old Quay from its towers.

The heaths surrounding Wareham figure as part of Thomas Hardy's 'Egdon Heath' in his Wessex novels.

WARMINSTER

Wiltshire
8 miles south of Trowbridge

Much of Warminster's past is retained in its wealth of houses, shops and inns built in the 18th and 19th centuries. Many of the houses are of local stone, some with mullioned windows, and three fine old inns are survivors of the days when Warminster was a coaching centre.

The 14th-century Minster Church contains an organ originally built for Salisbury Cathedral. Warminster School, built in 1707, was attended by Dr Thomas Arnold – later headmaster of Rugby School. The doorway on the school house was designed by Wren for Longleat House, but was later removed to its present site.

Longleat House, 4 miles southwest, the seat of the Marquis of Bath, was built in 1568–80. There are fine state rooms and collections of paintings, furniture and books. There is a safari park in the grounds.

In the 16th century, Warminster was a wool town and corn market. Today it is a military centre – site of the School of Infantry and the workshops of the Royal

Electrical and Mechanical Engineers. It has also become a popular look-out spot for UFOs, ever since a well-publicised siting in 1964.

A 2 mile drive west of the town centre leads to the foot of Cley Hill, 800 ft high, on the prehistoric Ridgeway which ran from South Devon to The Wash.

At Longbridge Deverill the Church of St Peter and St Paul is of a Norman origin, though it has work of various periods. There is a west tower, and at the end of the south aisle is some classical-style panelling. There are several interesting monuments and memorials.

WATCHET

Somerset
19 miles west of Bridgwater

The Ancient Mariner is thought to have set out on his 'fateful voyage' from Watchet's small and attractive port. The poet Samuel Taylor Coleridge (1772–1834) visited Watchet while staying in the area with William Wordsworth and his sister Dorothy. Coleridge almost certainly based his famous poem – *The Rime of the Ancient Mariner*, published in 1798 – on one of the old salts whom he met by the harbour.

The port was founded by the Saxons, and during the 19th century it flourished by exporting locally mined iron ore. But in 1894 the iron mines were closed and in the winter of 1900 the harbour was wrecked by a fierce storm, tidal waves washing away the wooden piers. Nonetheless, the present harbour was built immediately afterwards and today does a brisk trade. More than 100 ships a year bring mostly wood and pulp from the Baltic and wine from Spain and Portugal.

Watchet is a pleasing mixture of old stone houses and cottages, studded with handsome, late Georgian or early Victorian mansions. These include Market House on the corner of the harbour and Market Street, and the National Westminster Bank in Swain Street. The town climbs up to grassy high ground overlooking the seafront, on which stand a Baptist chapel and a 15th-century Anglican church.

The chapel was built in 1824 and is painted a fetching pale blue and cream. The church is dedicated to the 6th-century Welsh monk Decuman, who, according to legend, sailed to Somerset on a raft – accompanied by a cow which gave him milk during the voyage. Settling in the district, he lived the life of a hermit, bothering no one and communicating only with God. He is credited, however, with having performed the marriage ceremony uniting King Arthur and Queen Guinevere. One day, while kneeling at prayer, he was decapitated for no known reason by an unknown assassin. A figure of the murdered saint is set in a niche in the church tower.

St Decuman's has a fine Jacobean pulpit and a wagon roof supported by figures of angels. There are also monuments to the local Wyndham family, some of whom lived at nearby Kentsford Farm. The grandest monument is to Sir John Wyndham, who died in 1574.

To the southwest are the remains of 12th-century Cleeve Abbey, with its fine refectory and gatehouse.

WELLINGTON
Somerset
6 miles west of Taunton

An attractive town, Wellington has some fine Georgian houses. It was once noted for its ancient wool industry. The Squirrel Inn, nearly 400 years old, has been converted for residential and office use; and The Three Cups in Mantle Street was first recorded as carrying on business in 1694.

South of the town, on the highest point of the Blackdown Hills, an obelisk, begun in 1817 but only finished in 1854, commemorates the Duke of Wellington, victor of Waterloo in 1815, who took his title from the town.

WELLOW
Avon
4 miles south of Bath

Golden-stone cottages share Wellow's hillside main street with a handsome Manor House and ancient farm buildings. The oldest of them, Weavers Farm, has flanked the western side of the village square since the 14th century. Down Railway Lane from the square, the signal box for the disused Somerset and Dorset line marks the start of a footpath to Wellow Brook. Pedestrians can cross the brook by a medieval pack-horse bridge, its stone buttresses thick with moss. The watermill nearby, converted into a dwelling house, is said to date from Saxon times, although it was altered and added to in 1827.

The Manor House, along High Street, was the home of the Hungerford family, who bought Wellow Manor in the 1330s and held it until 1711. The present house was built in 1634, but its dovecote, around the corner in Farm Lane, dates from about 1250. It has nesting places for about 600 pigeons.

St Julian's Church, further east, was rebuilt about 1372 by Sir Thomas Hungerford, the first recorded Speaker of the House of Commons. In Wellow's heyday, as the centre of a sheep-rearing area, the church drew its congregation from neighbouring settlements as well as from the village. Fine wall-paintings in the north chapel, representing Christ and the apostles, date from about 1500. A statue over the south porch shows St Julian blessing the parish – with an oar in hand, because he was adopted as the patron saint of ferrymen. The church also has a fine pinnacled west tower and benches with poppy heads. Church Farmhouse, across the road, was built in 1620.

WELLS
Somerset
17 miles south of Bristol

The narrow and winding main street of Wells is noisy with cars and lorries, but the market square and cathedral precincts escape something of the din. Facing the spacious green is the famous cathedral. Its 13th-century west front is one of the finest in Britain, originally embellished with nearly 400 statues of saints, angels and prophets. Although there was a great deal of destruction during the 17th century, recent restoration has achieved a splendid result. The present cathedral was begun late in the 12th century, when the Bishop of Bath transferred his headquarters to Wells, and was completed before the middle of the 15th. Its many features of interest include the majestic north porch; the inverted arches, added in 1338 to strengthen the base of the central tower; the Chapter House; the humorous carved pillar-capitals in the south transept; and the superb Lady Chapel. The astronomical clock in the north transept is one of the oldest working clocks in the world. It has a dial some 6 ft across and moving models of jousting knights.

The Chain Gate, near the north porch, leads to Vicar's Close, a street of 15th-century houses, while south of the cathedral lies the fortified, moat-ringed Bishop's Palace. Its outer walls date back to 1206. It is claimed that the swans on the moat ring the bell by the bridge for food, as their ancestors were taught to do by a Victorian bishop's daughter.

The Quaker William Penn (1644–1718), who founded Pennsylvania in the USA, preached to a vast crowd before being arrested in the market place.

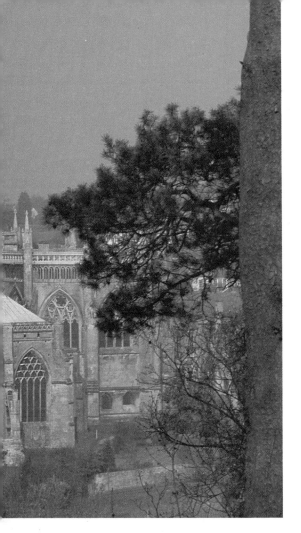

MATCHLESS WELLS *The cathedral is a symphony of arcaded walls, spandrelled roofs and great windows (above). The astronomical clock (below), whose second face can be seen on the north transept walk, has functioned since the 14th century.*

WESTBURY
Wiltshire
4 miles south of Trowbridge

The small weaving and glove-making town of Westbury has a little market place, good Georgian houses and an imposing town hall. Palace Green takes its name from the residence of the Kings of Wessex.

Two miles distant is the summit of Westbury Hill, reached by a road from Bratton village. Here Salisbury Plain ends its westward sweep in a climb to 755 ft before falling away dramatically to the Bristol Avon valley. The view is tremendous, with the steep, chalk slope dropping into a valley crisscrossed with roads and hedgerows and dotted with farmsteads and villages.

These are commanding heights indeed, which Iron Age men recognised when they built Bratton Castle on the summit. The fort covers 25 acres of the flat plateau, with its ramparts along the edges. Cut into the side of the hill is Wiltshire's oldest and best-known white horse, measuring 175 ft long and 107 ft high, with its head just below the castle's upper rampart. The Westbury horse dates from the 18th century, but it replaces an earlier figure said to have been carved to commemorate King Alfred's victory over the Danes at the Battle of Ethandun in AD 878.

The wide downland on the summit provides plenty of space for visitors to roam freely. In spring and summer, the yellow splash of bird's-foot trefoil attracts the chalkhill blue butterfly to lay its eggs.

WESTBURY-UPON-SEVERN
Gloucestershire
4 miles east of Cinderford

Canals bordered by yew hedges string together the lakes at Westbury Court, where the Dutch water garden is the only remaining one in England. The house itself no longer exists.

The garden, first laid out in about 1700 by supporters of William of Orange, has the original pavilions, and the canals are filled with water lilies.

DUTCH WATER GARDENS *A T-canal links the lakes at Westbury Court, maintained by the National Trust (overleaf).*

WESTON-SUPER-MARE
Avon
18 miles southwest of Bristol

Originally a small fishing village, now, after rapid growth in the last 100 years, Weston-super-Mare is one of the principal seaside resorts of the west coast. Other than the Church of All Saints, designed by G. F. Bodley between 1898 and 1902, it has little of historical interest but all the traditional features of a seaside town: piers, Winter Gardens, a Marine Parade extending for 2 miles, several parks and a wide sandy beach. There are regular boat trips from Birnbeck Pier at the north end of the front; donkeys, pony carriages and a Punch and Judy show on the beach.

A coastal toll-road through woods leads to Worlebury Hill, site of an Iron Age camp, with a superb view across the Bristol Channel to the Welsh coast. Finds from the camp are in Woodspring Museum.

Another fine view, northwest to Wales and southwest to the Quantocks, can be had from Brean Down, a headland 300 ft high reached by ferry across the River Axe from Uphill, a small village 1 mile south of Weston-super-Mare. There is a nature reserve and Uphill Manor, a picturesque Gothic mansion.

WESTONBIRT ABORETUM
Gloucestershire
3 miles southwest of Tetbury

The owners of Westonbirt House, the Holfords, planted the arboretum here in 1829 with hardy native and evergreen species such as oaks, Scots pines, beeches, holm oaks, yews and laurels, giving shelter to subsequent plantings of more exotic species. The noted landscape architect W. S. Gilpin had a hand in their arrangement. It is now the best collection of native and exotic trees in Europe. The Cotswold limestone gives way here to deeper, sandy loams – acid enough to grow rhododendrons and azaleas – and this sporadic geological deposit is a part of the Hinton Sand found elsewhere in pockets between Bath and Cirencester.

Westonbirt may be artificial, but in 150 years it has become so established that it appears almost natural. Trees simply like growing here. Many are the largest of their species anywhere in Britain, including maples, whitebeams and Caucasian oaks. There is now a Cherry Glade, glorious in spring; a collection of native British species (which number 25 only – Britain's wealth of tree species have almost all been imported); and a collection of willows. In autumn the maples set parts of Westonbirt ablaze with flame-red. In late spring the rhododendrons and azaleas are magnificent. There is complete freedom to walk anywhere in the woods, which cover some 116 acres, and the rides and paths are clearly marked by the Forestry Commission. The arboretum is open all year round.

WEYMOUTH
Dorset
26 miles west of Bournemouth

The ancient port of Weymouth was already busy in Roman times, with the mouth of the River Wey serving as one of the best safe anchorages in the south. Now a modern terminal for Channel Islands and Cherbourg steamers, Weymouth is also a popular resort with sweeping sand beaches. The town became a health and pleasure centre during the reign of George III, and pleasant groups of Georgian and early Victorian houses, some with fine ironwork balconies, some bow-windowed, stretch in a line from the harbour to the end of the promenade. In Trinity Street, two semi-detached Tudor cottages of 1600–10 are now a museum, housing typical furnishings of an Elizabethan sea-dog's house.

There are many unspoilt villages within easy reach, and a 4 mile walk eastwards to Osmington Mills can be rewarded by freshly cooked lobsters in any one of a number of little inns.

WHITCHURCH CANONICORUM
Dorset
4 miles northeast of Lyme Regis

A range of steep hills screens the village of Whitchurch Canonicorum from the English Channel, 2 miles away. The village lies in a valley and is reached by narrow, winding lanes plunging between hedgerows. The parish extends to the coast and contains about 50 farms, some of which date from the 17th century. In the centre of the village are thatched houses and cottages, standing in well-kept gardens.

The parish church of St Candida and Holy Cross is the jewel of the village. It was built in Norman times, and extended several times in the succeeding centuries. Its cruciform interior is something of a treasure-house. There are massive Norman pillars on the south arcade of the nave. In the north arcade, the capitals feature splendid Early English carvings of flowers and plants. The oaken pulpit is Jacobean, and the choir stalls are finely panelled. The church has a Perpendicular tower.

It is the only parish church in Britain to have what are thought to be the actual relics of the local patron. The bones of a woman, who may have been St Wite, are in a sealed casket contained in a 13th-century shrine built into the wall of the north transept. The casket was last opened in 1900 – and, centuries before that, medieval pilgrims used to thrust their crippled limbs into the three apertures built into the tomb in the hope of being healed.

Whitchurch Canonicorum is the capital of Marshwood Vale, the valley of the River Char which winds down to Lyme Bay at Charmouth. A network of meandering, high banked lanes wanders through villages of tawny sandstone patterned with grey-green lichen which shelter below heavily wooded hills such as Wootton and Lewesdon, some of them crowned with ancient hill-forts such as Lambert's Castle.

Three miles to the northwest lies Wootton Hill, where the road climbs through tunnels of beeches to a Forestry Commission car park in the shelter of tall Monterey pines. A gentle walk leads through Charmouth Forest, on the crown of the hill, where roe deer emerge from cover at dawn and dusk.

The forest road joins the B3165 which, 1 mile to the northeast, skirts the towering sides of Lambert's Castle, an Iron Age earthwork on the frontier between the territories of the Durotriges of Dorset and the Dumnovici, who gave their name to neighbouring Devon. From the southwest side the ascent is easy. The top is so spacious that horse races used to be run here in the 18th and 19th centuries. Now it is National

Trust property, with superb views over the Vale and northeast to the distinctive Pilsdon Pen (909 ft); the highest hill in Dorset, crowned by another hill-fort.

WHITCHURCH CANONICORUM *The small village with a large name lies among steep hills outside Lyme Regis.*

WILLS NECK
Somerset
7 miles southeast of Watchet

Triscombe Stone lies on the edge of the Quantock Hills and Forest, near Cockercombe. From a car park in the hamlet, a footpath leads to the 1260 ft summit of Wills Neck, the highest point in the Quantocks, from which the patchwork quilt of the west Somerset countryside unfolds in all its splendour. To the west, the Brendon Hills and the distant purple of Exmoor loom on the horizon; to the north, the South Wales mountains are visible on a clear day.

Wills Neck lies on a ridge – the name is derived from Old English and means 'Ridge of the Welshmen', referring to the Celtic tribe who probably fought a battle with the Saxons here; *walh* or *wealh* was an Anglo-Saxon word for foreigners or Welshmen. All around there is open moorland, dotted with clumps of gorse and bilberries rising from a carpet of bracken and heather. Sheep and ponies roam the paths, buzzards wheel overhead and, on sunny days in April and May, the emperor moth can be seen flitting over the heather, or in July and August the oak eggar moth.

On the south side of the hill the land falls away sharply to the tiny village of West Bagborough. In 1841, William Wordsworth and his wife, Mary, stayed as the guests of the Popham family at Bagborough House, a white, five-bayed Georgian house whose lawns are frosted with snowdrops in spring.

WILTON
Wiltshire
3 miles west of Salisbury

The carpets which have made Wilton, former capital of Saxon Wessex, world renowned are woven at the Royal Wilton Carpet Factory beside the Bath Road. The factory was given its royal charter by William III in 1699. The sheep whose wool is used in the carpets change hands at four annual fairs held in the town.

An 18th-century market-house stands on the town square, from which a series of ruined arches leads to the Gothic church, restored by a United States Ambassador in 1937 in memory of his ancestor and namesake, Robert Bingham, who was consecrated bishop here in 1229.

Wilton House, home of the Earls of Pembroke, stands on the site of an abbey founded by Alfred the Great. It was dissolved by Henry VIII, who gave the land to Sir William Herbert, created the Earl of Pembroke in 1551. Tradition has it that he consulted Holbein in the construction of the house. The house was largely destroyed by fire in 1647, and rebuilt by Inigo Jones. It contains fine furniture and paintings, including works by Rubens, Van Dyck and Tintoretto, and a collection of 7000 model soldiers. It is also noted for its elegant Double Cube Room, 60 ft long, 30 ft wide and 30 ft high. In the formal gardens, designed by Isaac de Caus, are several fine cedar trees, a Palladian bridge built in 1737 by Roger Morris and a casino by Sir William Chambers.

WIMBORNE MINSTER
Dorset
7 miles northwest of Bournemouth

There is a splendid approach from Blandford to this little market town, down a long avenue of beeches, which skirts the triple-banked Iron Age defensive earthworks of Badbury Rings.

The twin-towered, grey-and-brown chequered Minster Church of St Cuthberga gave the town the second part of its name. The first part comes from the River Wim, now called the Allen, which flows into the Stour on the outskirts.

The Minster, which may stand on the site of the nunnery founded by St Cuthberga around AD 700, embraces almost every style of architecture from Norman to late Gothic. It is faithfully reproduced in a model of the town, which is displayed off West Row. There are Norman tower arches, the nave arcade in Transitional Norman and 15th century. Among the tombs are that of the Duke and Duchess of Somerset, grandparents of Henry VII, and a brass to King Ethelred, King Alfred's brother.

In the streets around the square there are several old inns and hotels, and Wimborne is a good touring base for the surrounding countryside, vividly depicted in the writings of Thomas Hardy (1840–1928), who lived in Avenue Road for two years.

WINCHESTER
Hampshire
12 miles north of Southampton

Although outside the confines of modern-day West Country demarcations, the city is often still emotionally considered the capital of Wessex. Winchester – the old Roman city of Venta Belgarum – was made the capital of Saxon England by King Alfred in the 9th century. It remained the national capital for 200 years after the Norman Conquest, sharing the honour with London.

The magnificent Norman cathedral, at 556 ft one of the longest in Europe, took 300 years to complete. Building began in 1079 and the transept and crypt date from this period. The nave masonry is Norman, but is encased in stonework in the Perpendicular style. This is continued in the presbytery and Lady Chapel. The cathedral's many treasures include a black marble Norman font, medieval wall paintings and fine 19th-century stained glass. There is an abundance of carved wood. St Swithun, the chairmaker, one of the patrons of the church, has a shrine in the retrochoir.

Among the ancient buildings lining the close are the 13th-century Deanery, the 17th-century Pilgrims' School, and the Pilgrims' Hall with a 14th-century hammerbeam roof. The main access is via Priory Gate, an attractive 15th-century archway.

Castle Hall, in Castle Street, is all that survives of a 13th-century castle built by Henry III on the site of a Norman fortress. It was destroyed by Cromwell's troops in 1645. Henry V received the envoys of France here in 1415 before his Agincourt campaign; Sir Walter Raleigh was sentenced to death here in 1603, and it was here that Judge Jeffreys held a 'Bloody Assize' during the Monmouth Rebellion. A representation of King Arthur's Round Table, dating to about 1150, hangs on the west wall.

The oldest public school in the country, Winchester College, is also among the most respected. It was founded in 1382 and stands close to Kingsgate in one of the most medieval parts of the town.

BISHOP'S PALACE *Today's Bishop of Winchester lives in a residence built by Wren in 1684, incorporating a Tudor chapel.*

WINDMILL HILL

Wiltshire
2 miles northwest of Avebury

Windmill Hill, encircled by three concentric causewayed ditches with internal banks, was the site of regional gatherings and feasts during the Neolithic period, *c.* 3400 BC. It is an example of what is probably the earliest type of communal ritual monument built in Britain. Excavations revealed pottery and stone axes from all over Britain, showing wide contacts in this period. The summit is crowned by several Bronze Age barrows.

THE WINDRUSH VALLEY

Gloucestershire
6 miles west of Stow-on-the-Wold

In summer the Windrush is a beguiling little stream on its upper reaches, but in winter it has been known to flood, and so gave the name Guiting – from the Anglo-Saxon *gute* meaning 'flood' – to two of the peaceful villages lying in its valley, Temple Guiting and Guiting Power.

South of Temple Guiting lies Leigh Wood – a cool and shady place to explore on the footpaths. The woods are owned by Christchurch College, Oxford, and a Tudor manor at Temple Guiting was probably built as a summer residence for the Bishops of Oxford.

At Kineton, 1 mile south of Temple Guiting, a steep lane at the north end of the hamlet leads down eastwards through the cottages, and is marked Not Suitable for Motorists. It leads to a clear, gravelly ford and a narrow, high-hedged lane lying in the shadow of Leigh Wood. Further along the lane a track dips away to the south and crosses the Windrush again at another ford – sun-dappled under ancient trees, with a medieval packhorse bridge to make the crossing easier in flood.

A footpath winds south through the lush, wooded water-meadows at this spot, where the hills drop to create a still and sunlit place that feels strangely secret. The footpath is entangled in cow parsley, elder trees, hawthorns and blackthorns. In summer there are creamy curds of elder; in spring cowslips dapple the grassy banks; in autumn there are red hawthorn berries and sloes.

Deep within the watery woodland a narrow footbridge – a slab of ancient stone – crosses the chuckling Windrush. Grey wagtails flash their yellow chests as they dance in the air to take insects in flight, and warblers and thrushes nest in the willows, hazels and ash trees.

Guiting Power, 1½ miles south of Kineton, is a classic Cotswold village with a sloping, triangular green and honey-coloured stone houses. A footpath leads southwards past the church and then across open fields. The land is private, so keep to the public footpath. From it there are extensive views down the Windrush valley. Wild flowers and grasses cover the warm slopes where the occasional ancient oak tree stands sentinel.

After crossing a small tributary of the Windrush, the path continues on down the valley, partly by way of a minor road, to Naunton. The river here ambles behind the old stone cottages that line the street through this delightful backwater village. Further down the valley, across the A436 at Bourton-on-the-Water, there are many more visitors.

WINSFORD

Somerset
8 miles southwest of Minehead

All roads leading into Winsford are well worth travelling. None is more so than the lane that runs in from the south, from the Minehead to Tiverton road, through a wooded valley where massed rhododendrons bloom in June.

A handsome thatched inn, the Royal Oak, stands opposite a cobblestoned packhorse bridge over the River Winn, and there are seven more bridges and a ford in the village. The road from the ford leads up to an impressive church with a 90 ft tower.

The Church of St Mary Magdalene is of Norman origin, but now has architectural features and memorials of every century from the 12th to the 20th. The big west tower is 15th century, and at some point around that time the church roof seems to have been in danger of collapsing – the pillars in the south arcade of the nave slope outwards to support it. The massive door has timbers that are later than its heavy 13th-century ironwork, which is the product of a master blacksmith – probably a monk from Barlynch Priory, the scant remains of which lie to the south, near Dulverton.

Opposite Winsford's Wesleyan chapel, a plaque on a house records that this was the birthplace in 1881 of Ernest Bevin, the trade union leader and socialist MP who became Foreign Secretary in 1945. Bevin died in 1951, and his ashes are buried in Westminster Abbey.

Just off the road leading southwest from the village is the Caratacus Stone, with a battered inscription – *Carataci Nepus*, meaning 'descendant of Caratacus'. It has been dated between the 5th and 7th centuries.

About 4 miles southwest of Winsford are the famous Tarr Steps, a bridge of clapper stones strung across the River Barle. At one time considered Neolithic, they are now thought to have been constructed around the 13th century.

THE WINTERBORNES

Dorset
5 miles southwest of Blandford Forum

The streams which run from springs high up in the chalk hills of Wessex are not really streams at all in the conventional sense of the word, since they usually flow only when the water level is high after the autumn rains. They are called winterbourns, locally. Today, however, the spring waters which feed the Winterborne river near Blandford Forum have been tapped by wells drilled through the bedrock, and the stream flows freely throughout the year.

Before joining the River Stour, the Winterborne describes a semicircle along a small, sparsely wooded valley. For most of its journey it trickles beside the grass verges of the road, dissecting the pastureland and linking a series of villages and hamlets: Winterborne Houghton, where it rises, Winterbornes Stickland, Clenston, Whitechurch, Kingston, Muston, Tomson, and – appropriately at the end of the alphabet – Winterborne Zelston.

With the exception of Winterborne Zelston, none of the villages has the studied prettiness of some of the more famous Dorset villages. Apart from Winterborne Muston, each has its church and thatched cottages built of brick, stone or cob; but, because they are all workaday farming villages, they have modern houses too. This mixture is part of their charm.

All the Winterbornes have something special to offer – Winterborne Stickland has a 13th-century church, for instance – and each has a story to tell. The 11th-century Church of St Andrew in the middle of a farmyard at Tomson is the smallest in Dorset, measuring only 23 ft by 14 ft, and seating between 50 and 60 worshippers in Georgian box pews. It was much loved by the author Thomas Hardy, the sale of whose manuscripts raised money for its restoration in 1932. The Church of St Mary at Whitechurch has a fine 15th-century pulpit, a treasure discovered purely by chance a century ago. It had come originally from Milton Abbey where, during the Commonwealth, it has been plastered over to preserve it from destruction. When the abbey was restored two centuries later, the pulpit was thrown out into the yard as worthless. It was from here that the church at Whitechurch acquired the pulpit, still covered in plaster, in 1867. One day, as the rector tried to remove a nail from it, chalk and plaster came away in his hands, revealing the carving beneath.

Whitechurch is also the setting of the local legend regarding the Round Meadow which lies just outside. It is said to be cursed because it was once reaped on a Sunday. No crops would grow on it, and a church which villagers were trying to build on it was dismantled every night. Even today, however brilliant the sunshine, any attempt to plough it is sure to result in rain.

A series of manor houses lines the stream. At Clenston, the Tudor house has not been bought or sold since it was built, but has been passed down through the branches of the de Winterborne family. Next to it, beside the road, stands a magnificent barn with a hammerbeam roof of lavishly carved timbers. Higher Whatcombe lies a mile downstream and then, southeast of the main road, is Anderson Manor – a 17th-century mansion partly designed by Inigo Jones. Clenston Manor can be visited by arrangement and all the manors are clearly visible from the road.

Any journey through this group of Winterborne villages should end at Zelston – the most picturesque of them all. By this stage the stream which began as little more than a trickle is much broader. Willows arch gracefully over it as it passes between the Church of St Mary and Bridge Cottage – originally a row of three thatched 17th-century cottages.

WINTERBOURNE STOKE
Wiltshire
5 miles west of Amesbury

About 20 barrows or earthen burial mounds lie less than 1 mile west of Stonehenge at the crossroads of Winterbourne Stoke. Apart from a single Stone Age long barrow built about 3000 BC, they are round barrows made by the Beaker people who came to Britain from the Continent about 2000 BC.

The village itself is a collection of delectable stone cottages, tucked around winding lanes. The church has Norman doorways, box pews and many original 13th-century features, but it can easily be missed, tucked as it is down a dead-end road. The manor house is not open to the public, but its flint and stone facade can be appreciated from the bridge.

WITHAM FRIARY
Somerset
6 miles northeast of Bruton

The first Carthusian monastery in England was founded at Witham Friary by Henry II, as a penance for the murder of Archbishop Thomas Becket. The only remains are earthworks in a field northeast of the village. The church and a dovecote were converted into a village reading-room in the 19th century.

A lane crosses the course of a Roman road, which probably went as far as the Roman lead mines in the Mendips. Its course can be traced westwards a few hundred yards to a copse, and eastwards for 2 miles into Marston Wood.

THE WOODFORD VALLEY
Wiltshire
West Amesbury to Amesbury Down, north of Salisbury

The course of the River Avon, flowing south across Salisbury Plain, is diverted suddenly by the broad shoulder of Amesbury Down. Here the Avon makes a hairpin turn before entering the lovely Woodford Valley. From West Amesbury a road winds southwards through the valley, following almost every twist and turn of the west bank of the river and passing through straggling, picturesque villages of thatch and chequered stonework.

Sometimes the road climbs the valley side to give glimpses of water-meadows below the rows of weeping willows marking the river's course. Elsewhere, road and river almost touch, as at Middle Woodford where only a few yards of grassy bank divides them. The Avon here is wide, shallow and fast-flowing, with streamers of waterweed fanning out in the rippling current.

From Avon Bridge a road leads back up the valley, following the Avon's eastern bank for 4 miles to Great Durnford where there are riverside walks and a restored mill. The Durnford road passes Upper Woodford, which has the only road bridge across the river in the 7 mile stretch between West Amesbury and Avon Bridge. After Great Durnford the east bank road turns northeast, and passes Ogbury Iron Age camp before climbing to Amesbury Down.

WOODHENGE
Wiltshire
2 miles north of Amesbury

A Neolithic earthwork older than Stonehenge, Woodhenge was discovered – together with Durrington Walls Circle on its northeast side – in 1925. Six concentric rings of holes, now marked by concrete posts, appear to have been made for wooden posts and positioned, like Stonehenge, to indicate where the sun would rise on Midsummer Day. A circular ditch, some 220 ft in diameter, surrounds it. Woodhenge, and the circular earthworks of Durrington Walls, together probably formed a single religious centre which was moved to Stonehenge c. 1800 BC at the end of the Neolithic period. The Walls are almost bisected by the

WINTERBORNE CLENSTON *The bourne peacefully runs past the pretty little church at Winterborne Clenston in Dorset.*

Amesbury to Marlborough road. The bank, now large-ly eroded, enclosed a ditch some 80 ft wide and 20 ft deep, with two entrances. New road construction led to emergency excavation which showed that within the circle there were once many round buildings or arrangments constructed on a pattern similar to those at Woodhenge.

WOOKEY
Somerset
2 miles west of Wells

Some 2 miles northeast of this village is the famous group of caves known as Wookey Hole. (The name Wookey derives from the Old English word *wocig*, meaning a trap for animals.) The first three chambers of the caves are now floodlit; the River Axe flows through them before widening into a lake. A well-known feature of the caves is 'the Witch of Wookey', a huge stalagmite. The legend that a witch once lived in the caves was corroborated in 1912, when excava-tions revealed a woman's skeleton deep in the floor, close to a dagger, a sacrifical knife and a round stalagmite like a witch's crystal.

Wookey Hole was worn by the River Axe over a period of 50,000 years and was occupied in the Iron Age, while nearby Hyena Cave was occupied by Stone Age hunters when rhinoceros, mammoth, lion and bear roamed the Mendips.

Finds from the caves – including bone and flint tools from Prehistoric times, primitive jewellery and cooking articles from Celtic tribes, who lived in the cave c. 250 BC–AD 450, and medieval pottery and Bristol glass – are displayed in the local Wookey Hole Caves Museum and in Wells Museum. From Wookey Hole a footpath leads east to Upper Milton and then south to Wells.

Beside the access path to the caves stands an old paper mill that still produces paper as it was made in the early 17th century. Cotton fibre is pulped, tossed like a pancake, squeezed between two pieces of flannel in a press, dried, dipped in soap, alum and water and finally polished by being rolled between zinc sheets. This high-quality paper is used by water-colour artists and private press publishers.

WOOL
Dorset
5 miles west of Wareham

A village of mellow charm on the River Frome, Wool has one of the most beautiful 17th-century bridges in the county. The Elizabethan Woolbridge Manor was used by Thomas Hardy in *Tess of the D'Urbervilles* as the setting for Tess and Angel Clare's miserable wed-ding night. The mansion possesses a spectral coach-and-four which drives out at twilight, but only those of Turberville blood can see it, and for them it spells disaster. In the novel the unfortunate Tess sees the coach, and tragedy does indeed follow.

On the staircase of the manor, now a hotel, can be seen the faint tracings of two portraits of the real Turberville family; and the church where many of the family are buried is still standing. Half a mile east stand the ruins of 12th-century Bindon Abbey. It was into an open tomb in these grounds that, in Hardy's novel, a sleep-walking Angel Clare placed Tess.

WORBARROW AND KIMMERIDGE BAYS
Dorset
8 and 10 miles west of Swanage

A rich underwater life, flourishing on the low ledges of clay and shale that shelve into the sea, is one of the few qualities the neighbouring Worbarrow and Kim-meridge Bays have in common, together with the fact that they are both part of the Purbeck Marine Nature Reserve. Otherwise they contrast dramatically.

Worbarrow Bay is flanked on the east side by the towering limestone pyramid of Worbarrow Tout; to the west – across almost 2 miles of glistening water – is Mupe Bay and the tumbling Mupe Rocks. In between, the waves have cut back the softer disarray of rock to form cliffs that are green, grey, pink or ochre, and are broken in the middle by the shining white cove of Arish Mell, where the Purbeck-chalk range drops to the sea. A wooded gully leads to Worbarrow Bay, running down to the sea from the deserted village of Tyneham.

The Bay is within an army firing range, but it is open to the public most weekends and public holidays. Dates are given in the local press and on the army road boards. Marked paths lead to the bay from Tyneham car park, and it is essential to keep to the paths in case of unexploded shells.

Kimmeridge Bay is less dramatic, backed by low green downland and with modest cliffs whose crumbly, tawny rocks, rich in fossils, alternate with dark grey shale and clay. On the bay's eastern arm stands a tower commemorating Sir William Clavell of nearby Smedmore House; in the 17th century he came close to ruin trying to develop the commercial potential of the local sulphurous oil-shale, using it as a fuel first for producing alum, then for a glass works. The Celts were more successful with their use of the shale well into Romano-British times, and their bangles and ornaments made from hardened Kimmeridge oil-shale have been found as far away as Hadrian's Wall.

East of Kimmeridge Bay, towards St Anselm's Head, are the shattered cliffs of Kimmeridge Ledges, of dark grey-blue clay interspersed with bands of limestone and the omnipresent oil-shale. Sea erosion has caused

SAPPHIRE SEA *Pyramidal Worbarrow Tout may be the remains of a wall of limestone that kept Worbarrow Bay an islet until the sea cut through.*

many landslips on the cliff-face and the shore is littered with limestone blocks.

Just inland from the Ledges is Smedmore House, mentioned above. The property and, later, the house have passed through the family without a break since the 14th century.

WORTH MATRAVERS
Dorset
4 miles west of Swanage

For centuries Worth Matravers was one of the main centres for the quarrying of Purbeck marble, and surface workings of the old quarries can be seen in the hills around the village. The dark grey marble supports the tower and spire of Salisbury Cathedral.

The Church of St Nicholas, which stands close to

the centre of the stone-built village, is memorable for its Norman nave and chancel, and stunning modern east window. It was extensively restored in 1869 after it had become so dilapidated that services had to be held in the village school. In the churchyard is the grave of Benjamin Jesty, a Dorset yeoman reputed to be the first person to inoculate anyone with cowpox to ward off smallpox. Jesty is recorded as having carried out the experiments on his wife and two sons in 1774. It was not until 1798 that Dr Edward Jenner published his historic report concluding that cowpox inoculations serve as a protection against the fatal disease. The success of Jesty's experiment seems confirmed by the inscription on his wife's tombstone, which records that she died in 1824, aged 84.

The nearby seaside resort of Swanage was once merely a hamlet in the parish of Worth. A footpath over the downs, called the Priest's Way, links the two places. It was so called because it was the route used by the priest when he went to Swanage to hold services in the chapel there. To the south, another downland walk leads about 2 miles to a cave-riddled cape, known as St Alban's or St Aldhelm's Head, rising abruptly from the sea to a height of 354 ft.

Guillemots, razorbills and other seabirds make their nests on the precipices of the cape and carry on ceaseless traffic over the sea. On top of the headland is St Aldhelm's Chapel, a solid and perfectly square building erected around a central column supporting four Norman arches.

WOTTON-UNDER-EDGE

Gloucestershire
9 miles southwest of Stroud

The old market town of Wotton-under-Edge, on the edge of the Cotswolds, has some fine old buildings including a 14th-century school and a 14th- to 15th-century church. Among the interesting treasures in the church are some fine brasses and an 18th-century organ built by Christopher Schrider for St Martin-in-the-Fields, London, and played by Handel at a time when George I attended services there. The vicar of Wotton bought it when St Martin's discarded it. In Orchard Street is a house where Isaac Pitman (1813–97), a schoolmaster at Wotton, devised his system of shorthand. The almshouses date from 1632 and there is an imposing gabled woollen mill, with a clock tower and a great pond, dating from about 1800. Today it is a narrow fabrics and elastic factory, but its old buildings can be visited on appointment. Among them is a wool stove (now a stationery store), and a circular kiln in which washed wool was dried.

Immediately above and north of Wotton-under-Edge is Westridge Wood and the wooded Iron Age fort of Brackenbury Ditches. South of the fort, on the curving ridge of Wotton Hill, owned by the National Trust, are the remains of strip lynchets, ploughed terraces of Anglo-Saxon origin.

Northeast of Westridge Wood is Waterley Bottom, high-edged and lonely, in which the motorist may see nothing beyond the immense lane banks. Northeast of Wotton, reached by a narrow lane and the drive of a private house, is a footpath up Tyley Bottom into the narrow wooded head of the valley.

Most beautiful of all, and reached only on foot, is the head of Ozleworth Bottom, named after the Anglo-Saxon word for blackbird – and they are among the many birds found here. A narrow lane runs for 2 miles from the hamlet of Wortley to two cottages that span the stream below Ozleworth Park. From this shadowy bridge a muddy track on the south side of the stream climbs under trees to a field gate. There, a pathway climbs through grassy fields, streams, shady glades and warm, silent banks to Boxwell.

WRINGTON

Avon
2 miles east of Congresbury

Wrington church has a fine tower, visible for miles around. The River Yeo flows nearby, and wooded hills overlook the village from the north. Hannah More, the novelist and philanthropist, lived here for a time in a house called Barley Wood ($\frac{1}{2}$ mile northeast of the village) which she built in 1800. In the south porch of the church there are busts of her and of the philosopher John Locke, who was born here in 1632.

WYLYE

Wiltshire
16 miles northeast of Shaftesbury

Until the 1970s, Wylye was on the main road from London to Exeter. Now a bypass leaves the village in peace. It is a well-earned respite. For centuries Wylye was a major staging point between Amesbury and Mere. The Bell Inn, built in the 14th century, is now the only survivor of nine pubs in the village.

As the road winds into the village, it crosses the Wylye – the river which gave Wiltshire its name. From the bridge it is just possible to glimpse downstream a lead statue of a boy blowing a horn in the waters beside the red-brick mill building. This commemorates a post-boy who, in the days when there was a ford at this point, saved several of the passengers of a stage-coach which has overturned in the floods. He drowned in the act of doing so.

The road then curves into the main street and its row of cottages which lead to the 14th-century Wylands Cottage. Several have mullioned windows and the chequered walls of flint and Chilmark stone that are typical of this part of Wiltshire. Since 1924 many have had tiled roofs. In that year a blaze started at a farm in the village and, fanned by a strong westerly wind, set fire to the original thatched roofs as it raged along the street. Wylands Cottage hardly fits the dictionary definition of 'a small house'. Originally two cottages, it now dominates a road junction with its part stone, part timbered frontage, massive gable and steep, red-tiled roof.

The Perpendicular Church of St Mary the Virgin, which has a 15th-century tower, stands next to the Bell Inn. It has a richly carved oak pulpit dated 1628 and, by the south gate of the churchyard, an ostentatious tomb framed by wrought-iron railings. Tradition claims that it was built by a 'man of mean extraction' named Popjay, for his mother and sister. He left the village before he had paid for it and so, it is said, the rector settled the bill and had himself buried in the tomb.

There has long been a close association between the inn and the church; indeed, the 19th-century bell clappers from the church still hang in the fireplace of the Bell Inn.

Y

YARNBURY CASTLE
Wiltshire
3 miles west of Winterbourne Stoke

Few Wiltshire guidebooks mention Yarnbury, perhaps because it is overshadowed in renown by its neighbour, Stonehenge, 6 miles to the east. But Yarnbury Castle offers a haven of tranquillity, away from the crowds that flock to the great stone circle. It is an Iron Age hill-fort dating from 2nd century BC, with three grassy banks and three ditches enclosing an area of 28½ acres. In its centre are the just discernible traces of an earlier earthwork built between the 7th and 5th centuries BC, which was overlaid with sheep-pens in the 18th century.

Sheep still graze there, cropping the grass short and pausing only to stare indignantly at intruders who come up the short path from the A303 and climb the steep banks. This is an ideal place to rest awhile; to stretch out on the close-cropped grass and still be able to see the sweeping countryside in all directions. To the south the landscape is soft and gentle, for this is the southern edge of Salisbury Plain where it descends into the Wylye valley. To the north, east and west are the rolling uplands of the plain, the broad cornfields stretching to the horizon reminiscent of the wide open spaces of the American prairies.

YATTON
Avon
4 miles south of Clevedon

The old village of Yatton consists of a group of cottages, former almshouses and an old rectory clustered round an impressive church, dating back to the 14th century. The church is highly decorated and has a fine west front and the most elaborate south porch in Avon. Its Perpendicular tower is visible for many miles around. Inside are several monuments, spanning the centuries. A Chapter House was added in 1975.

YEOVIL
Somerset
21 miles east of Taunton

Yeovil was a small market town until the 18th century, but is now a busy industrial centre. It is noted for its 300-year-old glove-making industry as well as its more recent industries, which include one of the world's largest helicopter constructors. The large Perpendicular Church of St John the Baptist has a west tower, large windows and transepts. There is a vaulted crypt under the chancel and several monuments, one of which, to Robert Philips, c.1855, is a life-sized half figure.

The museum in Hendford Manor Hall, which is a converted coach house and stables, contains a noted collection of firearms and costumes, and also some remains of Roman mosaics.

Yeovil's Nine Springs, at the bottom of Hendford Hill, are reached by a waterside walk through woods – huge beeches and shaded paths, with nine springs flowing into an enchanting lake.

YEOVILTON
Somerset
6 miles north of Yeovil

Situated on the Royal Navy Air Station, the Fleet Air Arm museum at Yeovilton traces the history of naval aviation from 1903 to the present day. There are over 40 historic aircraft on display, some of which still fly; a unique collection of aircraft, aero-engines and ship models, as well as exhibitions of photographs, uniforms, medals and documents, and the Concord 002.

YETMINSTER
Dorset
5 miles southwest of Sherborne

The parish church of Yetminster, the Church of St Andrew, has a chancel built c. 1300, but the rest of the church, with a west tower, is 15th century. Inside, the roofs still retain some of their painted decoration. A brass with figure dates from c.1531, and there are a number of wall monuments, mainly of the 17th and 18th centuries. Some of the benches are 15th century.

ANCIENT EARTHWORKS *Yarnbury Castle lies on the southern fringe of Salisbury Plain, with downlands beyond.*

INDEX

Page numbers in **bold** type refer to main entries in the book. Numbers in *italic* refer to illustrations.

ACKNOWLEDGMENTS

The illustrations in this book were commissioned by Reader's Digest from the following photographers except those in italics.

8–9 Patrick Thurston; 10 Patrick Thurston; 12–13 Neil Holmes; 14 Susan Lund; 15 Susan Lund; 16–17 Neil Holmes; 19 Gordon Moore; 20 John Vigurs; 21 Philip Dowell; 22 Philip Llewellin; 24–25 Patrick Thurston; 28–29 Mike St. Maur Shiel; 30–31 Jon Wyand; 32 Patrick Thurston; 34–35 *G. Wilkins/Robert Harding Picture Library*; 36–37 Patrick Thurston; 39 Neil Holmes; 40 Neil Holmes; 42 Susan Lund; 43 Neil Holmes; 45 Patrick Thurston; 47 Patrick Thurston; 48–49 Philip Llewellin; 51 Jason Shenai; 52–53 Neil Holmes; 55 Neil Holmes; 56–57 Neil Holmes; 58–59 Susan Lund; 64 Clive Friend; 66–67 Jason Shenai; 68–69 Neil Holmes; 70–71 John Sims; 73 Eric Meacher; 75 Tim Woodcock; 77 Malcolm Aird; 80–81 Neil Holmes; 82 Patrick Thurston; 83 Patrick Thurston; 85 Susan Lund; 87 Patrick Thurston; 91 Susan Lund; 92–93 Neil Holmes; 95 Susan Lund; 95 Tim Woodcock; 99 Patrick Thurston; 100 Neil Holmes; 102 Jason Shenai; 104–105 Neil Holmes; 106–107 Tim Woodcock; 109 Jason Shenai; 112–113 Neil Holmes; 114–115 Neil Holmes; 116 Neil Holmes; 120–121 Jon Wyand; 122 Neil Holmes; 125 Neil Holmes; 128 Mike Taylor; 132–133 Trevor Wood; 134 Neil Holmes; 136 Susan Lund; 137 Philip Llewellin; 138 Neil Holmes; 139 Neil Holmes; 140 Tim Woodcock; 142–143 Neil Holmes; 144–145 Tim Woodcock; 147 Neil Holmes; 148 Malcolm Aird; 151 Jon Wyand; 152–153 *Robin Fletcher*; 155 Tim Woodcock.

The publishers express their thanks to local authorities, Tourist Boards and Tourist Information Centres in Gloucestershire, Avon, Somerset, Wiltshire and Dorset for their help in checking material, and to Hilary Bird who compiled the index.